INTRODUCTION TO COST-BENEFIT ANALYSIS

SECOND EDITION

INTRODUCTION TO COST-BENEFIT ANALYSIS

LOOKING FOR REASONABLE SHORTCUTS

GINÉS DE RUS

Professor of Applied Economics, University of Las Palmas de Gran Canaria, University Carlos III de Madrid and research affiliate, FEDEA, Spain

Cheltenham, UK • Northampton, MA, USA

Published by
Edward Elgar Publishing Limited
The Lypiatts
15 Lansdown Road
Cheltenham
Glos GL50 2JA
UK

Edward Elgar Publishing, Inc.
William Pratt House
9 Dewey Court
Northampton
Massachusetts 01060
USA

Paperback edition 2022

A catalogue record for this book
is available from the British Library

Library of Congress Control Number: 2020952706

ISBN 978 1 83910 374 2 (cased)
ISBN 978 1 83910 375 9 (eBook)
ISBN 978 1 80392 461 8 (paperback)

Typeset by Servis Filmsetting Ltd, Stockport, Cheshire
Printed and bound by CPI Group (UK) Ltd, Croydon, CR0 4□

CONTENTS IN BRIEF

FULL CONTENTS

PREFACE

Cost–benefit analysis is a powerful economic tool with which to inform responsible decisions taken within the public sector. It is rooted in welfare economics and its aim is to help the government to choose the best investment projects and public policies. The philosophy that underpins this appraisal methodology is consequentialist. Projects are evaluated by identifying and measuring their consequences, their benefits and costs expressed in monetary terms.

In writing this second edition, the intention remains the same: to assess whether public decisions, like investing in public infrastructure, subsidizing a product, or protecting a natural area, increase social welfare. Our experience in teaching undergraduate and postgraduate students, as well as advising public agencies, has revealed two key elements for the fulfilment of the original purpose of this technique, which is to help in taking informed public decisions for the benefit of the society.

One element is the importance of having a model. Cost–benefit analysis as a cookbook is quite dangerous if we do not understand where the recipes come from. There are many rules of thumb and recommendations for the application of cost–benefit analysis, but these rules are sometimes taken from different frameworks of analysis and could lead to serious errors. A basic model is needed to derive the rules for a sound assessment of the project, avoiding conceptual errors, double counting and the like.

The other element is the crucial role of the type of governance where the evaluation takes place. The separation between who decides and who evaluates, and the power and independence of the evaluating agency, are probably more important today than the methodology itself. One should not expect a significant influence of cost–benefit analysis on which projects and policies are approved unless the right institutional architecture has been previously established. A poor institutional design can stifle the power of the economic tool, limiting its role to an administrative procedure to get funding from a superior level of government.

We are very pleased with the reception of the first edition. The book is written not only for economists but also for anyone interested in the economic effects of projects and public policies, commonly financed with public money, and for the revision of the

book's second edition we have relied on the invaluable feedback of students and practitioners. In this new version we have corrected some errors, simplified some sections,
skipped some explanations, and updated the chapters with new material. We hope the
book is now more readable and useful.

People may be interested in cost–benefit analysis for different reasons. Some individuals must decide which projects will be undertaken; others must report to those
who decide on the social merit of these projects; or perhaps some might need stronger
arguments to defend their legitimate interest group position, to be better informed for
the next election or simply because they enjoy public economics.

One does not need to be an economist to understand the basics of cost–benefit
analysis but some previous knowledge of economics helps. A basic background in
microeconomics is clearly an advantage, not only to benefit more from this book but
also for the interpretation and better understanding of many aspects of the economy
and everyday life.

The book is not very technical, and the exposition is hopefully simple and easy to
follow. Its coverage is not comprehensive, but we hope the key elements for understanding and applying cost–benefit analysis are adequately treated. Although this is not a
theoretical book, it is analytic in the sense that it tries to follow the logic of arguments
using some basic models, which are made explicit in their assumptions, limitations and
implications.

The field of cost–benefit analysis has experienced a tremendous change in the last
decades but the main economic principles behind this tool remain unchanged for public
decision making. Moreover, despite the development of new techniques for the economic valuation of non-marketed goods, the refinement of demand forecasting or the
integration of wider economic benefits, current practitioners in the field share the same
aspiration as their colleagues in the past: to reach a reasonable degree of confidence
regarding the contribution of the project to social welfare.

This book began as course notes for undergraduate and postgraduate courses at the
University of Las Palmas de Gran Canaria and the University Carlos III de Madrid. I
wish to thank my students, and many other participants in short courses on cost–benefit
analysis, who read my class notes and helped me to decide how to convert them into
book form. I am indebted to many people in the writing of this book: Pino Betancor,
Ofelia Betancor, Javier Campos, Pilar Socorro, Eduardo Dávila, Doramas Jorge, Aday
Hernández, Gustavo Nombela and Enrique del Moral for their help during the production process of successive drafts. In the first and the second edition, my colleague
Jorge Valido has not only helped with corrections but also provided valuable feedback
through long and fruitful discussions.

My deepest gratitude goes to Chris Nash, Peter Mackie and Ken Guilliam of the
Institute for Transport Studies at the University of Leeds, and Per-Olov Johansson
of the Stockholm School of Economics. I owe Chris, Peter and Ken the passion for
economics as an instrument for a better society. Before I met Per-Olov, I used his book
Cost–Benefit Analysis of Environmental Change as the bible on the subject and admired
his work, so it is easy to realize how lucky I feel for our academic collaboration and

friendship. Chris and Per-Olov have provided valuable comments and invaluable advice on draft chapters, and in many discussions on the subject. I am indebted to them for their patience, generosity and encouragement.

For all the people named above and for quite a few colleagues from whom I have learned during all these years of teaching and practising cost–benefit analysis, I cite the words of George Stigler (1988, p. 36) on university life:

> Association with a group of able colleagues is a strong advantage that a professor usually has over a non-academic economist. Frequent exchanges with strong minds and powerful scientific imaginations that have a deep understanding of the problem one is struggling with are invaluable in discovering errors and eliminating strange perspectives that creep into one's work.

Finally, I wish to thank the staff at Edward Elgar Publishing for their encouragement and advice as I prepared the manuscript. I am the only one responsible for all the remaining errors.

1

Introduction

In principle cost–benefit analysis is straightforward. Any investment project can be viewed as representing a perturbation of the economy from what it would have been had the project not been undertaken. To evaluate whether the project should be undertaken, we need to look at the levels of consumption of all the individuals of all commodities at all dates under the two different situations. If all individuals are better off with the project than without it, then it should be adopted (if there is an individualistic social welfare function). If all the individuals are worse off, then it should be rejected. If some individuals are better off and some worse off, whether we should adopt it depends on how we weight the gains and losses of different individuals. Although this is obviously the 'correct' procedure to follow in evaluating projects, it is not a practical one; the problem of cost–benefit analysis is simply whether we can find reasonable shortcuts.

(Atkinson and Stiglitz, 2015, p. 398)

1.1 THE RATIONALE OF COST–BENEFIT ANALYSIS

Cost–benefit analysis is not about money. It is not about inputs or outputs either. It is about welfare. The value of this economic tool is to help in the selection of the best projects and policies for the benefit of society. Money is central to financial analysis but only instrumental in the economic appraisal of projects. Money is the common unit in which economists express the social costs and benefits of projects.[1]

Volume of drinking water, accidents avoided, time savings and energy and labour consumed are measured in different units, and we need a common unit of measure to express all these heterogeneous items in a homogeneous flow. This is the key role of money in cost–benefit analysis. It solves the problem of converting something unobservable (well-being) into something measurable (willingness to pay) but the process is not without difficulty, as the individual level of income is not uniform in society and hence 'voting with money' both reflects the intensity of preferences and the individual's income level.

---

[1] In this book, the term 'project' refers interchangeably to projects and policies.

The creation of jobs is frequently presented as a benefit of a project, but labour is an input not an output. A motorway, for example, is not constructed to create jobs but to move people and goods. Workers building and maintaining a motorway represent a social cost equal to their social opportunity cost – that is, the net value lost in the next best use of this input. It is true that if a worker is unemployed, society does not lose as much as in the case of a similar worker already employed, but this only shows that the opportunity cost is context dependent.

The output of a project is easier to measure than its welfare effects. Public agencies report their activities with indicators such as passengers, water, electricity, or the number of students taught within a training programme, but cost–benefit analysis sees output as a means to increase welfare. The success of a new facility cannot be explained by the number of users, as it is possible, for example, to subsidize prices to induce people to use the new facility without increasing social welfare. Therefore, cost–benefit analysis is interested in the social value achieved from the outputs of the project compared with the value of other goods sacrificed elsewhere for the sake of the project.

Cost–benefit analysis is about the well-being of individuals affected by the project and not about the number of users or water consumption. The change in welfare is what economists want to measure, and this is quite a challenging task because welfare cannot be directly measured. To solve this problem, economists have found an alternative: to use money as an expression of welfare. I do not know how great the utility[2] of a particular individual is when driving his car from here to there at a particular date and time, but if I am able to determine the amount of money to charge for this trip that makes him indifferent between driving or not, then interesting things can be said. Cost–benefit analysis is not about money, but money helps.

Cost–benefit analysis conceived as a toolkit for the selection of projects, in the general interest of society, presupposes the existence of a social planner, a benevolent government that compares benefits and costs before the implementation of projects. Many economists and non-economists would consider such a view naive, to say the least. An alternative view explains a government's action by the political power of different interest groups.[3] Subsidies to agriculture, for example, could be better explained by the pressure from farmers than by an independent assessment of the social benefits and costs of agricultural policy.

Do we need to believe in the goodwill of the government to practise cost–benefit analysis? The answer is no. If we believe that a government's acts are better explained by the influence of interest groups, cost–benefit analysis can show who benefits and who loses as a result of particular projects, and the magnitudes of the gains and losses. This assessment can be very helpful in explaining which policies are adopted, or even in influencing a government's decision. 'Cost–benefit analysis may be in the battle against misleading information spread by self-interested political pressure groups. Still, these

---

[2] We use the terms utility, individual well-being and individual welfare as synonymous.

[3] George Stigler, Gary Becker and Sam Peltzman are among the top economists promoting the 'interest group competition model'.

analysts can influence political outcomes by making enough voters aware of the true effects of different policies' (Becker, 2001, p. 316).

To present the conceptual foundations and methods of cost–benefit analysis we will proceed 'as if' the government would aim for the best projects in the general interest of society. Although we know of many cases that show that such an assumption is unrealistic, the simplification is harmless. As we proceed to identify benefits and costs, winners and losers, and try to measure and value the main effects of the project under evaluation, the analysis is not going to change whatever our particular beliefs on the government's behaviour are.[4]

We have begun by assuming the existence of a benevolent government. This is not the only assumption and simplification in this book; in fact, there is no way to deal with the analysis of the economy but through the use of simplifying assumptions, replacing the actual world with a model that reflects the essence of the more complex reality we want to understand.

To move forward, we need to clarify what is understood by acting in the general interest of society. Let us consider that our benevolent government is evaluating the construction of a dam and a hydroelectric power station. The government doubts whether it should accept the project. By undertaking the project, the region would obtain electricity at a lower cost than without the project, recreation benefits, both in the stock of water (e.g., fishing and boating) and in the flow of reservoir release (e.g., fishing and rafting). Moreover, some jobs would be created at the time of its construction and during the lifetime of the project. Furthermore, there might be a multiplier effect, as the project would create new economic activity induced by the expenditure associated with the construction and operation of the project.

Economists point out that from the benefits described above, some costs must be deducted. First, the construction and maintenance costs, equal to the net benefits of alternative needs that have not been attended to because the public money has been assigned to the dam and power station. They also argue that labour is an input, not an output, so it is a cost of the project, though its magnitude will depend on what is lost when the worker is employed within the project. Surprisingly, for many, the multiplier effect, if it exists, turns out to be irrelevant, as it is usually also associated with the alternatives.

Second, all the other costs related to the relocation of the inhabitants of the village in the area where the dam would be built and to the people negatively affected by the alteration of the flow and course of the river should be accounted for. The magnitude of these costs could be substantial.

The government considers all the relevant benefits and costs regardless, in principle, of who the beneficiaries and the losers are (assume for simplicity that all the effects are inside the country) and the government decides to undertake the project if, given the available information, society improves. Its decision is not based on the arguments of

---

[4] Nevertheless, if we are interested in the relevance of cost–benefit analysis in the real world, we need to address explicitly the institutional design and the possible conflicting objectives (see Chapter 10).

the private companies that will build the dam and power station, nor on the campaign of the opponents. The decision takes into account the whole of society, with social welfare as the main goal. The challenge for our benevolent government is how to value all the benefits and costs and how to compare them, given that beneficiaries and losers are individuals with different income, education, health, and so on, and are affected at different moments during the lifespan of the project.

This water project, like any other public infrastructure such as parks, high-speed rail (HSR), highways, ports or the introduction of policies such as environmental regulations, can be interpreted as perturbations in the economy affecting the welfare of different individuals at different moments in time compared with the situation without the project or policy, which does not necessarily mean the status quo but what would have happened in the absence of the project or policy. Hence, the assessment of the effects of the project requires a benchmark. It is necessary to compare the world *with* and *without* the project: to recreate an alternative world, or the so-called counterfactual.

Cost–benefit analysis practitioners must solve two main problems. First, they must build the counterfactual, and this means to replicate the world without the project, a dynamic world that evolves without the perturbation introduced by the project. This is not an easy task because the time period for this exercise may be quite long – 30, 50 years or more – and the values of key variables will possibly change in each of these years. Second, the practitioner must imagine the world with the project, forecasting the main changes with respect to the counterfactual that she has previously created.

The expected changes when the project is implemented are then the result of the comparison with the counterfactual: the worse the counterfactual, the better the project. Hence, it is important to present all the assumptions and the data used to complete this exercise. Transparency and ex post evaluation can help to avoid both innocent errors and strategic misrepresentation.

Suppose the counterfactual and the world with the project have been properly designed and the expected changes have been estimated: time savings, improved water quality or a reduction in the number of fatal accidents. Now, the analyst must convert these values into monetary units ($),[5] assuming that this is technically possible and morally acceptable.

Summarizing, we want to measure changes in the welfare of the individuals in society. However, individuals' utility cannot be measured in the same way as the amount of electricity produced or the number of people displaced to build the dam. To decide on the merit of the project, we need to measure something that is unobservable. Furthermore, what is observable – the production of electricity, number of individuals involved, extension of flooded surface, and so on – is not very useful if we do not translate the physical units into a common measure related to changes in individual utility, which allows the comparison between what is gained and what is lost.

---

[5] We use the dollar symbol, $, as representing an undefined monetary unit without any relation to its actual market value.

Table 1.1 Benefits and costs of a hydroelectric power station (values in $)

Individual	Benefits	Costs	Net benefits
A	7	0	7
B	2	8	−6
C	3	4	−1
D	9	1	8
E	1	6	−5

Hence, though the ideal way of measuring the impact of our project is through utility functions (we would measure the change in utility of each individual), the problem is that these utility functions and the associated utility changes are unobservable. Converting the unobservable utility changes through an 'exchange rate' between utility and income to observable monetary units gives us a way of calculating the impact of the project.

Economists know that the monetary valuation of utility changes is not without difficulty, basically because the 'exchange rate' is different for different individuals. The monetary price individual A is willing to pay for the construction of the hydroelectric power station both reflects the change in the marginal utility and his level of income.

An alternative might be to submit the project to a referendum and to accept the outcome – that is, accept the view of the majority. Let us have a look at this in more detail. Table 1.1 shows the benefits and costs (expressed in monetary units) of those affected by the construction of the dam and the hydroelectric power station. Our society consists of five individuals.[6]

Individual B, for example, benefits from cheaper energy (+$2) but he also fishes downstream and the dam prevents him from practising his favourite sport in the initial conditions (–$8). The result is a net loss of $6 for individual B. We could interpret the values in the 'net benefits' column as the monetary compensation that will be needed with the project to leave each individual indifferent without the project: for example, individual B would be willing to accept $6 and individual A would be willing to pay $7.[7]

The 'net benefits' column allows us to anticipate that the project would be rejected in a referendum. Individuals A and D would vote in favour, but individuals B, C and E would vote against it. Would it be a good decision to reject the construction of this project? To answer this question, we must check whether the construction of the dam is a social improvement and for this purpose we need a decision criterion.

A possible criterion is the strong Pareto improvement. To move from one situation to another is a social improvement (in the sense of Pareto) if at least one person is better

---

[6] We assume the individual is the best judge of his or her own interests, hence we ignore problems derived from lack of information, bounded rationality or distorted preferences (see, for example, Adler and Posner, 2001; Sunstein, 2014).

[7] We assume for simplicity here that willingness to pay and willingness to accept coincide. For a technical discussion on why these monetary measures of utility differ, see Chapter 11.

off without making anyone else worse off. There are winners and nobody loses. We have seen that the referendum would result in the rejection of the project. Would it be possible, in these circumstances, to reach a Pareto improvement despite the outcome of the ballot?

Although it seems clear that the project under discussion would not be approved in a referendum, society may gain from the project if, as it happens to be in this case, the benefits ($22) outweigh the costs ($19). Suppose the project is carried out and part of the benefits is used to compensate individuals B, C and E, so that their net benefit is zero, leaving them indifferent. Table 1.1 shows that, after compensation, there is a net benefit of $3 to share out as deemed appropriate. If the project is rejected, this net gain would be lost.

On the other hand, when comparing the benefits and costs of the project, the magnitude of gains and losses counts. Individual C is against the project because it costs her $1, while D is in favour because she obtains benefits of $8. If we ignore the intensity of preferences, like in a referendum, we lose the potential gains arising from the project.

As we have seen, the Pareto improvement criterion requires no losers (i.e., there is full compensation to those initially harmed by the project). This rarely happens in the real world since, in many cases, the situation is similar to that described, but without full compensation to the losers.[8] If a project produces a positive balance of benefits to society as a whole and there are losers who, for some reason, cannot be fully compensated, it is normal practice to undertake such a project (the winners could have compensated the losers and still remain winners).

This criterion, in which the compensation is only hypothetical, is known as the potential compensation criterion, or Kaldor–Hicks criterion.[9] If the losers are compensated, it would result in a Pareto improvement. In practice, unless the project has unacceptable distributional consequences, the economic evaluation basically rests on the criterion of potential compensation just described.

To be more precise, we need to weigh individual (or group) i's monetary gain with the marginal utility of income of individual i, and with the social welfare weight attributed to individual i reflecting the social welfare function. Hence, the marginal social utility of income (see Chapters 2 and 11) attributed to i depends on what social welfare function[10] we assume and the income distribution.

We can multiply the social marginal utility of income by the monetary valuation of the project (willingness to pay or willingness to accept) of individual i and sum over all individuals. So, if the initial welfare distribution is optimal the marginal social

---

[8] As is the usual case with legal expropriation.

[9] This is a simplification of the Kaldor–Hicks hypothetical compensation. Boadway pointed out that a positive sum of compensating variations, for example, is not equivalent to gainers being able to compensate losers. The problem known as the Boadway Paradox is that the act of compensation might affect relative prices and hence utility (see Boadway, 1974; Jones, 2002).

[10] For a utilitarian society, the marginal social utility or welfare weight is unity for all i; for a Rawlsian society, it is equal to zero for all but the worst-off individual or group.

utility of income is the same for everyone.[11] Then a project so small that it leaves the welfare distribution unchanged can be evaluated simply by summing willingness to pay or willingness to accept across individuals/groups. The common justification of the Kaldor–Hicks compensation criterion in practice is based on the argument that redistribution can be performed more efficiently through the fiscal system and that, overall, given the large number of different projects being carried out, the positive and negative distributional effects tend to offset each other, and everybody wins in the long run; or the distributional effects are insignificant, or the costs of identifying winners and losers, and paying compensation, are higher than the benefits.

1.2 STEPS OF COST–BENEFIT ANALYSIS AND OVERVIEW OF THE BOOK

The economic appraisal of investment projects and public policies must be flexible enough to capture the specific characteristics of each case study. However, there are some steps that must be followed independently of the particular aspects of the project under evaluation. These are described below.

1 Objective of the project and examination of the relevant alternatives

Before evaluating the project, its objective – that is, the problem to be solved – must be clearly defined and the relevant alternatives identified. To analyse an isolated project without considering its role within the programme or policy where it belongs can lead to wrong conclusions. Moreover, before working with data and applying the methodology of economic evaluation, it is essential to consider the relevant alternatives that allow the achievement of the same objective. Overlooking some relevant alternatives can lead to important errors.

There are two starting points in the appraisal of projects: first, when the analyst must evaluate a specific project, for example, a price reduction in a public service sustained with public subsidies; second, when the goal of the project is to reduce prices but there are different alternatives. In this case, the subsidization of prices is an option. However, there are also other policies with which to achieve the objective. An alternative could consist of introducing a system of incentives that compensate for efforts in the reduction of costs that allow price cuts. Another policy could be a private concession of the public service.

The consideration of different projects to achieve the same goal is a previous stage to the identification and quantification of benefits and costs in the evaluation, given that the omission of more efficient alternatives is to lose the opportunity to gain better results. It is not enough to have positive social benefits; it is necessary that those

---

[11] The marginal utility of income might vary across individuals since they might have very different utility functions.

benefits are greater than the benefits in the best available alternative. The same happens with investment projects. The question 'Is the investment the best way of solving the problem?' must be answered. Other possible reversible and less costly options should be analysed, such as different management of the facility.

At the stage of searching for relevant alternatives, it is very useful for the economist to interact with and receive feedback from other specialists more familiar with the technology or field related to the project. The objective of this step is to avoid errors because of a lack of precise information about more efficient methods to achieve the same goal. The greater refinement in the evaluation methodology would be useless if better alternatives had not been taken into consideration.

Finally, it is wrong to define projects with too broad a scope because a positive evaluation of the aggregate can conceal separable projects that may have negative expected returns. Therefore, their inclusion, without differentiation, in a programme or a more global project, can lead to the wrong conclusions. To establish the limits of a project is not always easy, but a careful discussion of the project with experts can allow us to distinguish intrinsic complexity and complementarities from the inclusion of independent projects that are perfectly separable.

On the other hand, it is incorrect, to say the least, to evaluate a project so narrowly defined in the sense that its existence is not possible without complementary actions. Suppose that an investment project is composed of two main parts (e.g., a port and an access road) and the social net present value (NPV) is negative. The strategy of promoters could be to evaluate only the first part (the construction of the port) and, once it has been built, to present another project consisting of the complementary infrastructure to connect the port with the road network. In this case, the road project will probably be socially worthy because the investment cost of the already existing port is now irrelevant in the evaluation of the construction of the road, a principle that is not applicable to the lost benefits if the port cannot be operated.

2 Identification of costs and benefits

Once the project is defined, it is necessary to identify the benefits and costs derived from its implementation. In some cases, this step is immediate and should not create great difficulties when the project only has significant direct effects (Chapter 2) and the secondary effects can be overlooked. On the contrary, the identification of the costs and benefits of a project with major effects on secondary markets is more complicated.

The more reasonable approximation, when the analysis is not conducted within a general equilibrium framework, consists of identifying the main secondary markets affected by the project, as would be the case with the evaluation of a new railway line that reduces the demand for an existing airport (Chapter 3).

In financial analysis, the identification is much simpler: benefits are revenues and costs are the payment of inputs valued at market prices. However, in economic analysis, benefits are those that are enjoyed by any individual independently of their conversion into revenues, and costs are net social benefits lost in the next best alternative.

Finally, it is necessary to decide 'who stands' in cost–benefit analysis. Generally, country frontiers delimitate who should be included. Citizenship is the reference point when the project has no global or controversial effects beyond national boundaries. Sometimes it depends on who finances the project. In a co-financed project with supranational funds it would not be acceptable to exclude citizens of countries that contribute with their taxes to financing the project.

3 The counterfactual

In cost–benefit analysis, we must compare two situations: *with* the project and *without* the project. The situation without the project is called the counterfactual, the changing world in the absence of the project. For this task it is important to avoid a comparison of the project with an irrelevant counterfactual. For example, when comparing with the situation *before* the project, the *NPV* can be high because it may hide the fact that without the project that situation does not remain constant. There are maintenance policies or a minimum renewal of equipment, and so on, that could be implemented without the project. Thus, in the evaluation – for example, of the construction of an HSR line – we must compare with a counterfactual where the demand changes and the supply of conventional rail and competing modes of transport also changes.[12]

The situation without the project is also known as the *base case*. We must distinguish between *do nothing* and *do minimum*, the latter consisting of the minimum intervention that is foreseen without the project. The distinction can be made clearer with an example. Consider that the objective is to replace the water pipes that supply water to the city because of excessive water leaks. In this project, the reasonable base case is a *do minimum* because, without the project, there will be maintenance operations and selective actions to avoid greater damage. Now consider that the project consists of a maintenance plan instead of investing in a new pipe network. In this case the base case would be a *do nothing*.

4 Measurement of costs and benefits

Projects' benefits can be measured through individuals' willingness to pay (or willingness to accept). Sometimes a monetary measure of the utility change that is derived from the project can be obtained by observing the behaviour of consumers in the market – that is, from market data. This is the case with the measurement of direct benefits in the primary market affected by the project (Chapter 2), the indirect effects in the secondary markets related to the primary market (Chapter 3) and in the valuation of non-marketed goods when the analyst can find an 'ally' market where some useful information is revealed about the willingness to pay of the individuals (Chapters 7 and 8).

---

[12] The comparison with an irrelevant alternative can be an analyst's error or a strategy for getting the project through.

On other occasions, economists must estimate project benefits by asking the individuals directly about their willingness to pay (stated preferences). This consists of asking individuals about monetary quantities that reflect the change in their well-being thanks to the project. This approximation is used for non-marketed goods like environmental impacts or safety changes (Chapter 8).

In general, projects and public policies that are subject to evaluation imply the use or saving of resources. The costs of a standard investment project can be classified as: construction, maintenance, labour, equipment and energy – costs that are measured from the quantity of the inputs valued by their respective prices. From an economic point of view, the cost of an input is the net social benefit lost in the next best alternative. Market prices will sometimes be a good approximation of the opportunity cost, but in other cases it will be necessary to introduce some adjustment in market prices to approximate the social opportunity cost of the inputs, and this is what is called shadow pricing (Chapter 4).

5 Benefits and costs aggregation

Benefits and costs occur in different periods of time and affect different individuals. The aggregation requires homogeneity, but benefits and costs that occur in successive years or affect individuals with different social conditions are far from being homogeneous. If they are directly added, the implicit weight associated with each benefit or cost is the unity: a unit of net benefit is treated equally disregarding the year or the individual.

Many infrastructure projects have lifetimes of over 30 years. Moreover, in the case of public policies like educational or health programmes, the ex ante lifespan is, in principle, infinite. To discount future benefits and costs is a process of homogenizing to allow comparison. The discounting is performed using a discount rate greater than zero. This implies that the value of the benefits and costs decreases with time. The basic idea consists of the fact that individuals generally place more value on present than future consumption and, therefore, future units of consumption are counted with a lower present value (Chapters 5 and 6).

Project costs and benefits affect individuals' utility. To go from net individual benefits to aggregate social benefits implies redistributive effects. If society gives, for example, more weight to the income of poor people, then the benefits and costs of a project cannot be added without social weighting. The net social benefit of the project should ideally be obtained as the weighted sum of the individual net benefits (Chapters 2 and 11).

6 Interpretation of results and decision criteria

The task of the practitioner of cost–benefit analysis is to obtain a figure that summarizes the flows of benefits and costs. This figure is the *NPV* of the project and helps with the decision to accept/reject or to choose between a set of projects.

To obtain a unique figure is not always easy. There are positive or negative impacts that resist conversion into a monetary figure, as happens to be the case with some environmental impacts. There are situations in which it can be appropriate to make a qualitative description of some effects, and then to attach this information to the *NPV* obtained with the effects that can be unambiguously measured. Another useful approach is to take some related monetary benchmarks to compare the qualitative benefits or costs with those values.

When the flows of benefits and costs of a project are discounted and the *NPV* is positive, the implementation of that project will increase social welfare, particularly when its redistributive effects are positive or insignificant. Nevertheless, a positive *NPV* is not a sufficient condition to approve a project, nor is a higher *NPV* a sufficient condition to choose between two mutually exclusive projects. It may be necessary to homogenize before choosing the project with the higher *NPV*; or in the case when delaying a project is possible it may be necessary to consider the optimal timing (Chapters 5 and 6).

Results should be subject to a risk analysis to determine the sensitivity of the *NPV* to changes in key variables. Ideally, it is preferable to compute a probability distribution of *NPV* instead of obtaining a unique *NPV* figure. Risk analysis allows the decision maker to obtain some information about the likelihood of the possible results. Risk analysis does not eliminate the risk of the project but makes the actual risk of the project to the decision maker more evident (Chapter 9).

7 Economic return and financial feasibility

Cost–benefit analysis deals with the social profitability of projects in contrast with financial analysis, which uses revenues instead of social benefits and private costs instead of social costs. However, it is very important for the analyst to deliver a report that not only includes the economic return of the project but also the financial result or commercial feasibility of the project.

It is perfectly possible for a project or public policy to generate social benefits that exceed social costs and, at the same time, to present a negative financial result. Let us consider, for example, the case of a reforesting policy that reduces land erosion and delivers new space for recreation. Moreover, the responsible public agency obtains some revenues from charging for parking close to the recreation area. It is likely that this project presents a positive social *NPV* and a negative financial result. The analyst must present both results to the decision maker for two main reasons.

First, the real world is characterized by the presence of budget constraints. Therefore, it is really useful for the public agency to have information on the social net benefit of the project as well as on the proportion of costs that are covered by revenues. Second, many projects produce a range of *NPV*s as a function, for example, of the pricing policy applied. It is usual for projects that admit the possibility of charging users to present different possible combinations of social *NPV* and financial *NPV*. For example, a road project can be evaluated as a free-access or as a toll road. If the second option is chosen, several possible price structures exist: it is possible to discriminate by time, vehicle type or use intensity. It is likely that social benefits diminish with the toll. However, collected revenues can contribute to fixed costs. To report the different options available and their social and financial NPV increases the usefulness of cost–benefit analysis.

The economic evaluation of projects and policies requires estimating the effects of the public intervention. To give up present resources in exchange for expected net future benefits requires a rigorous exercise of identification and valuation of these net future benefits. The attempt to predict future changes caused by the project is full of difficulties. The practitioner must compare two different worlds – *with* and *without* the project. Both are hypothetical. Both happen in the future. It is true that we can gather information from previous projects to try to recognize the ranges where the variables are expected to move and reduce the likelihood of making big mistakes, but the nature of the exercise is somehow speculative, particularly in the cases of projects with a long lifetime. One way to deal with this problem is to work with random variables. Instead of using deterministic values for some key variables (e.g., demand), it is better to work with some plausible ranges for those variables and their probabilities of occurrence, as we do in Chapter 9.

1.3 EX POST COST-BENEFIT ANALYSIS

The calculation of the social profitability of the project can be conducted once the project life has been completed, or its life is already long enough to see the actual effects of the intervention. This is called ex post cost–benefit analysis and it is quite useful even for the ex ante exercise as it provides empirical evidence when a similar new project is under evaluation.

The ex post exercise can be done by repeating the ex ante cost–benefit with the observed instead of the predicted values. This ex post assessment is useful for providing information for future evaluation in the case that the project is completed, as well as to introduce corrections in the case of ongoing projects. The ex post evaluation of projects has shown a common pattern in many projects consisting of the underestimation of costs and the overestimation of benefits, resulting in a biased expected social profitability.[13]

The weakness of this ex post cost–benefit analysis is that we are using the same theoretical framework (Graham, 2014) and hence the re-evaluation with the actual data cannot reveal the validity of the underlying model to explain the relevant economic effects of the project. Alternatively, it is possible to make an econometric estimation using observed data and to look for causality to understand the effects of past interventions.

---

[13] This has been called strategic bias and consists of non-random deviations from predicted values that result in an inflated ex ante social profitability with the aim of getting financial support from the corresponding public agency (see, for example, Flyvbjerg, 2014).

Nevertheless, the statistical ex post exercise also has its own difficulties. The first and most challenging task is that we are not so much interested in what happens with the project but in what happens compared with what might have happened without the project – that is, we are interested in the incremental change.[14]

In his famous paper on railways and American growth, Fogel (1962, pp. 165–6) pointed out that the high correlation between new railway construction and economic and population growth was simply that the correlation does not necessarily imply causality:

> The evidence is impressive. But it demonstrates only an association between the growth of the rail network and the growth of the economy. It fails to establish a causal relationship between the railroad and the regional reorganization of trade, the change in the structure of output, the rise in per capita income, or the various other strategic changes that characterized the American economy of the last century. It does not establish even *prima facie* that the railroad was a necessary condition for these developments. Such a conclusion depends not merely on the traditional evidence, but also on implicit assumptions in its interpretation.

According to Fogel, the victory of railways over channels (the existing alternative) only required providing the service at a lower cost to the buyer and this is the only inference we can gather from the data. Only with a marginal price reduction can the deviation of traffic be very large, but this does not mean that the effect on the economy is going to be significant as this depends on the absolute value of the savings in transport costs.

Something similar happens nowadays with the effects of HSR investment. The facts that many lines have diverted most passengers from air transport and that cities with HSR stations are associated with higher employment and economic activity do not demonstrate the social profitability of those lines. Fogel's insight points to the compatibility of massive deviation from the competing modes of transport with negative social benefits. A simple reduction in the ticket price (through subsidies) of enough magnitude to change the balance marginally in favour of the train will change modal split even if the deviation from one mode of transport to the other involves a social loss (de Rus, 2011).

Causal inference requires comparing the situation with and without the project and this requires comparing individuals or geographic areas affected by the project with a control group to unveil causality. Ex post cost–benefit analysis based on statistical

---

[14] 'Is it legitimate for the historian to consider alternative possibilities to events which have happened? ... To say that a thing happened the way it did is not at all illuminating. We can understand the significance of what did happen only if we contrast it with what might have happened'. This is the opening quote by Morris Raphael Cohen, the philosopher, lawyer and jurist, in Fogel (1962, p. 163) on the role of railways in the American economic growth. It is instructive on how the analyst should look at the reality when searching for the social value of public interventions.

causal inference needs to compare cities with HSR (the treatment group) and cities without HSR (the control group). The problem is that in this search the analyst will face selection bias, and we cannot make use of randomized trials with large infrastructure projects and the like. Fortunately, we have a set of econometric tools to deal with the effects of projects where random assignments are not available.[15]

THINGS TO REMEMBER

1. Cost–benefit analysis is a tool to help in the selection of projects that increase social welfare. This is the final goal – the well-being of individuals. As the change in utility cannot be measured, economists use a monetary valuation of that change. This is the role of money in cost–benefit analysis.
2. The economic evaluation of a project is a challenging task. Benefits and costs must be identified and valued, and their aggregation implies the comparison of gains and losses to different individuals and different moments of time.
3. In the assessment of a project, it is necessary to compare the world with and without the project: to envisage an alternative world – the counterfactual. The analyst faces two challenges: to build the counterfactual, an imagined dynamic world that evolves without the perturbation introduced by the project, and to foresee the world with the project, predicting the changes with respect to the counterfactual she has previously created. Transparency and ex post evaluation can help to avoid innocent errors and strategic misrepresentation.
4. The basic criterion with which to decide whether a project is socially desirable is the Kaldor–Hicks compensation criterion. Its logic is simple: the project is socially worthy if the winners could have compensated the losers and still remain winners. The compensation is hypothetical. The potential compensation criterion overlooks equity. A project passing the test could have undesirable distributional consequences.
5. The common justification for the Kaldor–Hicks criterion is based on two ideas: redistribution can be achieved more efficiently through the fiscal system and the large number of different projects implemented by the public sector will end up benefiting everybody in the long run. In any case, the net present value of a project can be supplemented with a list of the likely winners and losers, though the identification of the final ones is not an easy task.
6. Cost–benefit analysis is to the government what financial analysis is to a private firm. While the first compares the social benefits and costs, the second concentrates on revenue and cost of the firm, disregarding any effect on other agents. Nevertheless, the analyst should in general report both the economic and financial result of the project as budget constraints are normally present.

---

[15] See Angrist and Pischke (2015) and Athey and Imbens (2017) for the econometric tools with which to estimate from observational data the effects of projects and policies on outcomes.

7.   Both ex ante and ex post cost–benefit analyses have a role to play in public policy. The estimation of the net social benefit of the government intervention is a key input in the selection of projects and policies. The ex post analysis is also useful to gather information of the actual effects of projects and to improve the ex ante evaluation.

2

The economic evaluation of social benefits

We like the cost–benefit criterion first because we think its application makes almost everybody better off over the long haul, and second because it is easy to apply. In other words, the benefits are high and the costs are low. The reasoning may be slightly circular, but the cost–benefit criterion recommends itself highly.

(Steven E. Landsburg, 1993, p. 105)

2.1 INTRODUCTION

The measurement of changes in social welfare and the decision criteria for the economic assessment of projects can be approached by modelling the economy as a set of individuals who, given their preferences, try to maximize their utility, subject to two constraints: the available resources and the technology. A project changes the equilibrium in the markets in which individuals participate as consumers, owners of production factors, taxpayers, or affected by externalities, and cost–benefit analysis tries to measure the change in their well-being to assess whether the project represents an improvement for an aggregate called society.

Given the scarcity of resources, people are typically forced to choose between different uses, and the available technology limits the quantity, variety and quality of goods produced from those resources. In a society where what matters is the welfare of its individuals, the focus is not on increasing production but the well-being of individuals. In this sense, preferences limit the utility that they can obtain for a given endowment of resources and technology, which is particularly relevant in the decisions that the public sector take outside the discipline of the market.

In addition to the decisions of the individuals, the government also intervenes with projects that alter the equilibrium of some markets and affect social welfare. Its decisions affect the quantity, quality and composition of goods and services and their distribution. This chapter presents some economic concepts to build a basic framework for practical cost–benefit analysis.[1]

The basic model is described in Section 2.2, where we simplify society into several groups: consumer, taxpayers, the owners of production factors and the individuals

---

[1] For a formal treatment see Chapter 11.

affected by the externalities, named here as the 'rest of society', to account for the external effects of the project. Consumer surplus and producer surplus, key concepts in cost–benefit analysis, are explained in Section 2.3, where the crucial distinction between price, cost and value is addressed.

To decide whether a project should be approved, we must compare its social benefits with its social costs, previously identified and measured. We need, first, to quantify in monetary terms the changes in individuals' utility with respect to the counterfactual – that is, the world without the project; second, to use some criteria for the aggregation of the benefits and costs affecting different individuals and at different points in time; and, finally, to use some decision criteria to accept/reject, postpone, or select from among a set of them.

In this chapter we focus attention mainly on the benefits, although we refer to the costs when it helps the argument (the detailed treatment of costs is in Chapter 4). One of the main points in this chapter is the distinction between two alternative procedures for assessing the net benefits in Section 2.4: the sum of the changes in surpluses of individuals and the sum of the changes in the willingness to pay and in real resources, ignoring transfers. This distinction turns out to be quite useful in cost–benefit analysis, and carefully following one approach or the other can help to avoid common mistakes in the evaluation of projects.

Efficiency is not the only reference in society, and who wins and who loses with a project is very important for public decision making. Section 2.5 discusses the conversion of income into individual utility and of individual utility into social welfare.

The evaluation procedures contained in this chapter apply to projects that are 'small'.[2] This requirement is necessary to simplify – to focus on the project's impact mainly on the primary market and on the most directly affected secondary markets. The construction of a residual water treatment plant is a project whose effects on inflation and government deficit are not generally expected to be significant. 'Large' projects that affect the macroeconomic variables should be analysed, where possible, with general equilibrium models.

When not specified, we will deal with market demand functions. Although the ideal would be to work with compensated demands, the results obtained using the observed quantities in the market are somewhat acceptable in many cases (see Chapter 11). In this book we assume that the conditions required for using market demands for the monetary measurements of utility changes are satisfied.

---

[2] One definition of a small project is that it is virtually infinitesimally small. One can then draw on the envelope theorem implying that secondary effects 'net out'. For example, if we change an output price (*ceteris paribus*) we obtain the supply function (from the profit function) minus the demand function, both multiplied by the marginal utility of income if we have a single-individual (or Robinson Crusoe) economy. Other supplies and demands are affected by the price change but these effects net out. At least, this is so in the absence of tax wedges. Alternatively, one might consider a perturbation as a linear approximation. The project is so small that higher-order effects can be ignored. This produces the same general equilibrium cost–benefit rule.

2.2 THE BASIC FRAMEWORK

A simplified economy

A project can be contemplated as a perturbation in the economy that affects the well-being of individuals. The project's impact occurs in the primary market (the directly affected market), and also in the so-called secondary markets, which are related to the primary because their products are complements or substitutes (see Chapter 3). Furthermore, the effects generally last for a long period of time, as in the case of civil engineering projects, environmental impacts and policies that modify market structure.

What the construction of a water irrigation project or transport infrastructure, investment in education and the improvement of air quality have in common is an effect on the welfare of individuals. Some individuals are better off and others worse off; they are all located somewhere and where they are located is relevant to the decision whether to include their change in welfare or to ignore it. This is the question of standing – the issue of who counts in cost–benefit analysis. Usually, the nation establishes the boundaries to who counts but sometimes it is the type of project, as in the case of the preservation of worldwide endangered species. On other occasions co-financing by supranational organizations determines the countries that should be included. Although common sense may help in many cases, the difficulties of standing could be significant in some projects with global externalities.

To make the problem manageable, we will simplify as much as we can and work with a very simple model of the economy, as described below.[3] In our simplified economy, in which we are going to evaluate projects, there are three owners of production factors: first, the 'owners of capital' (O), generally called producers, who have a variety of equipment, infrastructure and facilities where goods and services are produced; second, the 'owners of labour' (L), including employees of different skills and productivity levels, but in our basic model they all belong to the only existing group of owners of labour or 'workers'; and, finally, the landowners (R).

The factor of production 'land' is defined in a wide sense, including not only the soil for agriculture or the land for residential or productive uses, but also natural and environmental resources such as climate, water, air, flora and fauna and landscapes, which may be affected by projects. We must distinguish between the land under private ownership and the natural resources that are common property. We differentiate the 'landowners' (R) from the common property of natural and environmental resources (also called 'natural capital'), which when affected by externalities we will include in the 'rest of society' group (E).

---

[3] Sometimes individuals might be altruists in the sense that they care about damage caused by their activities on human beings or other species, or on the environment in other countries. For example, suppose country A replaces hydropower electricity with country B's electricity produced by coal-fired plants. A's citizens might – but need not necessarily – include the negative environmental impact in their utility functions (see Chapters 7 and 8). For a discussion of who 'stands' in cost–benefit analysis, see Johansson and de Rus (2019) and Zerbe (2018).

The combination of production factors creates a flow of goods and services. The income paid to those factors of production allows us to include additional agents: 'consumers' (C) and 'taxpayers' (G), so that society is composed of six groups of individuals. Obviously, one can be a member of more than one. Moreover, our simplified society has another feature: the value of a unit of benefit (or cost) is the same regardless of to whom it may accrue (this assumption will be relaxed in Section 2.5).

In this unsophisticated world, the social surplus (SS) is the sum of individual surplus:

$$SS = CS + OS + LS + RS + GS + ES, \tag{2.1}$$

where consumer surplus (CS) is the difference between what consumers are willing to pay for the goods and what they pay. The surplus of the owners of capital (OS) is equal to firm revenues minus variable costs. The surpluses of workers (LS) and landowners (RS) are equal to the wage and land income, respectively, less the minimum payment they are willing to accept for the use of the factor – that is, its private opportunity cost. Interestingly, payment for land, like any other fixed factor, is usually what individuals are willing to pay for the activity that requires the use of that fixed factor in competitive markets.

Taxpayer surplus (GS) equals tax revenues less public expenditure. Finally, the surplus of the 'rest of society' (ES) includes the value for the individuals of non-marketed goods such as the effects of the project on landscape, clean air, climate, or even safety levels, which may change when a project is carried out net of compensation payments – for example, the negative externality of a power plant that contributes to global warming, or the positive externality of an investment in alternative energy sources that reduces it, net of any compensation.

The government's decision to invest in a project aimed at changing prices, costs or quality, affects the surplus of the social groups over the years for which the project continues producing its positive and negative effects, so that the total impact of the project can be expressed as the aggregate of changes in the surpluses of the individuals:

$$\Delta SS = \sum_{t=0}^{T} \delta^t (\Delta CS_t + \Delta OS_t + \Delta LS_t + \Delta RS_t + \Delta GS_t + \Delta ES_t), \tag{2.2}$$

where Δ denotes an increase or decrease in the surplus of the various agents and δ^t is the discount factor that allows us to express in present value the flow of benefits and costs over the lifespan of the project. This is a key issue in cost–benefit analysis because individuals usually prefer one unit of consumption today than in the future. For example, if individuals are indifferent between \$95 in the present (year zero) and \$100 within a year (without inflation), the discount factor that converts the benefit in year one into units comparable to the benefits in year zero is equal to 0.95 (see Chapters 5 and 6).

The existence of a fixed factor such as land, though it does not change the value of the final result of equation (2.2), may completely modify the distribution of the social surplus. It is well known that land can capitalize on most of the benefits of transport improvements. In the case of an infinitely elastic supply of homogeneous workers, the surplus of each group, landowners excepted, would be zero in expression (2.2), as landowners would take the total surplus through higher land prices. This is a warning to avoid double counting or benefits and also the deceptive prediction of who gets the net surplus.

In the case of urban surplus generated by transport projects increasing proximity to the city centre, Collier and Venables (2018) have shown that with heterogeneity, both in labour productivity and demand for housing, workers can get a significant part of the surplus. The implication for the economic evaluation of transport improvements is that, although the project increases the land values around the locations affected by the improvement, only in some extreme case would the increase in land values reflect the total benefits of the projects because a share of those benefits are captured by workers.

Therefore, when the assumption of an infinitely elastic supply of homogeneous workers does not hold, the benefits of projects improving accessibility cannot be measured by exclusively looking at the changes in land prices in competitive land markets. The capitalization of the benefits of the project in land prices is incomplete and would underestimate the social surplus of the project.

The case of a regulated public service operated by a private concessionaire, as shown in Figure 2.1, can help to illustrate the change in social surplus. The service's (e.g., a sports facility) annual costs have a fixed component (K) – that is, independent of the volume of service – and variable costs (wL), where L is the quantity of labour and w the wage. Under these assumptions, the average variable cost (c) shown in Figure 2.1 is equal to wL/x, where x is the number of users. For simplicity, we assume a single period.

Demand D has a negative slope, indicating that if the price p goes down (up), the number of users x increases (decreases). The superscript indexes 0 and 1 represent the situation without and with the project, respectively.

The government plans to reduce the regulated price from p^0 to p^1. Let us look at the expected change in social surplus once this reduction is implemented. Without the project, the initial price is p^0 and the demand equals x^0. The total revenue is represented

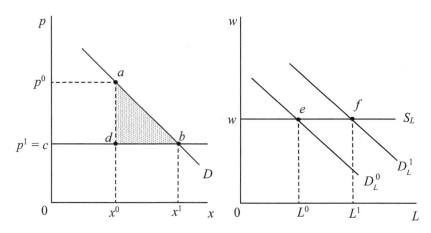

Figure 2.1 Price reduction in a public service

by the area p^0ax^00 and the total cost by cdx^00 plus the fixed cost K. Therefore, the net profits of the firm providing the public service are represented by p^0adc minus K.

Consider the change in social surplus with the project. The increase in consumer surplus is equal to p^0abc and the reduction in producer surplus is represented by p^0adc. The change in social surplus is therefore equal to abd.[4] If the government compensates the producer for the loss of surplus with the project, the change in social surplus (abd) remains constant because the change in producer surplus is equal to zero, and the change in taxpayer surplus (ΔGS) is negative and equal to the amount of the compensation (p^0adc). The change in consumer surplus is unaffected. Therefore, the change in social surplus is still represented by the area abd once the change in taxpayer surplus is included. Income transfers do not change the results if the additional taxes required for the income transfer can be made without additional costs (e.g., the distortionary effects of taxation).

What about worker surplus? Looking at what happens in Figure 2.1 (right), the increase in production causes a shift in labour demand from D_L^0 to D_L^1, generating an increase in the number of employees ($L^1 - L^0$). Should we count the earnings of the additional workers as an increase in the social surplus? If the answer is yes, we would have to add efL^1L^0 to the area abd in Figure 2.1 (left). However, the answer is no, because while these additional workers receive a wage that they did not receive previously, they now lose the net value of what they were doing before they were employed – their opportunity cost that in the conditions represented by the labour supply S_L is exactly equal to the wages being paid (efL^1L^0). In the described circumstances, workers are indifferent between working and not working at wage w, and therefore the change in their surplus (ΔLS) is zero.[5]

2.3 PRIVATE AND SOCIAL BENEFITS

Price, cost and value

It is worth exploring further the concept of willingness to pay and costs used in Section 2.2, in relation to the calculus of the surplus of each group and with the demand and costs functions in Figure 2.1.

When a private company operating in a competitive market assesses whether a particular activity is profitable it compares the revenues and costs attributable to such

---

[4] An individual can belong to any group in expression (2.1). We assume that the individual is able to distinguish, when asked about his willingness to pay for a project that affects the price of a product (and company profits), the effect on his surplus as, for example, a consumer and a producer, so by adding the change in the consumer surplus and the producer surplus we do not incur double counting. For the effect of this bias on stated preferences, see Johansson (1993).

[5] Worker surplus increases when the wage is higher than the private opportunity cost for the new workers (see Chapter 4).

an activity (financial analysis). It can be argued that, in general, the value per unit of product for the firm matches the net price of the product sold, and the unit cost is equal to the internal cost to the firm in terms of the use of materials, labour and other inputs. However, price is not necessarily equal to value, private value does not necessarily coincide with social value, and private cost is not necessarily equal to social cost.

An open-access natural park has a cost of maintenance and management and, although nothing is charged for its enjoyment, its use has value for the individuals who visit the park.[6] The distinction between price, value and cost, and between private and social in the last two concepts, facilitates the task of valuing goods in order to evaluate projects.

Although the maximum that an individual is willing to pay for a good that can be purchased in the market reflects the economic value, expressed in monetary terms, of the good for the individual, the maximum willingness to pay does not necessarily coincide with what is actually paid: the user of a sports centre may be willing to pay an amount of money higher than the existing fee for the use of the facilities. The user of a healthcare service with free access may be willing to pay a certain amount of money for the use of this service, were the access conditional on the payment of a fee.

The private value of the good to an individual coincides with the social value of the good unless there are external costs or benefits. Continuing with the example of the health service, a vaccination campaign is beneficial not only to the users of the service but also to society as a whole, given the reduction in the spread of the disease. This is what is called a positive externality.

We must also distinguish between total and marginal value. The first concept refers to what an individual would be willing to pay for the consumption of all units, while the second refers to the value of the last unit consumed. The case of water illustrates the difference between the two concepts: the total value is very high for any individual, while the marginal value of the last unit consumed is usually very low, at least in societies without scarcity problems. In a first approximation, the total value for society is obtained by adding the willingness to pay of the individuals (for distributional issues, see Section 2.5).

The price of a good is what is charged in the market for its consumption. If there is no price discrimination, the price does not coincide with the valuation of the individuals of any unit of the good consumed but the last one, whose marginal value does coincide with the price because, with decreasing demand curves, individuals are willing to pay more than the market price for each of the previous units. The fact that the market price equals only the marginal value of the last unit exchanged in the market points to the inaccuracy of using revenues as social benefits. When a single price is charged, the total value or social benefit of the good is therefore higher than total revenues.

---

[6] The total value of environmental goods includes the value of that use, and also the non-use or passive use value. Passive use value reflects what individuals are willing to pay for the good being available now or in the future, or simply for the mere fact of its existence. The economic interpretation of these concepts and their measurement is discussed in Chapters 7 and 8.

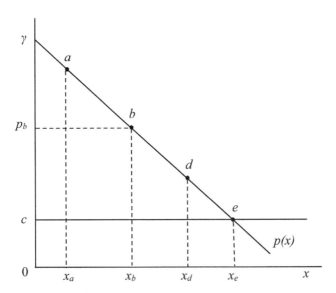

Figure 2.2 Value, price and cost

The cost of a good is the benefit lost in the next best alternative – that is, the net value of other goods that one must give up to obtain the good (the opportunity cost). In competitive markets, not distorted by subsidies or taxes, for example, the price of the production factors used in producing the good is the opportunity cost of that good. The distinction between private cost and social cost is also necessary in cases where the production requires not only inputs traded in the market, but also non-marketed goods (e.g., environmental resources), or when it generates positive or negative externalities that the firm does not internalize – that is, fall on the 'rest of society'.

The difference between these concepts can be illustrated by the following example. A water supply firm serves a city, incurring a total cost that has two components: a fixed cost for the entire system of production and distribution (K) and a constant variable cost per unit of water produced and distributed (c). Figure 2.2 shows the water demand of the company[7] and how at price p_b consumers demand quantity x_b. It also shows how each unit of water has a different valuation.

The first units of water are possibly used to meet basic needs, so that their valuation is very high. The maximum reservation price (γ), at which the company would not sell any water, might be the price of an alternative supply system – for example, a price somewhat higher than delivering water in a road tanker. As water consumption increases, the value of each additional unit decreases, indicating that the following units of water are intended to cover less valuable needs.

Every unit of water to the left of x_b is valued above the price p_b, hence the user valuation of a unit of water only matches the price in the case of the last unit of the quantity x_b. As the variable cost of supplying one unit of water is equal to c, the

---

[7] We assume that the market demand for water coincides with the compensated demand (see Chapter 11).

difference between revenue, social benefits and private costs is evident. The value of use of the water consumed, equal to the sum of the values of each unit, is represented by the distance between the horizontal axis and the demand ($\gamma + \ldots + a + \ldots + b + \ldots + e + \ldots$). With a price equal to p_b, the sum of all the unit values equals the area between 0 and x_b below the market demand $p = p(x)$ – that is, the area $\gamma b x_b 0$. The revenue ($p_b b x_b 0$) is part of the total value, and the private cost is equal to $K + c x_b$.

To calculate the social benefit of a policy that changes the consumption of water, it is generally incorrect to use revenues as social benefits since we have seen that revenues are only part of them. Observe that, to the right of x_b in Figure 2.2, there are consumers whose marginal valuations are above the cost (for example, at point d). When the price is equal to marginal cost, the marginal value coincides with the average variable cost and the price, given that the marginal cost is constant in Figure 2.2, but fixed costs are not covered. Beyond point e, individuals value the units of the good below their marginal cost. Producing at the right of x_e is inefficient since the value of the good is below its opportunity cost.

Consumer surplus and producer surplus in a competitive market

Figure 2.3 shows a competitive market in equilibrium. Firms in the market are price takers and there are no barriers to entry or exit. The market demand $x_d = x(p_d)$ is the horizontal sum of individual demands and collects information on the amounts that consumers are willing to buy at different prices. The inverse of this function, $p_d = p(x_d)$, represents what consumers are willing to pay for different units of the good. This function approximately reflects the subjective valuations of the good and, in the absence of externalities, other distortions and problems of equity, the social benefit of exchanging different quantities of that good.[8]

In Figure 2.3, consumers are willing to pay for the quantity x_m the area $\gamma_d x_m 0$. If the price is p_0, the maximum they are willing to pay is represented by the area $\gamma_d b x_0 0$. It can be seen that the price chosen determines the total value of the good for the individuals. In the case of Figure 2.3, consumers pay p_0, consume x_0, and the total value of the good to them is $\gamma_d b x_0 0$. Since they pay $p_0 b x_0 0$, they obtain a surplus $\gamma_d b p_0$. This is the concept of consumer surplus (CS), which is equal to the difference between what individuals are willing to pay (WTP) and what they actually pay (revenue represented by the price multiplied by the quantity). For the quantity x_0 and the corresponding price $p_0(x_0)$:

$$CS(x_0) = WTP(x_0) - p_0 x_0. \tag{2.3}$$

The supply curve $x_s = x(p_s)$ represents what producers are willing to offer at different prices. It is given by the horizonal summation of supply curves of the individual firms in the market. The inverse of this function $p_s = p(x_s)$ represents the marginal cost of production. Between 0 and x_0, the total cost of production (for simplicity we assume

---

[8] Assuming the income effect is very small.

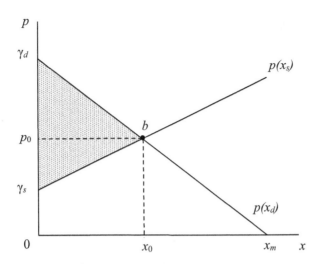

Figure 2.3 Social surplus in a competitive market

that all costs are variable) is represented by the area under the supply function between 0 and x_0. This area ($\gamma_s bx_0 0$) represents the opportunity cost of producing the quantity x_0. Producers sell x_0 at a price p_0, resulting in producer surplus equal to the area $p_0 bx_0 0 - \gamma_s bx_0 0$. The producer surplus (*PS*), which corresponds to x_0, is equal to the area $p_0 b\gamma_s$ and it can be expressed as:

$$PS(x_0) = p_0 x_0 - C_0, \tag{2.4}$$

where C_0 is the variable cost of producing x_0.

If the industry is in long-term equilibrium, profits tend to zero and the surplus of the producer that appears on the figure could be the compensation for some factor that remains fixed in the long term – for example, land. Producers have zero profits, since firms would bid for the fixed factor. The price of land would rise to absorb the producer surplus. Therefore, to obtain the social surplus, we would have to add the surplus of the owners of the fixed factors. Both procedures lead to the same result as long as the surplus is not counted twice.

In perfect competitive markets, the social surplus in equation (2.1) can be expressed as the sum of the surpluses of consumers and producers, or, alternatively, as the willingness to pay net of resource costs:

$$SS(x_0) = CS(x_0) + PS(x_0) = WTP(x_0) - C_0, \tag{2.5}$$

where the term $p_0 x_0$ in equations (2.3) and (2.4) nets out since it is an expenditure for consumers and a revenue for producers (i.e., income transfer).

Expression (2.5) is represented in Figure 2.4, showing the net social surplus that is generated in the market represented by the shaded area in Figure 2.3. In the absence of

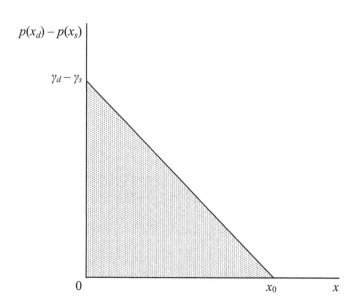

Figure 2.4 Social surplus

distortions, the area represented in Figure 2.4 is the maximum surplus that society can gain from this market given the preferences of consumers and the level of income and technology. Therefore, any distortion, such as the introduction of a tax or the presence of market power, reduces the maximum surplus. This reduction is the social cost of the distortion.[9]

Although Figure 2.4 looks like a demand function, it represents the net social value all the units consumed. Note that the difference between what consumers are willing to pay per unit and the opportunity cost of these units is what Figure 2.4 represents. The relationship with Figure 2.3 is the following: the first unit exchanged in Figure 2.3 provides a social surplus equal to the difference $\gamma d - \gamma s$. In Figure 2.4 this difference is the intercept. When supply equals demand, x_0 in Figure 2.3, society obtains no further benefits of the last unit, as the net social benefit of this last unit is zero, as shown in Figure 2.4. If we go beyond x_0 then the (marginal) surplus becomes negative. That is why x_0 is optimal. In Chapter 3 we use this argument to justify not accounting for the indirect effects of the projects when these effects involve only marginal changes in competitive markets.

The previous analysis is also useful for seeing the two main effects of the introduction of a tax: income transfer and efficiency loss. Assuming that the administrative costs of tax collection are zero, the introduction of a specific tax (τ) in the previous competitive market can be seen in Figure 2.5, which shows the cost in terms of the surplus lost (bx_0x_1) that society incurs to raise tax revenue ($\tau bx_1 0$). This illustrates what is called the

---

[9] Plus the additional costs of the chosen mechanism – for example, in the case of the tax, the time lost in making the statements, the payment to staff dedicated to tax collection, fraud prosecution, and so on.

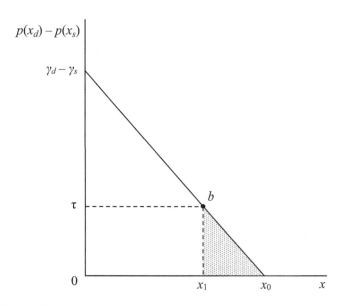

Figure 2.5 The social cost of a tax

deadweight loss of a tax and why project investment costs financed by taxes are sometimes multiplied by some conversion factors to reflect their opportunity costs (in Figure
2.5 investment costs represented by a tax revenue equal to $\tau b x_1 0$ have an additional
social cost of $b x_0 x_1$).

We now assume that the tax is zero and analyse the social cost of negative externalities with the help of Figure 2.6. The consumption and production of goods not only
generate benefits and costs for the individuals who consume or produce them; the supply
of a good can also produce positive or negative externalities on other individuals and
firms (e.g., the producer that pollutes a river reduces the welfare of fishers and walkers).

In this case, the sum of the changes in consumer surplus and producer surplus over-
states the social surplus. We must add the change in the surplus of the 'rest of society'
represented by ΔES in expression (2.2) to take into account the loss of welfare for individuals affected by the negative externalities associated with the production of the good.

To represent the impact of a negative external effect that we assume to be constant
per unit and equal to φ on the social surplus in Figure 2.6, we only need to add the
externality to the private unit cost. Given that the equilibrium quantity does not change
(firms do not internalize the externality), the effect on the surplus can be represented by
shifting the curve of the surplus in the amount of the externality.

The externality φ has the effect of reducing the social surplus in the area dx_0be. Note
that by subtracting the loss to the initial area dx_00, the resulting surplus is equal to the
difference in areas $(ex_10) - (x_1x_0b)$. From x_1 to x_0, the production of the good or service
in this market has a negative impact on welfare because what consumers are willing to
pay is below the social opportunity cost. Then, why is it produced? Because producers
do not internalize the cost of the external effect, making their market decisions with a

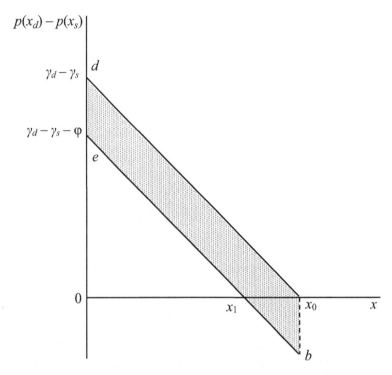

Figure 2.6 Loss of social surplus because of an externality

cost function that does not reflect the social opportunity cost (this is what is called a market failure).

2.4 ALTERNATIVE APPROACHES FOR THE MEASUREMENT OF SOCIAL BENEFITS

Real and monetary values

Cost–benefit analysis aims to compare the flow of benefits and costs over the lifetime of a project. The relevant concepts are the social benefits derived from the increase in individuals' utility and the opportunity cost of the resources.

The flow of benefits and costs can be presented in current or constant terms. The result of the evaluation will not change because the variables are expressed in real or monetary terms. In general, the flow of benefits and costs is usually expressed in constant units of the base year – that is, in real terms, ignoring inflation. We are not concerned with the evolution of nominal values, but with the use of resources and the flow of real benefits associated with the project.

However, the analyst might work with data expressed in current units. Sometimes the variables are expressed in these units (reflecting real changes and inflation), as happens to be the case in infrastructure projects where users pay for the use and the private sector is involved as a manager or concessionaire.

Whatever the reason for the flows being expressed in real or nominal terms, the only recommendation is to be consistent. If the data are expressed in current units of each year, we must use a nominal interest rate. If the data are expressed in monetary units of the base year, the real discount rate is the right one.

It may happen that the prices of some items evolve over or below general inflation. In this case we must account for the difference. For example, suppose that the expected annual inflation over the 20 years of project life is 2 per cent, and the expected changes in the price of a raw material used in significant quantities for the project amount to 5 per cent, reflecting inflation and opportunity cost. By expressing the variables in monetary units of the base year, we only correct the element of general inflation (2 per cent), hence allowing the price of the raw material to grow to reflect the change in the real value of the resources. Although this approach is the right one, for projects lasting more than 20 years, figuring out the evolution of prices for each element of costs and benefits is not always possible.

The relationship between the real and nominal net present value (NPV) is:

$$\sum_{t=0}^{T} \frac{B_t - C_t}{(1+i)^t} = \sum_{t=0}^{T} \frac{(B_t - C_t)(1+\psi)^t}{(1+i_n)^t},$$ (2.6)

where:

B_t, C_t: annual benefits and costs in real terms;
ψ: inflation rate;
i: real discount rate;
i_n: nominal discount rate.

From equation (2.6):

$$\frac{1}{1+i} = \frac{1+\psi}{1+i_n}.$$ (2.7)

Solving for i we obtain the formula to calculate the real discount rate:

$$i = \frac{i_n - \psi}{1+\psi}.$$ (2.8)

Expression (2.8) is often approximated as $i_n - \psi$. For a nominal rate of 6 per cent and inflation of 3 per cent, the real rate is 2.9 per cent according to equation (2.8) instead of 3 per cent, which is obtained directly by subtracting inflation from the nominal rate. We assume for simplicity that i and ψ are constant over time.

Sum of change in surpluses or change in willingness to pay and resources

Let us assume we have decided to measure the flow of benefits and costs in constant terms. There is still another choice between two alternative approaches. The first is the sum of changes in the surpluses of the different social agents. The second is to calculate the changes in willingness to pay and in the resources, ignoring income transfers. Both methods, properly used, lead to the same result. One of the most common errors in cost–benefit analysis is the double counting of benefits, and one of the best remedies to prevent it is to be systematic once one of the two methods described above has been chosen.

In Figure 2.1, the evaluation of a policy consisting of the price reduction of a public service was conducted through the changes in the surpluses of producers, consumers and workers. Let us now follow the alternative approach, adding in the willingness to pay and the change in resources. To the left of x^0 nothing happens. The change in willingness to pay is the result of the increase in demand quantity from x^0 to x^1. The change in willingness to pay in this market coming from the additional units sold is represented by the area abx^1x^0. To gain this additional willingness to pay, the quantity of labour $L^1 - L^0$ is required and the opportunity cost of these workers is represented by the area efL^1L^0 (the value of leisure). This area is equal to area dbx^1x^0 and, hence, the net social benefit is equal to area abd.

The experience in the economic evaluation of projects shows how important it is not to mix the two approaches. The following case illustrates another example of this key issue in the application of the evaluation methodology. Consider the case of a competitive market, as depicted in Figure 2.7, in a country with full employment. The demand curve shows the annual quantities demanded at each price, and the supply curve represents the annual quantities offered at each price. There are no other effects on the economy beyond those reflected in the market represented in the figure. Without the project, the exchanged quantity is equal to x^0, where the superscript zero denotes 'without project' and the price is equal to p^0. Note that with this price the quantity offered is equal to the quantity demanded, the market is in equilibrium, and the consumer surplus (area $\gamma_d bp^0$) and the producer surplus (area $p^0 b\gamma_s$) generate the maximum social surplus.

What kind of project could improve society in the described circumstances? In Figure 2.7, without the project $p^0 = c^0$. Suppose now that if the government spends public money (I) on a new technology, the marginal cost of production is reduced from c^0 to c^1 regardless of the quantity produced. If the government invests I at zero cost to firms, it is then possible to produce in two ways: either with the costs represented by the original supply curve (S_N) or with the new supply curve (S_I). Assume that the two technologies are compatible. It can be seen that it is cheaper to produce with the new technology only from x_N^1.

To determine whether the project's benefits (B) outweigh its costs (C), we must compare the government investment (I) at the beginning of year one with the social benefits over the lifetime of the project (T), assuming a discount rate equal to i and that B and C are situated at the end of the year, and at discount rate i, if the condition (2.9) holds, the project is socially profitable:

$$\sum_{t=1}^{T} \frac{B_t - C_t}{(1+i)^t} > I. \tag{2.9}$$

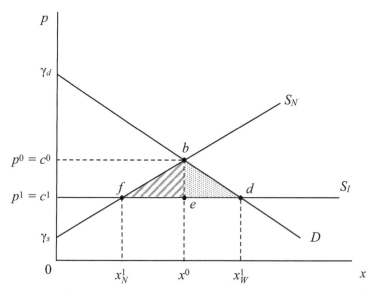

Figure 2.7 The effects of a project

The introduction of the new technology reduces the market price to p^1, as Figure 2.7 shows, which is the new marginal cost of production, and the annual quantity increases to x^1_W, as all the consumers who are willing to pay the opportunity cost c^1 find someone who sells. It is interesting to note that the new quantity exchanged (x^1_W) is not all from the new technology, as it is still more efficient to produce the quantity (x^1_N) with the previous technology.

Consider the change in the surpluses of different agents. Consumer surplus changes from the situation without the project (area $\gamma_d b p^0$) to the situation with the project (area $\gamma_d d p^1$), so the increase in consumer surplus is equal to the area $p^0 b d p^1$. Producer surplus without the project equals area $p^0 b \gamma_s$, and with the project $p^1 f \gamma_s$, so there is a reduction equal to $p^0 b f p^1$. Adding the change in the surplus of producers and consumers, we have a net gain equal to the area bdf.

The change in consumer surplus can be expressed as:

$$\left(p^0 - p^1\right) x^0 + \frac{1}{2}\left(p^0 - p^1\right)\left(x^1_W - x^0\right).\tag{2.10}$$

Equation (2.10) shows the two components of the consumer surplus. The first term represents the surplus thanks to the reduction of the price affecting the initial quantity (x^0). The second term (the additional quantity demanded when the price decreases) is multiplied by ½, because the surplus of the first unit is the difference between the initial and the final price, and the surplus of the last unit is zero (the willingness to pay equals the price).

Operating in equation (2.10) we obtain what is known in practical cost–benefit analysis as the 'rule of a half':[10]

$$\frac{1}{2}\left(p^0 - p^1\right)\left(x^0 + x_W^1\right).$$ (2.11)

The change in the producer surplus is:

$$p^1 x_W^1 - p^0 x^0 - C^1 + C^0,$$ (2.12)

where C^0 is the cost without the project and C^1 the cost with the project.

Adding expressions (2.11) and (2.12) we obtain the change in consumer and producer surplus:

$$\frac{1}{2}\left(p^0 - p^1\right)\left(x_W^1 - x_N^1\right).$$ (2.13)

Let us examine in more detail the origin of this benefit. Recall that the price fall has increased the surplus of consumers in the area $p^0 bdp^1$. However, part $(p^0 bfp^1)$ of that gain is a transfer from producers to consumers that leaves the social surplus unaffected. This does not happen with the benefit represented by area bdf, which does not exist without the project. This benefit has two sources. The first is by increasing the quantity produced $(x_W^1 - x^0)$, which does not increase the surplus of the producers because it is priced at a marginal cost, but it increases the surplus of the consumers (bde), who are willing to pay $bdx_W^1 x^0$ but only pay $edx_W^1 x^0$.

The second source of project benefits is the cost savings of producing the quantity $x^0 - x_N^1$ that was previously produced at cost $fbx^0 x_N^1$ and now is produced at cost $fex^0 x_N^1$. The cost savings go entirely to the consumers since we are in a competitive market. To the change in the present value of consumer and producer surpluses, during the lifespan of the project, we must add the change in taxpayer surplus $(-I)$.

Alternatively, the second approach is based on the changes in the willingness to pay and resources, ignoring transfers. The increase in willingness to pay (area $bdx_W^1 x^0$) comes from the additional units sold in the market, and the change in resources equals the incremental cost of the new production (area $edx_W^1 x^0$) and the savings of producing $x^0 - x_N^1$ with the new technology (area fbe). The annual gross benefit is represented by area bdf. Once we have summed the discounted annual benefits during the lifetime of the project, we must subtract the investment costs $(-I)$.

Assuming that the annual net social benefit (denoted $\overline{B}$) is constant over time and equal to area bdf in Figure 2.7 and that T goes to infinity,[11] then the NPV is:

$$NPV = \sum_{t=1}^{T} \frac{B_t - C_t}{\left(1+i\right)^t} - I = \frac{\overline{B}}{i} - I.$$ (2.14)

---

[10] The rule of a half assumes that all other prices remain unchanged, otherwise the demand curve (as well as the supply curve) might shift. Moreover, it assumes a linear demand curve.

[11] For a constant benefit B to perpetuity, the discounted present value is equal to B/i (see Chapter 5).

When $\dfrac{\overline{B}}{i} > I$, the NPV is positive and the project is socially desirable. The case represented in Figure 2.7 can equally be applied to a public policy. Suppose, for example, that the market in Figure 2.7 corresponds to an economy without international trade, initially in equilibrium with price p^0 and production (completely national) equal to x^0. The evaluated public policy consists of opening the economy and allowing imports at a lower price (p^1). Since imports are allowed, demand increases for the same reason as in the case of the investment project in new technology discussed earlier. The only difference between the two cases is that the NPV is greater now than in the case of the introduction of a new technology. The net social benefit of opening the economy to external trade is equal to $\dfrac{\overline{B}}{i}$. We can produce more cheaply and allocate resources (initially used to produce $x^0 - x_N^1$) to more productive activities. From x_N^1 it is cheaper to import than to produce in the country. If the opportunity cost of the resources is represented by S_N, this policy is like the introduction of a new costless technology that allows an increase in welfare.

The treatment of taxes

We can apply the two alternative approaches described above in the presence of taxes. With the sum of surpluses, taxpayer surplus should now be included. Through the change in willingness to pay and in real resources, we must ignore transfers and include the willingness to pay that corresponds to the additional units sold independently of the fact that this 'new' willingness to pay is partly transferred to taxpayers through the tax.[12]

Let us see how the presence of taxes affects the change in surpluses by introducing a specific tax on production in a market with price (p^0) equal to constant marginal cost (c^0). The market price is equal to marginal cost plus the specific tax (τ). The change with the project consists of a reduction in price, resulting from a reduction in the unit cost of production ($c^1 < c^0$), and the subsequent change in the quantity demanded ($x^1 > x^0$).

Without the project, $p^0 = c^0 + \tau$; with the project, the price ($p^1 = c^1 + \tau$) is below the initial price (p^0) with a difference equal to the unit cost ($c^0 - c^1$). The change in social surplus is equal to the change in consumer surplus, the change in producer surplus (equal to zero in this case) and the change in the surplus of the taxpayers.

Applying the rule of a half, the change in consumer surplus (CS) can be expressed as:

$$\Delta CS = \frac{1}{2}\left(p^0 - p^1\right)\left(x^0 + x^1\right). \tag{2.15}$$

As the price is equal to the unit cost plus the tax, and the tax does not change:

$$\Delta CS = \frac{1}{2}\left(c^0 - c^1\right)\left(x^0 + x^1\right). \tag{2.16}$$

---

[12] See the last paragraph of this section.

The change in producer surplus (*PS*) is equal to the change in profits (equal to zero in this case):

$$\Delta PS = \left(p^1 - c^1 - \tau \right) x^1 - \left(p^0 - c^0 - \tau \right) x^0. \tag{2.17}$$

The change in taxpayer surplus (*GS*) is limited to the increase in tax revenue as a result of increasing the quantity sold (the unit tax remains unchanged):

$$\Delta GS = \tau \left(x^1 - x^0 \right). \tag{2.18}$$

The change in social surplus (*SS*) is equal to:

$$\Delta SS = \frac{1}{2} \left(c^0 - c^1 \right) \left(x^0 + x^1 \right) + \tau \left(x^1 - x^0 \right). \tag{2.19}$$

If the calculation of the benefit is realized through the change in willingness to pay and the use of resources, we have a reduction in the cost of producing the initial quantity without the project and an increase in the willingness to pay minus the cost of the resources used in the new production, as expressed in equation (2.20):

$$\Delta SS = \left(c^0 - c^1 \right) x^0 + \left[\frac{1}{2} \left(p^0 + p^1 \right) - c^1 \right] \left(x^1 - x^0 \right). \tag{2.20}$$

Expressions (2.19) and (2.20) represent two alternative ways to obtain the same result, as the reader can easily check.

The previous argument holds provided that the additional demand comes from income increases and not from the diversion of demand from other existing activities. If the increase in the quantity demanded ($x^1 - x^0$) has been diverted from other activities, it must be borne in mind that in these activities tax revenues will be reduced, so the surplus of the taxpayers is unaffected, unless the tax rate is different, in which case only the difference matters. This shows that applying general rules such as 'taxes should be ignored because they are income transfers' can sometimes be misleading. When the new quantity is not diverted from other activities or, if it is, these activities are taxed at a lower/higher rate, the indirect tax (wholly or partially) is a benefit/loss in the same sense as profits or consumer surplus.

2.5 WINNERS AND LOSERS

Virtually all investment projects and public policies unevenly affect the different groups of individuals that compose society. It is quite unlikely for a project to distribute its costs and benefits uniformly. There are many projects whose costs are borne entirely by taxpayers, while the benefits are concentrated in a particular group. For example, the construction of a park in a residential area benefits the landowners in this area, and visitors and those passing by. In other cases, such as the construction of a power plant for a region, larger groups benefit, but their negative external effects, through, for example, emissions, are primarily borne by the population living close to the plant.

Sometimes the benefits go beyond the limits of the target group, and the generated externality distributes its effects across a wider population. This is the case with an immunization campaign improving the general health of all people, including the unvaccinated, because of the reduction in the probability of infection.

A challenging task is to find out the final beneficiaries of the project. A water policy that reduces the cost of irrigation can benefit producers who now have a lower cost of production, or consumers of agricultural products if the market is competitive. However, if land is scarce, it is likely that the owners of the fixed factor are the beneficiaries because of changes in the price of the land.

Why should we worry about the distributional issues in cost–benefit analysis? The rationale is that if society attaches more value to the utility of individual A than that of B, and the project distributes its net benefits so that A wins $100 and B loses $100 with the same increase in individuals' utility, the government considers that this project is not a zero sum game. Furthermore, even assuming that a unit of utility to A is socially equal to B, one unit of income does not produce the same increase in utility unless the marginal utility of income is the same for A and B.

Conversion of income changes into welfare

When conducting a cost–benefit analysis instead of a financial analysis, the practitioner is looking for the net benefit for the whole society, resulting from the aggregation of the changes in utility of winners and losers. The result would be a good measure of the change in social welfare arising from the implementation of the project, if it were possible to measure and compare these changes in utility.

According to the analysis performed in Chapter 11, the change in social welfare (ΔW) from a variation in the quantities of the n goods consumed by the m individuals who form society can be somewhat expressed as:

$$\Delta W = \sum_{j=1}^{n} \sum_{i=1}^{m} \frac{\Delta W}{\Delta U_i} \frac{\Delta U_i}{\Delta x_{ij}} \Delta x_{ij}. \tag{2.21}$$

Reading from right to left in equation (2.21), we can see the process through which an increase in the amount of good j consumed by individual i ultimately affects social welfare. First, the project increases the amount of good j for the individual i, by the amount Δx_{ij}. This consumption increases the utility (U) of that individual to a greater or lesser extent depending on the value of $\Delta U_i / \Delta x_{ij}$, which is the marginal utility of the good for the individual and whose value depends on the preferences of the individual with respect to the good delivered by the project and the amount of the endowment that the individual already had. By multiplying the amount of good j by the marginal utility of that good ($\Delta x_{ij} (\Delta U_i / \Delta x_{ij})$), it can be seen that we convert the physical units of the project into units of utility. Then we multiply by the social marginal utility ($\Delta W / \Delta U_i$) – that is, the social value of a unit of individual utility – leading to the change in social welfare. To make the measurement of social benefits in equation (2.21) operational and taking into account that individual utility is not observable, we replace $\Delta U_i / \Delta x_{ij}$ with $((\Delta U_i / \Delta M_i)p_j)$, since we know[13] that for the individual i, to maximize her utility, $\Delta U_i / \Delta x_{ij} = (\Delta U_i / \Delta M_i)p_j$, where $\Delta U_i / \Delta M_i$ is the individual marginal utility of income, and equation (2.21) is then equivalent to:

$$\Delta W = \sum_{j=1}^{n}\sum_{i=1}^{m} \frac{\Delta W}{\Delta U_i} \frac{\Delta U_i}{\Delta M_i} p_j \Delta x_{ij}. \qquad (2.22)$$

Expression (2.22) shows how the change in goods consumed by the individuals as a result of the project originates a change in welfare. Reading from right to left, an increase in the quantity of the good is converted into monetary units multiplying for the willingness to pay (the price for small changes). It is not enough to estimate the changes in the quantities of goods consumed by individuals; we also need to know the variation in the utility when income changes ($\Delta U_i / \Delta M_i$) and how much society values the change in well-being improvement experienced by the individual ($\Delta W/\Delta U_i$).

Taking into account that $(\Delta W / \Delta U_i)(\Delta U_i / \Delta M_i)$ is the social marginal utility of income for the individual i (which we call β_i), expression (2.23) is a weighted sum of the benefits (positive or negative) that individuals receive:

$$\Delta W = \sum_{j=1}^{n}\sum_{i=1}^{m} \beta_i p_j \Delta x_{ij}. \qquad (2.23)$$

The introduction of weights, to account for income differences, alters the net social benefit of the project (provided that the weights are different from one). By making the weights depend on the level of income or other criteria, we could obtain different values of β, so that the greater the β_i, the greater the weight that society attaches to the benefits and costs of individual i.

The problem with this approach is that we do not know the values of β_i, and the result of the economic evaluation of projects will depend on the values we choose. The introduction of weights changes the result of the project since the benefits and costs of the individuals involved will change depending on the value of a parameter that is quite difficult to estimate. Moreover, the introduction of the weights presumes the identification of the final beneficiaries and this is far from being the case when fixed factors are capitalizing the positive effects of projects (e.g., land rents). The question is: what does the decision maker gain when altering the efficiency result by introducing the weights according to expression (2.23)?

---

[13] We assume an interior solution (see Chapter 11).

A practical approach

It is likely that an unweighted NPV jointly presented with a breakdown of benefits and costs by income levels, geographical areas and some other characteristic of interest can be more helpful to the decision maker than a single figure obtained by applying social weights. Moreover, a socially unworthy project, in terms of efficiency, could be approved if the weights for certain individuals are sufficiently high, which makes no sense before comparing it with a direct transfer of income. If redistribution is the objective, it pays to select the most efficient method of distribution.

The use of the potential compensation criterion, implicit in the NPV calculation, implies that the value of the social marginal utility of income is assumed to be equal to one, because distribution is optimal, or society has at its disposal means for unlimited and costless redistributions and therefore we simply need to compare benefits with costs in order to determine whether the project is socially desirable or not. Moreover, redistribution is not necessarily costless since, for example, it might affect incentives in a negative way. In this case, the actual income distribution may not be far from the constrained optimal one. This means that the actual situation represents a kind of constrained optimum and possibly we can just sum gains and losses across individuals. This is also sufficient if relative prices are left more or less unchanged (Johansson and Kriström, 2016).

Although omitting the distributional effects of the project simplifies the evaluation, we run the risk of obtaining misleading results, but the redistributive effects are not always significant enough for their inclusion in the analysis. Moreover, many projects include imperfect compensation schemes (i.e., compensation in a legal expropriation) that, although incomplete, ameliorate the undesirable redistribution effects of the projects.

Many public policies (health, primary education) and investment projects (electricity, telecommunications) will probably benefit the majority of the population when the final effects are considered. A public investment that lowers the cost of telephone services in a competitive market ultimately benefits the final users, which can be practically the whole population in a developed economy. In assessing a policy of this nature, redistributive effects might be negligible.

Redistributive effects could be significant, but the cost of identifying the final winners and losers, and how much they win and lose, could be high enough to outweigh the gains arising from the information on the distributional effects. This is especially true when those affected are many and heterogeneous and when the identification of the final beneficiaries is complicated with the presence of fixed factors.

In the practice of cost–benefit analysis, equity weights are rarely included, it being much more common that the public agency that evaluates or commissions the evaluation is interested in disaggregating the effects of the project in terms of the relevant groups affected, and also in having an estimate of the jobs that will be created as a result of the project. However, remember the risk of double counting if labour has already been priced at its opportunity cost in the calculation of the project benefits (see Chapter 4).

Finally, the characteristics of the project may suggest the way to face the problem of adding surpluses. An example can help. Suppose a policy aimed to help poor consumers through an *ad valorem* subsidy applied to the price of a product in a market with imperfect competition. With an *ad valorem* subsidy and market power we know that a significant part of the subsidy will go to the firm. The policy is not designed to increase the profit of the firms, but this is going to be a consequence of the new equilibrium. It would be sensible in this case to present the *NPV* of the policy both including and excluding the producer surplus, explaining that a transfer from taxpayers to firms was not the objective of the subsidy. Moreover, the analysts should include the alternative of introducing a specific subsidy.

THINGS TO REMEMBER

1. It is worth having a simplified model of society and a clear idea of the main impacts of the project before measurement. Time devoted to thinking about the characteristics of the problem and to assessing whether its appraisal can be reasonably dealt with in that simplified framework is a prerequisite to a sound identification and measurement of benefits.
2. Revenues are not synonymous with social benefit. In general, the willingness to pay for the project is the social benefit, and revenues (as well as taxes) are part of this benefit. The rest is called consumer surplus and is a social benefit of the same nature as the revenue or additional tax collection. Free-access facilities do not generate revenue, but social benefits are there, in the hands of the social agents.
3. Two main alternative approaches are available for measurement: the sum of changes in the surpluses of economic agents and the sum of changes in willingness to pay and in real resources, ignoring transfers. Both lead to the same result, but they should always be kept apart. Be careful with taxes. Taxes can sometimes, but not always, be treated as income transfers.
4. Cost–benefit analysis deals with real values. The change in real things is what really matters: saving lives, improving the quality of water, reducing the resources required to produce the same amount of food, and so on. The unit to measure real values is not important, so the only warning is to be consistent. The net present value of the project is not going to change whether inflation is included or not.
5. Identify winners and losers when feasible. The net present value of the project accompanied by a list of who benefits and who is harmed can be helpful for the decision maker, though the identification of the final beneficiaries is not an easy task. At least one should not forget that the net present value, in the typical evaluation reports, only represents an efficiency measure that gives the same value to a unit of benefit and a unit of cost, regardless of who the affected party is.

3
Indirect effects and wider economic impacts

... Any project is likely to have some perceptible effect on the demand and supply of goods produced by other industries, the main effects of this type being in the industries which supply the materials used by the project, and the industries which supply goods which are either complementary to or competitive with the project's output. If, as a consequence of a project, changes occur in the output of an industry for which, at the margin, social benefits equal social costs, no adjustment need be made.

(Arnold C. Harberger [1965] 1972, p. 47)

3.1 INTRODUCTION

Calculating the social net present value (*NPV*) of a project, through changes in the primary market, and ignoring other impacts on the economy beyond the observable effects in the primary market, may be inadequate once the condition of price equal to marginal cost in the rest of the economy, mentioned by Harberger in the opening quote, does not hold. A project may imply the reduction of production costs or an increase in the quality of the environment. Besides these direct effects, the project may boost the economic activity in other markets and bring an increase in labour productivity and changes in firms' location, among other effects of a broader scope than the effects in the primary market analysed in the previous chapter. These other impacts are called indirect effects and wider economic benefits, though we could better call them wider economic impacts without assuming a priori the final sign – that is, positive or negative.

Does cost–benefit analysis include all the relevant economic benefits of investment projects or does it ignore some important indirect effects on the economy? Indirect effects are those induced by the project beyond the primary market. When building a wind farm that reduces the price of energy, the direct effect occurs in the electricity market, but it also affects the firms that build the windmills or supply inputs for the wind farm.

There are other indirect effects, since the product of the primary market, the supply of electricity, is related to other markets whose products are complements to, or substitutes for, the electricity produced by windmills: the electricity produced by a fuel-burning plant is a substitute for the electricity from the windmills, and appliances are a complement (e.g., the demand for electric stoves increases if the price of electricity falls).

We therefore have a broad set of candidate markets for measuring the effects of the project beyond the primary market. In general, and this significantly simplifies the job of the analyst, the indirect effects can be ignored provided that, in the markets where they occur, the marginal social benefit equals the marginal social cost. We deal with the analysis of the indirect effects in Section 3.2.

An interesting issue is when the product of the primary market is an input for other markets. This case is another relationship of the primary market with other markets but different from the one discussed in Section 3.2. The relationship is established when the product of the primary market affected by the project, such as electricity or transport, is an input for the production of other goods. In Section 3.3 we discuss the measurement of the direct benefits using an input-derived demand and in Section 3.4 how the results should be modified in markets with imperfect competition. This section also analyses the so-called wider economic effects. Finally, in Section 3.5, we address the territorial effects and regional development induced by infrastructure investment projects.

3.2 INDIRECT EFFECTS

An investment project for outdoor recreation in a natural area (with activities like bird watching, hiking, fishing and swimming) increases the demand for hotels and restaurants in a nearby village. This effect is one of the many indirect effects of the project. It does not occur in the primary market in which we have measured the willingness to pay of the individuals who enjoy the outdoor activities. These effects occur in the secondary markets and the question is whether they should be included in the calculation of the NPV of the project. The answer depends on the existence of distortions in these markets (price is not equal to marginal costs).

Expression (3.1) accounts for the indirect effects, assuming prices are left unchanged:

$$\sum_{t=1}^{T}\sum_{j=1}^{n} \frac{\left(p_{jt} - c_{jt}\right)\left(x_{jt}^1 - x_{jt}^0\right)}{\left(1+i\right)^t}, \tag{3.1}$$

where the first term in parentheses in the numerator is the difference between price and marginal cost in each secondary market j at a given period of time t, and the second term the increase or decrease in the quantity produced in the secondary market as a result of the change produced by the project in the primary market. The two sums indicate that these effects are accounted for in the n secondary markets in the economy over the T years of the project, discounted at the discount rate i. Assuming for simplicity that there is a single secondary market and the effect occurs only in the present, expression (3.1) simplifies to:

$$(p - c)\Delta x. \tag{3.2}$$

It is important to emphasize that the indirect effects are sometimes a simple relocation of a previously existing economic activity and therefore the increase in the occupancy of hotel rooms ($\Delta x > 0$) in a particular city should be accounted for (we will see immediately how) in exactly the same manner as the decline in hotel occupancy ($\Delta x < 0$) that happens somewhere else, or any other activity that without the project received the expenditure of those visitors.

When the marginal social benefit equals the marginal social cost ($p = c$), an increase or reduction in production in the secondary market, following the shift in demand with the project, does not change the social surplus. In competitive markets, without changes in prices, the indirect effects should not be included because the price equals the marginal cost of production. In these conditions, an increase or decrease in the quantity induced by the relations of complementarity or substitutability with the primary market does not change the social surplus since the willingness to pay for the increase in production in the secondary market is equal to its opportunity cost.

When there are distortions in the secondary markets ($p \neq c$) and the products of these markets are complements to or substitutes for the product of the primary market, the indirect effect may increase or decrease the benefits of the project. The ultimate sign of these effects on the *NPV* of the project will depend on whether the price in the secondary market is higher or lower than the marginal social cost and the combination of one of these cases with the fact that goods are complements or substitutes.

The figures in this section are built, for simplicity, under the assumptions of demand shifts to the right in the secondary market ($\Delta x > 0$ in equation (3.2)). Depending on what happens in the primary market (rising or falling prices, changes in quality, etc.) and the relations of complementarity or substitutability with the secondary markets, demand shifts may be to the right or to the left. Assuming that price is equal to marginal cost in the primary market, we have several cases depending on whether the secondary market price is equal to marginal cost.[1]

Indirect effects in competitive markets

Suppose that the price of electricity falls, increasing the demand for electricity (primary market) and shifting the demand for electric stoves (secondary market). This indirect effect of reducing the price of electricity is represented in Figure 3.1.

The reduction in the price of electricity increases the demand for electric stoves in this secondary market, and demand changes from D^0 to D^1 in Figure 3.1, without changes in utility since, in the primary market, the willingness to pay for the electricity incorporates the utility of its use, and the price of electric stoves is unchanged because the supply is perfectly elastic, as assumed in Figure 3.1; or in the case of a positive slope

---

[1] If price is not equal to marginal social cost in the primary market, the number of possible cases increases.

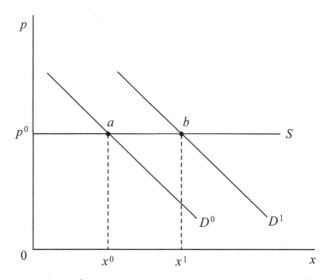

Figure 3.1 Indirect effects (without price changes and distortions)

supply, because the shift in demand is marginal in the market for electric stoves, leaving the price constant.

Let us see what happens with the producer surplus. In the market for electric stoves, the increase in demand induced by the price reduction of electricity does not change the price of the good in the secondary market (whose supply is perfectly elastic, as Figure 3.1 shows), with incremental revenue equal to incremental costs (area abx^1x^0). Therefore, the producer surplus remains unchanged in this market.

The case illustrated in Figure 3.1 is the case of a complement of the good directly affected by the project. In the case of a substitute the analysis is similar, changing the direction of the demand shift, now to the left but with the same result: as the social surplus does not change in the secondary market we can also ignore the indirect effect as these changes do not affect welfare.

Negative externalities and subsidies

When the price is lower than the marginal social in the secondary market (e.g., a negative externality or a subsidy), as shown in Figure 3.2, the indirect effect can be significant and may affect the social profitability of the project.

Consider the case of a negative externality (atmospheric pollution, noise, and the like). Initially, we are located at the equilibrium point e of a secondary market where there is a constant negative externality equal to φ per unit. While the increase in demand does not affect the price, the social cost is now higher than the private cost. In the initial equilibrium, the marginal social cost exceeds the price paid by users in φ. With the increase in demand from D^0 to D^1, there is no change in the utility of consumers or producers (revenue edx^1x^0 equals private cost), but there is an additional increase in

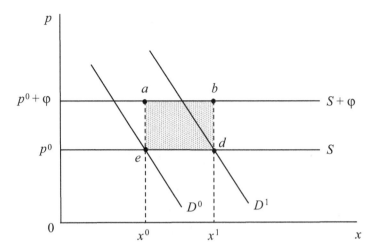

Figure 3.2 Secondary market with externality or subsidy

social cost represented by the area *abde*, which reduces the surplus of the 'rest of society' and therefore has to be included.

Interpreting φ as a subsidy in Figure 3.2, the analysis is similar to the previous one. The marginal social cost is $p^0 + φ$ but the firm produces as if the cost is equal to p^0. When the demand shifts to the right in the secondary market, there is no change in consumer and producer surpluses; on the contrary, taxpayer surplus is reduced in the area *abde*.[2]

This analysis is valid provided there are no other distortions in the economy (or those other distorted markets are unaffected by the project under consideration) – that is, if all other affected markets are of the type illustrated in Figure 3.1.

Taxes and unemployment

In the cases contemplated in Figure 3.2, the increase in production in the secondary market reduced the social benefits of the project. In the cases of revenue-collecting taxes and involuntary unemployment, the price is higher than marginal cost and the indirect effects of additional production in the secondary market have a positive effect on the social profitability of the project.

Consider the case of a unitary tax included in the market price of electric stoves, as represented in Figure 3.3. The marginal cost is now $p^0 - τ$ instead of p^0, and therefore the increase in the demand for electric stoves in this secondary market, induced by the reduction in the price of electricity in the primary market, produces an increase in the social surplus equal to the tax revenue *abde*.

---

[2] For simplicity we ignore the deadweight loss produced by the taxes required to subsidize the amount *abde* (see Section 4.6 in Chapter 4).

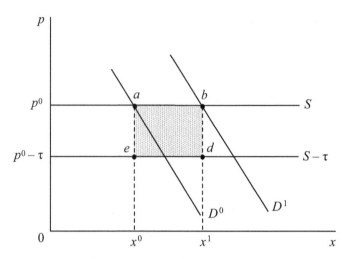

Figure 3.3 Secondary market with taxes

The demand shift does not change the price, but the social cost of the additional units is lower than the private cost. Initially, the social marginal cost is equal to $p^0 - \tau$. Given the increase in demand from D^0 to D^1, with no change in the utility of consumers or producers (revenue abx^1x^0 equals private costs), there is an increase in the surplus of taxpayers equal to the area $abde$. In this case, tax revenue is a benefit of the project. In this case, taxes are not a transfer of income to be ignored in order to avoid double counting (unless in another secondary market a similar reduction in tax collection occurs).

In the event that there is unemployment and the opportunity cost of labour is less than the market wage, $p^0 - \tau$ could be interpreted as the social opportunity cost of producing electric stoves in a situation of unemployment and minimum wage regulation, and p^0 as its market price. The area $abde$ should be counted as a social benefit (an increase in the surplus of workers) since, given the increase in demand in the secondary market, the real cost of the resources used to increase production is equal to edx^1x^0 (the opportunity cost of production). The area $abde$ would be measuring the benefit of job creation (see Section 4.5 in Chapter 4 for a more detailed treatment).

3.3 DIRECT EFFECTS MEASURED WITH A DERIVED DEMAND

A project that reduces the cost of an input used by many firms can be measured in the market of that input, instead of calculating the change in the producer surplus and the consumer surplus of all producers and consumers. When building a new infrastructure that reduces transport costs, the effects are enjoyed by many firms whose profits may increase, or by consumers who travel at a lower generalized price or consume goods at a lower price.

Although the content of this section is in fact the measurement of direct benefits with an input-derived demand used for all the firms, its understanding under the assumption of perfect competition is key for the analysis of wider economic benefits, as presented in Section 3.4.

Practically all firms require transport for the commuting of their workers and/ or for access to input markets and the distribution of their goods and services to their customers. In the case of manufacturing, transport demand is derived from the needs in the markets for final goods and services. This is called *derived demand* and it helps to circumvent the difficulties in the measurement of the benefits of the reduction in transport costs. The evaluation of investment projects that reduce transport costs is simplified when the measurement of the benefits is carried out in the transport market, without having to deal with changes in many other markets using the transport service. The shortcut requires those markets to be perfectly competitive.

By concentrating the effort on measuring the benefits with the demand for transport we avoid the identification and measurement of changes in the surpluses of a large number of firms and their consumers. This does not mean that companies in other markets using the transport services do not benefit from the project that reduces the cost of transport, or that consumers do not benefit from lower prices; it is simply to avoid counting the same effect twice, because the benefits of reducing such a cost have been measured in the input market.

The upper part of Figure 3.4 shows the impact of the reduction of transport costs on the supply of a product and its effects on producer and consumer surpluses. S^{0+} and S^{0-} are the supply curves without the project, gross and net of transport costs, respectively. The situation without the project shows a competitive market in equilibrium where we assume that producers are located at the same point in the space but consumers are located at different distances from producers, which offer the product according to the supply function S^{0+}. The supply (S^{0+}) and the demand determine the equilibrium without the project at price p^0 and the quantity produced x^0.

The market price paid by the consumers p^0 is not fully received by the producers since the cost of transport (assume price equals marginal cost in the transport market) reduces the price that producers receive (p^{0-}). All the units produced are transported to their ultimate consumers and therefore at the cost of transport without the project c^0 (equal to $p^0 - p^{0-}$) the quantity produced is equal to that effectively transported.

So far, this figure provides little help. However, when we assume a reduction in the cost of transport with the project, Figure 3.4 shows how the derived demand for transport is very useful for measuring welfare changes. With the project, the cost of transport is reduced, and in the upper part of the figure the supply function is shifted to the right, so that the new equilibrium is determined by the supply function S^{1+} and the demand. The new price with the project is p^1 and the quantity produced x^1. In the lower part of the figure x^0 increases to x^1.

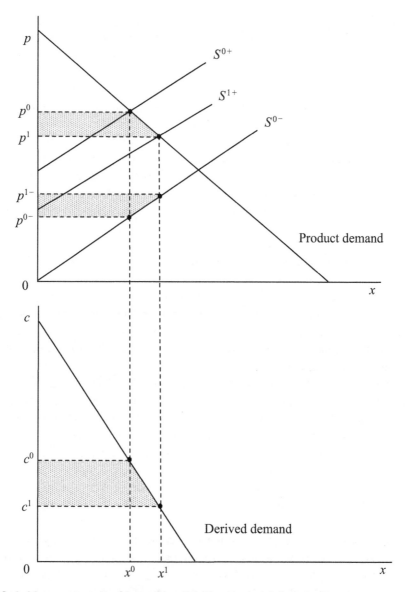

Figure 3.4 Measurement of benefits with the derived demand

The change in social surplus, in the upper part of the figure, is composed of the change in the surplus of consumers and producers. Applying the rule of a half (see Chapter 2), the change in consumer surplus is equal to:

$$\frac{1}{2}\left(p^0 - p^1\right)\left(x^0 + x^1\right),\tag{3.3}$$

and in producer surplus:

$$\frac{1}{2}(p^{1-} - p^{0-})(x^0 + x^1).\tag{3.4}$$

These are the effects of the reduction in transport costs (under the assumption of perfect competition). The difficulty of measuring such surpluses in the markets for final goods is significant but the demand for transport, as represented in the lower part of Figure 3.4, shows a shortcut to the measurement of the change in social surplus by applying the rule of a half with the transportation costs and trips realized.

$$\frac{1}{2}(c^0 - c^1)(x^0 + x^1).\tag{3.5}$$

Expression (3.5) is equal to the sum of expressions (3.3) and (3.4). Measuring the change in social surplus with the derived demand for transport following expression (3.5), we cannot add as benefits the benefits of the cost of transport in the market for goods using transport as an input. If we do so, we would double count the benefits.

3.4 WIDER ECONOMIC EFFECTS

Indirect effects are those that occur in the secondary markets linked to the primary market by relations of complementarity or substitutability and have already been analysed in Section 3.2, concluding that they must be included whenever there is a distortion in these markets and the magnitude of effects is significant. The impossibility of concluding a priori whether the final sign of the indirect effects would be positive or negative, depending on the circumstances of the affected markets, was also highlighted.

Market distortions produce other effects, the so-called *wider economic benefits*, which in principle should be included in the calculation of the social profitability of the project because they are not double counting and can be important in certain contexts. With no intention of being exhaustive we discuss the case of imperfect competition in markets that use transport as an input, the benefits derived from agglomeration economies and the effect of increasing competition as a result of the implementation of the project.

Imperfect competition in markets that use transport as an input

To estimate the welfare gains of a project that reduces the cost of transport it is advisable, as we saw earlier, to use the derived demand in order to circumvent the difficulties of measuring the effects on every market affected by the project. A necessary condition for the final effects to be calculated in the transport market was that product markets were perfectly competitive. What happens in the presence of market power?

In markets with imperfect competition the price is higher than the opportunity cost, and firms are in equilibrium at a point where consumers are willing to pay above the marginal cost. This is the typical textbook case of a monopoly. If the producer is unable

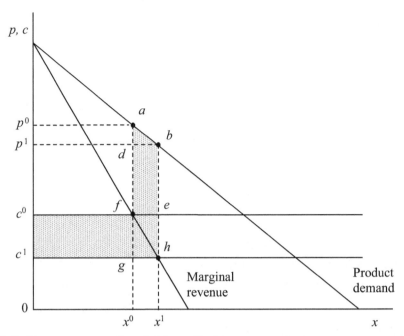

Figure 3.5 Measurement of social benefits in a monopoly

to price discriminate, a price reduction to attract new customers reduces revenues on the existing units and thus what the monopolist compares with the marginal cost when deciding to increase or decrease its output is the marginal revenue (the revenue of the new units minus the lost revenue of the existing ones), not the price.

The economic consequence of a profit-maximizing monopolist is well known: a suboptimal equilibrium quantity and the corresponding loss of efficiency. How does this fact affect the evaluation of a project that reduces the cost of transport for firms with market power? Figure 3.5 shows the effect of a reduction in transport cost on the marginal cost of a profit-maximizing monopolistic firm whose unit cost changes from c^0 to c^1. Initially, the firm is in equilibrium at point a, and now the equilibrium is at point b with a reduction in consumer prices from p^0 to p^1. The increase in producer surplus is represented by the area $c^0 f h c^1$. The consumer surplus increases in the area $p^0 a b p^1$.

One might think that in the transport market these areas are measured by the change in total surplus in Figure 3.4 by applying the rule of a half, as reflected in expression (3.5). However, although this is the case for competitive markets, where the marginal change in output has zero value, this does not happen in markets with imperfect competition, where the price–marginal cost margin is positive.

To see this intuitively, we can think of a very small change in Figure 3.4, so the areas in the figure reduce to the following expression:

$$-x\Delta c + (p - c)\Delta x. \tag{3.6}$$

If the product market that uses transport as an input is competitive, the social value of the last unit exchanged is close to zero as the price is equal to the marginal cost (as shown in Figure 3.4) and therefore expression (3.6) is equivalent to expression (3.5), whereas in the imperfect competition case, the value of the last unit equals the price minus the marginal cost (greater than zero, as shown in Figure 3.5) and therefore the application of expression (3.5) ignores the second term of expression (3.6). Although consumers are not willing to pay more than the equilibrium price for an additional unit and nor are producers willing to produce it (because its marginal revenue equals the marginal cost), there is an additional benefit by producing that marginal unit that the transport project makes possible and it is equal to ($p - c$).

Ignoring transfers, the change in total surplus equals the cost reduction in the production of x^0 (area c^0fgc^1) plus the willingness to pay (net of costs) of Δx (area $abhg$).

Besides the increase in social surplus, measured with the rule of a half in the transport market, we now have an additional benefit, equal to the reduction in the deadweight loss, because of the existence of imperfect competition, equivalent to the increase in production multiplied by the difference between the price and the marginal cost (Venables and Gasoriek, 1999). It should be noted that the effect can be negative if, in some secondary markets, firms with market power sell less because the reduction in transport costs positively affects, for example, a product that is a substitute for the product in the secondary markets.

Agglomeration economies

Agglomeration economies are in fact a positive externality that firms generate when they locate close to other firms. Once we relax the assumption of perfect competition, the pecuniary externalities associated with the concentration of firms in space increase welfare. In the presence of imperfect competition and increasing returns to scale the interaction among firms creates positive externalities like technology (Krugman, 1991).

If productivity increases with the density of firms, productivity depends on the location decision of each firm. A company, when deciding where to install the plant, considers its own benefits but not the increase in the profits of other firms. There are several reasons that firms in areas with a higher firm density are more productive, and why firms choose these locations despite the higher labour and land costs, among other drawbacks. These include access to wider markets, the availability of a more specialized labour market that matches the needs of firms and the access to technologies and the production processes of firms in the area.

One key element is the direction of the causality between the density of the area (city size) and the gains of productivity:

We are left with the view that cities exist because they are areas with high levels of productivity, which might occur because people come to places that are innately more productive or because density itself enhances productivity because of agglomeration economies. The strong correlation between urban size and

productivity ... supports this view. Does that link reflect agglomeration economies, where size creates productivity, or heterogeneous local productivity levels
that then cause agglomeration? (Glaeser and Gottlieb, 2009, p. 1000)

For the economic evaluation of projects such as investment in transport infrastructure,
or in city amenities, it is useful to consider that a complete urban model has three
equilibrium conditions that determine three local variables. The three equilibrium conditions are the indifference of workers across space; firms maximize profits and hence
wages are equal to the value of the marginal productivity of labour; and supply equal
demand in the housing market. Spatial differences in productivity, amenities and the
building industry explain differences in population density, wages and prices. Again,
agglomeration economies can be the result of these differences or the consequence of
labour density (Glaeser and Gottlieb, 2009).

Whatever the direction of causality, the existence of differences in productivity
between locations and the fact that the mentioned equilibria imply that workers are
indifferent across space create a source of additional benefits (beyond time savings)
when a transport project reduces commuting time from the periphery to the city centre.

The benefits of time savings of a transport project are valued by the firms, which
now change the location and increase the density of firms in a city or an industrial park
(as measured by the derived demand function), but would be lower than the increases
in productivity enjoyed by all the firms. Following the same reasoning, the reduction
in the density of firms in the area where the companies were initially located reduces
productivity and therefore it is a negative effect that should be accounted for.

There is empirical evidence of the positive effect of a higher *effective density* on productivity, understanding effective density as an indicator of the degree of agglomeration,
such as employment in the area and its surrounding areas (weighted by the generalized
cost of transport), so that it appears that an increase in effective density increases the
average productivity of the area. Nevertheless, it is important to look to the net effect in
the economy, as the decrease in density in the surrounding areas is part of the process.

A project that reduces transport costs may also induce an increase in the concentration of jobs in an area where there are economies of agglomeration by reducing the cost
of commuting for workers who, with the project, are now more willing to move to the
city or the industrial park. However, the opposite might also occur if the reduction in
transport costs encourages the dispersion of economic activity. For an urban project
that reduces the costs of travel within the city, it is more likely that the positive effect will
dominate, while for an intercity transport project the possibility that the dispersion will
increase cannot be ruled out, depending on a set of local factors such as land prices,
wage differences between areas, and so on (see Duranton and Puga, 2004; Graham,
2007; Venables, 2007).

The benefits derived from productivity changes arising from economies of agglomeration should include the additional tax revenues that are collected because of the
increase in economic activity. Additional gains – for example, that workers value when
they take their decision to migrate to the area of highest density of employment – are

net of taxes; nevertheless, additional tax revenues are also productivity gains (Venables, 2007). This is another example, by the way, that taxes are sometimes mere transfers and at other times represent welfare gains.

Wider economic benefits: caution ahead

Research on wider economic impacts has revealed that conventional cost–benefit analysis may underestimate the benefits of large infrastructure projects. At the same time, the recent popularity of wider economic benefits, as well as the use of impact studies, also reveals the interest of promoters to get the approval of projects with insufficient direct benefits. There are some general principles in order to avoid a too mechanical and misleading use of wider economic benefits (Venables, 2019):

- *Narrative:* There should be a clear narrative of the main problem that policy is intended to address and the key market failure(s) that motivate the policy.
- *Transparency:* The mechanisms underpinning both the quantity changes and their social value should be clear and explained in a manner that enables the key magnitudes to be understood from straightforward back-of-the-envelope calculation.
- *Sensitivity:* There should be an analysis of the dependence of the quantity effects and their valuation on key assumptions about the economic environment. Scenarios outlining the quantitative importance of failure of these assumptions should be outlined.
- *Complementary policies:* There should be a thorough consideration of complementary measures that are needed for a successful implementation of a project.
- *Alternatives:* Any project should make a strong case that it provides the most cost-effective way to solve the main problem described in the narrative.

Recent research on the nature and magnitude of *wider economic benefits* is still far from producing practical rules for the economic evaluation of transport projects subject to the usual constraints of time, money and technical resources. Some recommendations are suggested (OECD, 2007). The additional economic effects not captured in conventional cost–benefit analysis exist, and they have their origin in the existence of increasing returns, agglomeration economies, market power or the benefits of a broader labour market. Moreover, firms and households take long-term decisions in reacting to the changes in transport costs. Therefore, the sign and magnitude of these effects are very different between projects and it is not possible to transfer them to new projects being evaluated.

A practical idea for small projects is to work under the assumption that the wider economic benefits do not exist or are unimportant. Although this approach runs the risk of ignoring them in the case where they are significant, there is consensus on the fact that this risk is offset by the elimination of the risk of double counting and delays in project evaluation. For large projects or for the evaluation of investment programmes it may be justified to undertake more sophisticated analyses.

Aggregate studies that focus on global impacts have problems detecting the direction of causality. Moreover, they do not contain information with a sufficient level of detail that makes the results useful in evaluating projects. In addition, there is some confusion about whether these studies measure wider economic effects, ignored in standard cost–benefit analysis, or whether they only measure the final impact of the direct effects already measured.

More detailed 'microscopic' studies seeking to capture the effects of transport cost reductions on the internal reorganization of firms and families are scarce. This is not surprising since this type of longer-term response is difficult to integrate into micro-focused modelling that analyses the interaction in the markets. However, it is known that companies and households make reorganization decisions in response to new transport conditions.

Ex post studies are also scarce. Existing ones have found no robust evidence on the existence of wider economic benefits. The latest research suggests that if one wants to go beyond the conventional cost–benefit analysis to include any possible additional benefits, one should distinguish between direct benefits and impacts on productivity, competition and the labour market. Furthermore, when there are spatial spillover effects, regardless of including the wider benefits, we should expect different results in the evaluation if the size of the geographic area analysed varies. Moreover, the economies of agglomeration may also have negative effects because of the increase in traffic congestion that may even lead to negative wider economic benefits.

In the modelling of agglomeration effects, as with the spillover effects, there is concern about using a 'black box' of questionable utility in the evaluation of projects. Advancing with the 'microscopic' analysis of the agglomeration benefits would be very useful for a better understanding of the effects on production, product distribution and access to inputs, and for a better understanding of mechanisms that tend to spread the activity because of the reduction in transport costs through just-in-time processes or the advantages of having separate plants to avoid upward pressures on wages.

The existence of spatial spillovers requires extreme care in estimating the effects of local agglomeration. For example, the study of the London Crossrail link concluded that the benefits of conventional cost–benefit analysis had to be increased by 20 per cent to include the effects of agglomeration, but it could not demonstrate the extent to which these wider benefits were losses in other geographical areas. For example, when qualified labour leaves their area looking for more productive jobs, the losses in productivity in the periphery must be included in the analysis plus the long-term negative economic effects triggered by this labour migration.

From the available empirical evidence and the evaluation of the experts on whether conventional cost–benefit analysis is sufficient to estimate the social profitability of a project, the general recommendation is to be extremely cautious since, although economists are advancing with the knowledge and measurement of wider economic effects, they are still far from turning the results into practical rules for their inclusion in cost–benefit analysis.

The risk of double counting is so high that the best approach is not to include wider economic benefits in small projects and focus the efforts on the direct effects. With the available evidence, it does not seem reasonable to transfer the results from other studies, using percentages or similar procedures, if we take into account the variability in the magnitude of the wider economic effects, and even the sign, which could be negative when congestion and other negative externalities are present. When investment induces agglomeration, it may also induce additional negative externalities not fully captured in the analysis.

Finally, there is an additional practical element concerning the use of the wider benefits in the evaluation of socially unprofitable projects. Promoters might make distorted use of the wider economic benefits approach to provide additional justification for weak projects; the application of such methods therefore requires a thorough examination of the underpinning justification.

Higher competition

When transport costs are high, projects that reduce them can facilitate the entry of new firms who find it profitable to offer their products compared with the situation without the project when the incumbent firms were protected by the barriers to entry that in fact represent the transport costs. This effect should not be confused with welfare gains arising from the expansion of output in imperfectly competitive markets after a reduction in transport costs.

The pure competition effect, with the entry of new firms, is less likely to occur in countries with a mature infrastructure network. In these countries, significant increases in competition resulting from the fact that a transport project reduces travel time are not expected. However, it is an effect that could be important in any project that affects a part of the country that is poorly connected and in which some firms enjoy market power because of poor accessibility.

3.5 LOCATION EFFECTS AND REGIONAL DEVELOPMENT

The location of firms and the induced increase in economic activity is one of the arguments used in the defence of investment projects in public infrastructure. It is assumed, for example, that the construction of highways or railway lines, which reduce transport costs from a poor region to more developed one, will enable greater economic growth for the former thanks to the higher attraction of the poor region for the location of firms.

The empirical evidence shows that benefits for the poor region are far from being guaranteed. Roads can be used to export goods from the poor region to the rich region but also from the rich to the poor. Therefore, in principle, a reduction in transport costs between the two regions does not guarantee the desired location effects. In the presence of agglomeration economies, a reduction in transport costs can facilitate a greater concentration of activity in the rich region, which could now export its products at a lower cost to the poor region, rather than directly produce in the poor region.

The emphasis on the location effects of firms in deprived areas may be of interest to governments or lobby groups who want the project to be approved. However, from the point of view of the economy as a whole, it does not seem reasonable to introduce as benefits the more than doubtful location effects of firms that could even materialize in the opposite direction than the one originally planned.

The so-called new economic geography has shown that the effects of reducing transport costs in the less developed regions not only depend on the characteristics of the project but also on the economic context.[3] A simplified explanation of the difficulty of establishing a priori the location effect of an infrastructure is as follows.

Let us consider a country with two regions, the rich (R) and the poor (P), separated by an inadequate transport infrastructure (we will call the initial quality level – travel time, route conservation, safety, etc. – 'bad'). There is only one factor of production, labour, and wages are initially identical in the two regions.

Economic activity and the location of firms between region R and region P are in equilibrium. There are more companies in R and more unemployment in P. The equilibrium is explained by several factors including the level of infrastructure. First, producing in R and exporting to P, using the infrastructure, has the advantage of reaping the economies of agglomeration (economies of scale and access to specialized inputs, for example) that give rise to a lower unit cost in R than in P. Locating the firm in P has the advantage of avoiding the transport costs incurred when producing in R and exporting to P.

The trade-off between the pros and cons of producing in one region has been resolved with an initial level of activity and location of firms that we take as a starting point and that allows us to call one region 'rich' and the other one 'poor'.

Suppose we are going to evaluate a project that allows the infrastructure to pass from level 'bad' to 'good', reducing the transport costs between the two regions. How will this project affect the location of firms between the two regions? It is often argued that investment projects in infrastructure improve the situation of the poor region by allowing its development. The empirical evidence is not so optimistic, with several possible outcomes.

In the simplified world described here, the availability of a better infrastructure changes the initial equilibrium. The only change that has occurred is a reduction in the transport cost, hence it is more profitable to produce in R, take advantage of economies of agglomeration and export to P using the improved infrastructure. The result is the relocation of firms in R. The new economic activity raises wages in R and attracts the labour force from P to R, which allows the containment of wages and the reinforcement of the relocation in R.

---

[3] See, among others, Krugman and Venables (1996) and Puga (2002).

Suppose now that a new project improves the infrastructure from level 'good' to 'very good' and that transport costs are further reduced. We can visualize two plausible scenarios. In the first, wage agreements are negotiated at the national level. If so, the cheaper costs will intensify the relocation effect benefiting region R. The second scenario involves regional wage bargaining. In this case wages will rise in region R and fall or remain constant in P.

If the wage differential is sufficiently high and transport costs are sufficiently low, it may happen that companies move to the poor region and export to the rich. Everything will depend on the trade-off between the benefits of agglomeration economies in R and the lower labour costs in P.

The previous example is a warning of the difficulty of predicting the final location effects, or regional development effects, of infrastructure investments projects without incorporating other factors, sometimes more critical than the infrastructure per se, such as the labour market situation. Companies, when making their location decisions, take into account a set of factors, one of which is transport cost. A reduction in one factor changes the equilibrium and may foster agglomeration or dispersion, depending on the combined effects of the set of relevant factors.

THINGS TO REMEMBER

1. Secondary markets are affected by the change in the primary market, the one where the direct effects of the project take place. Indirect effects and wider economic benefits may be significant.
2. In competitive markets the indirect effects are equal to zero. In the case of distortions, such as externalities or taxes, the indirect effects should be considered.
3. The existence of indirect effects does not necessarily mean an increase in social benefits. Indirect effects may be positive or negative depending on the relationship of complementarity or substitutability between the goods in the primary and the secondary markets, and the existence of distortions.
4. The measurement of direct benefits can sometimes be performed with an input-derived demand, as in the case of the transport project. Derived demand has the advantage of concentrating valuable economic information that simplifies the calculus of the direct benefits.
5. Wider economic benefits can also be present because of, for example, economies of agglomeration that induce productivity increases when a project helps to increase the employment density in an area. Some of the positive effects derived from agglomeration economies also have the side-effect of congestion or the reduction of similar benefits in those areas losing firms and workers.
6. A reasonable line of action is to concentrate attention and effort on the identification and measurement of the direct effects, and the closest substitutes and complements in distorted markets, ignoring the minor adjustment in many markets where measurement would be too costly to justify the additional benefits in terms of precision in the calculation of the NPV.

7. Regional development is one of the arguments used in the defence of major infra-structure projects in poor regions, but this argument is not supported by empirical evidence. Transport infrastructure can be used in both ways and a reduction in transport costs between two regions does not guarantee the desired location effects.

4
Opportunity costs, market and shadow prices

Please circle the best answer to the following question

You won a free ticket to see an Eric Clapton concert (which has no resale value). Bob Dylan is performing on the same night and is your next-best alternative activity. Tickets to see Dylan cost $40. On any given day, you would be willing to pay up to $50 to see Dylan. Assume there are no other costs of seeing either performer. Based on this information, what is the opportunity cost of seeing Eric Clapton?

A. $0; B. $10; C. $40; D. $50[1]

4.1 INTRODUCTION

Policies and projects evaluated within the public sector are undertaken because their social benefits are expected to exceed their social costs (at least this would be desirable). It is difficult to find situations where there are benefits without any cost. In general, to obtain benefits, it is necessary to use production factors whose opportunity costs are usually greater than zero. In other words, one must give up some goods to acquire others.[2]

The correct measure of costs is essential to any economic assessment. The market price of the production factors employed in the implementation of any project does not always reflect the opportunity cost. The costs of projects can derive from the use of already produced goods, land and other natural resources, plus labour and capital. From an economic point of view, the cost of the input is the social benefit in the best available alternative, which has been lost for the sake of the project.

Frequently, when the demand for an input for the project is small with respect to the market size of the input, its market price is a good approximation of the social cost resulting from its use. If the project involves a change in the market price of the input

---

[1] Ferraro and Taylor (2005). Check your answer in section 4.2.

[2] And sometimes to incur losses of efficiency in some markets to obtain an overall socially desirable result. In certain circumstances it may be optimal to set a price below or above the marginal cost in a regulated market when there are substitutes or complements in related markets for which marginal cost pricing is not feasible. This policy is derived from the theory of second best (Lypsey and Lancaster, 1956).

(e.g., in the case of a specific input available in short supply), the economic valuation of this input requires us to distinguish between resources of new supply and resources diverted from other uses as a consequence of the price rise derived from the shift of the demand in the factor market.

In Sections 4.2 and 4.3 we analyse the circumstances when the market price of inputs is a reasonable approximation for the opportunity cost of production factors, and the situations in which it is advisable to correct them and estimate the so-called shadow prices. Section 4.4 describes some practical problems when the analyst deals with the measurement of the social cost in the presence of taxes. Section 4.5 discusses the shadow price of labour through the interaction of supply and demand in the labour market under different conditions. Section 4.6 deals with the cost of public funds as many projects are partially or totally financed by distortionary taxes.

4.2 THE FACTOR PRICE AS AN APPROXIMATION OF THE OPPORTUNITY COST

What is the opportunity cost of seeing Eric Clapton? The opening quote of this chapter was the only question included in a survey carried out with students in an academic meeting in Philadelphia. Of the 200 respondents, 45 per cent were from institutions currently ranked in the top 30 US economics departments, one-third of the sample were students and around 60 per cent of the respondents had taught an introductory economics course at university level. Before checking your answer, it is worth noting that the distribution of answer was the following:

A. $0 (25.1%); B. $10 (21.6%); C. $40 (25.6%); D. $50 (27.6%)

The figures show that the respondents appear to be randomly distributed across the possible answers. Roughly, only one out of five gave the correct answer – $10. Let us see why $10 is the right one. By going to see Eric Clapton you give up $50, the sum you value going to see Bob Dylan (which is the next best alternative), but if you go to the Dylan concert you have to pay $40, and hence the net value lost when you go to Eric Clapton is $10. The opportunity cost is sensitive to any change in the circumstances. If, for example, Dylan's concert were free, the opportunity cost goes up to $50.

It is worth emphasizing that the value you give to the Clapton concert is irrelevant to answering the question of the opportunity cost of this concert. Moreover, we do not know whether you will go to the Clapton concert or not. The only thing we do know is that if you go, the value for you of the Clapton concert is at least $10.

The cost of a project is what society loses by giving up a particular set of goods because of its implementation. Such costs are not the goods that we must renounce, but the utility lost by renouncing these goods. This value is, expressed in monetary terms, the amount that individuals are willing to pay for the goods that are no longer produced.

If a bridge is built, its cost is the net value of all the goods we have renounced in return for the new infrastructure. The cost of the bridge would be, in a strict sense, the utility lost by the individuals because of the loss of goods that could have been produced had the factors of production employed in its construction been employed in the best available alternative, instead of the construction of the bridge. Expression (4.1) reflects this idea:

$$C_j = \sum_{k=1}^{s} p_k dx_k, \qquad (4.1)$$

where C_j is the total cost of producing the good j (i.e., the bridge) and dx_k is the marginal reduction in the quantity produced of the k good lost to produce good j multiplied by the marginal willingness to pay for those goods (p_k, under the assumption of a small project).

In practical terms it is very difficult to identify which goods are no longer produced because a project is carried out. One solution to this informational problem is to find an approximation in the factor market, where the demand is derived from what is happening in the market for goods, and the factor supply represents the opportunity cost of the factor. In the case of good k we will assume for simplicity that its production function depends on two production factors z_1 and z_2:

$$x_k = f_k(z_1, z_2). \qquad (4.2)$$

The total differential of expression (4.2) shows that any output variation depends on the change in the quantity of the inputs used multiplied by their marginal productivities:

$$dx_k = \frac{\partial x_k}{\partial z_1} dz_1 + \frac{\partial x_k}{\partial z_2} dz_2. \qquad (4.3)$$

Substituting equation (4.3) into equation (4.1) and recalling that any profit-maximizing firm uses additional units of input until their market price (w) equals the value of its marginal productivity, $w = p(\partial x/\partial z)$, the cost of the project can be re-expressed as:

$$C_j = \sum_{k=1}^{s} (w_1 dz_1 + w_2 dz_2). \qquad (4.4)$$

The cost of the project, initially expressed in equation (4.1) as the social value of the diverted goods, appears now in (4.4) as the quantities of the inputs (dz_1 and dz_2) required for the production of those goods, multiplied by their respective prices (w_1 and w_2).

In practice, the validity and usefulness of expression (4.4) for identifying and assessing the costs of a project is conditioned by three underlying assumptions. First, all the changes in input markets are marginal; second, input and output markets are perfectly competitive, without distortions, like indirect or income taxes; and third, all the resources are fully utilized. However, once these assumptions are abandoned to deal with more realistic project assessment situations (which include, among others, the presence of subsidies or taxes, or the use of unemployed labour in the project), expression (4.4) is no longer valid to calculate the opportunity costs of the project. This is what shadow pricing is about – adjusting market prices to reflect the opportunity costs.

4.3 MARKET AND SHADOW PRICE OF INPUTS

A typical project requires the use of some produced goods (x) and inputs (z). The cost of this project (C) can be expressed as:

$$C = pdx + w_z dz + wdL, \tag{4.5}$$

where, p is the vector of market prices (including taxes) of the goods used by the project, w_z the vector of market prices of inputs other than labour (L), and w the wage rate.

The distinction between goods and inputs in expression (4.5) is somehow blurred in practice as the inputs to be purchased for the project are basically produced inputs (i.e., goods). Nevertheless, we keep the distinction for a later discussion of the shadow price of inputs, where those inputs are deviated from the private sector.

Figure 4.1 illustrates these ideas by showing the supply and demand in equilibrium of any input z, where (w_z^0, z^0) represents the market equilibrium under different supply schemes and there is an *ad valorem* indirect tax (τ). Whereas the demand function is the same for the three cases, the supply is perfectly elastic in the left panel, showing the (infinite) availability of any quantity at the market price w_z^0. In the central panel, the input supply function is upward sloping, indicating than to supply more than z^0 requires an increase in w_z. In the right panel, the supply is perfectly inelastic, meaning that the available amount of the input is fixed at z^0 and cannot be increased.

Now consider that the project shifts (marginally) the input demand to the right. In the case of a perfectly elastic supply, the input price w_z^0 remains constant and the suppliers provide the additional amount of z – that is, dz in expression (4.5). Note that w_z^0 is not the opportunity cost of an additional unit of z, as the indirect tax (τ) is a mere transfer. Therefore, the shadow price of z for our project is the market price of the input net of taxes: $w_z^0/(1+\tau)$.

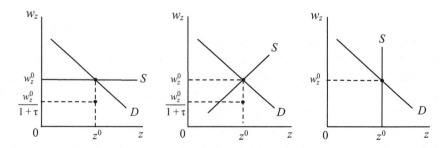

Figure 4.1 Market and shadow prices of inputs

In general, the shadow price of any of the inputs used in the project are the market price of the input, net of taxes. This principle is applicable to the majority of projects whose demand is marginal in the input markets, even for the central case of Figure 4.1 as long as the quantity of inputs demanded by the project is marginal with respect to national or international markets. In all these cases, the demand shift is negligible, and the equilibrium price w_z^0 only changes marginally.

The central panel of Figure 4.1 is also useful to go deeper in the identification of the opportunity cost of the project. Suppose now that the quantity of z demanded for the project shifts the demand curve outwards a discrete amount, and the input price w_z goes up to clear the market. This increase in w_z induces a marginal increase in the supply of z (to the right of z^0) and also a deviation of z from the private sector to the project (to the left of z^0) when some firms find it no longer profitable to purchase z^0 at a higher price than w_z^0.

The opportunity cost of the quantity of the input z purchased for the project has a lower and an upper bound depending on where that amount of dz comes from. When one unit of z comes from the additional production of z, the opportunity cost is the social marginal cost of producing the input – that is, the market price of the input net of the indirect tax. Alternatively, when one unit of z is deviated from the production of other goods in the private sector, the opportunity cost of one unit of z is the value of the production associated with that input in the private sector. In this case, the social marginal cost of z is higher and only for infinitesimal changes, close to w_z^0 in the central panel of Figure 4.1.

Moreover, the opportunity cost of the input deviated from the private sector to the project could be higher than w_z^0 for two reasons. On the one hand, the market clearing price w_z will be higher than w_z^0 when the input demand increases; on the other hand, for example, if the private sector is paying an *ad valorem* tax (θ) for the production of a good crowded out by the diverted input, the opportunity cost of one unit of z is equal to $w_z(1 + \theta)$, where θ is the value-added tax and where $w_z > w_z^0$. Thus, $w_z(1 + \theta)$ is equal to the value of the marginal productivity of the input.

An example clarifies this idea. Let us assume a perfect competitive market where the marginal cost of 1 litre of petrol is \$0.5 and there is a specific revenue-collecting tax on petrol of \$0.5, its market price (w_z) is \$1 per litre. In these circumstances, the social opportunity cost of using an additional litre of petrol in the project is 0.5, when the litre comes from new production (as in the left panel of Figure 4.1), and \$1.2 when the litre of petrol is deviated from a private transport company paying a 20 per cent indirect tax in its goods market. Hence, the lower bound of the shadow price of 1 litre of petrol is \$0.5, and the upper bound \$1.2. In practice, inputs are generally available, as in the left panel of Figure 4.1, and their shadow price is, simply, their market prices net of taxes.

Finally, note that the derivation of the rules to convert market into shadow prices was obtained with indirect taxes or commodity-specific taxes designed to raise revenue. In the case of Pigouvian taxes – that is, taxes designed to internalize externalities – the social opportunity cost includes the tax, as the tax is correcting an external cost instead of a way to collect revenue, as in the case of the value-added tax and the like.

A wide range of projects requires land and sometimes this land is situated in locations with limited possibilities for substitution. This is the case, for example, of power plants, dams and airports. In principle, determining the cost of the land required for an infrastructure investment project should not present major problems as long as the land market operates under competitive conditions and there are no distortions causing the market price to differ from the true opportunity cost of the input.

The opportunity cost of land used in the construction of new infrastructure is the net benefit lost in the best possible alternative use of that land. For example, when the best alternative use is in agriculture, the market price of land will reflect the discounted market value (net of variable cost) of agricultural production during the time of use of the land for the project. This price will be higher the more valued the production is in that piece of land and the smaller the possibility of substitution for other pieces of land. Therefore, if the market is competitive, the price of the land will reliably reflect its opportunity cost.

The payment of this fixed factor is called economic rent, meaning that the payment of the factor is above the minimum price to have the factor offered in the market. This is represented in the right panel of Figure 4.1, with a fixed supply in the long run and with an equilibrium price w_z^0 determined by the value of the demand for the factors. The social value of the land is simply a reflection of the value of the goods obtained using the land, including any tax paid by the landowner.

The cost of the land for the project is based on a simple idea. If the land market is competitive, the opportunity cost of land required for a project is its market price (w_z^0), reflecting the net benefit lost in the best possible alternative use of that land. When the project increases the demand for land, the equilibrium represented in the right panel of Figure 4.1 is no longer compatible with the initial price w_z^0. The quantity of land demanded by the project shifts the demand curve outwards in the amount dz, and the price of land goes up to clear the market. When the price of land rises, the quantity of land demanded by the private sector goes down, releasing the land required by the project. Hence, the opportunity cost of the land for the project is the value lost when the project displaces the economic activity in that piece of land, and for small quantities of land it can be approximated by the market price of land.

In those cases where the project represents a significant change in the demand for land, the outward shift of the demand curve (in the amount of land required by the project) will increase the price from w_z^0 to w_z^1, and the cost of the land required for the project can be calculated with the average of both prices, $(w_z^0 + w_z^1)/2$, multiplied by dz. Finally, it should be underlined that the social opportunity cost of land is rarely the payment for its expropriation, which is based on some official values that are not necessarily equal to individuals' willingness to voluntarily accept the land's release for the project.

4.4 OPPORTUNITY COSTS, TAXES AND INCOME TRANSFERS

When the practitioner of cost–benefit analysis deals with real-world situations, where the social and private costs differ due to the existence of taxes, it is crucial to follow one of the two approaches when estimating the net social benefit: adding the change in surpluses or adding the change in willingness to pay and change in real resources, ignoring transfers. The following case illustrates the consequences of private decisions on social welfare in the presence of taxes, as well as the importance of following one of two alternative approaches in the evaluation.

Consider the case of a public project with the goal of deviating freight from road to rail. Assume that in both transport modes price is equal to marginal cost plus taxes, and service quality is identical. The full price (inclusive of time costs) without and with the project is shown in Table 4.1.

The project investment cost is $100 million, and it reduces the time cost by rail by $6 per unit (from $15 to $9), keeping the monetary price and the marginal costs unchanged. There are no externalities in both modes or any other direct or indirect benefit or cost. Project length is one year, and the discount rate is equal to zero. Without the project, 200 million units of freight are shipped exclusively by road, as the generalized price by road is $15 and by rail is $20. The user chooses the cheaper mode of transport (no differences in quality). With the project, the time cost by rail is cut by $6 and the generalized cost goes down to $14. This causes the deviation of the 200 million units from road to rail. Is this project socially worthy?

The situation is the following. We have a project costing $100 million and in return the time cost by train goes down from $15 to $9. The new generalized price by train is $14, and it causes 200 million units to shift from road to rail. If we look at the market, the users move freely to rail because rail is now cheaper, and doing so they get a benefit of $200 million,[3] twice the investment costs. Nevertheless, other economic agents stand in cost–benefit analysis, so we have to add their surpluses to obtain the social benefits.

Table 4.1 Real costs and income transfers

Full price of a unit by road ($) (without the project)	Full price of a unit by rail ($) (without the project)	Full price of a unit by rail ($) (with the project)
Marginal cost: 5	Marginal cost: 5	Marginal cost: 5
Tax: 5	Tax: 0	Tax: 0
Time cost: 5	Time cost: 15	Time cost: 9
Total: 15	Total: 20	Total: 14

---

[3] We assume every unit of deviated traffic obtain the same benefit.

With price equal to private marginal cost (cost plus tax) the producer surplus is zero with and without the project. The change in taxpayers' surplus is negative and equal to $1100 million ($100 million of the investment cost, and $1000 million loss of tax revenue). Adding this up to the consumer surplus ($200 million) the result is a negative social benefit equal to $900 million.

Alternatively, we can add the change in willingness to pay and change in resources. The only change here is that every unit shifting from road to rail involves a loss of $4, as there is no change in marginal cost and time cost rises from $5 to $9, and the specific tax is a mere transfer. Hence, a loss of $800 million in time costs plus the investment costs ($100 million) is equal to a negative net social benefit of $900 million.

Suppose now that the specific tax in Table 4.1 is a Pigouvian tax – that is, a tax to internalize an externality (e.g., pollution). Is this project socially desirable? Let us add the change in surpluses. The change in consumer surplus, producer surplus and taxpayer surplus is the same as before, but going back to expression (2.2) in Chapter 2, we have to add the change in surplus of a group that we called 'rest of society'. This group is better off now when 200 units deviate from road to rail, resulting in a reduction of pollution equal to $5 per unit of traffic. Multiplying by the total traffic deviated to rail we have a positive change in the surplus of the rest of society equal to $1000 million (the monetary value of the reduction in pollution).

Adding the surplus of consumers (+$200 million), taxpayers (–$1000 million of tax revenue lost and –$100 million investment costs), and the rest of society (+$1000 million), we obtain a positive net social surplus of $100 million. Alternatively, we add the change in willingness to pay and the change in resources. In this case, society loses $800 million of time with the shift from road to rail, save $1000 million of pollution, and give up $100 million of additional resources to implement the project, resulting in a net social benefit of $100 million.

4.5 THE SOCIAL OPPORTUNITY COST OF LABOUR

Virtually any investment project requires labour. The construction of public infrastructure, as well as in educational or health-related projects, needs workers with different skills. Moreover, once the construction is finished, additional labour is required for maintenance and operation during the lifetime of the project.

Once we have estimated the number of workers required for the project, we need a price to calculate the total cost of labour. Should we use the gross or the net wage? How should we account for the creation of new jobs in areas of high unemployment?

The opportunity cost of labour in expression (4.5) is valued at its market price (w), but again this is only valid under several restrictive assumptions that usually do not hold in actual project assessments, particularly in conditions of high unemployment. Thus, once the number of workers required for the project is known, the next step is to identify where these workers come from. Were they already working in the private sector? Were they previously unemployed? Were they receiving unemployment benefits?

In the analysis of the shadow price of labour it is advisable to distinguish three main possible sources of the labour demanded by a project: (1) workers already employed in other productive activities; (2) voluntarily unemployed at the current wage; and (3) involuntarily unemployed, willing to work at the current wage.

Figure 4.2 illustrates the necessary adjustments to go from the labour market wage rate to the social opportunity cost of labour in each of these cases. We will assume that the project will have a significant effect on the demand for labour and that there is a proportional income tax (τ_w). Initially, without the project, the labour market is in equilibrium, with the supply (S) and the demand (D^0) determining a wage rate of w^0 and a quantity of labour of L^0. The existence of a proportional income tax (τ_w) introduces a distinction between the market supply function (S) and the opportunity cost of the labour supplier, $S(1 - \tau_w)$. The supply function $S(1 - \tau_w)$ shows the marginal value of leisure of the workers and the demand function the value of the marginal productivity of labour for the firm. At the equilibrium wage rate (w^0), the value of marginal productivity of labour for the firm is equal to the value of leisure for the marginal worker plus the income tax.

With the project, the demand for labour shifts from D^0 to D^1 (the horizontal distance between these two parallel demands is exactly the amount of labour required for the project), the wage rate goes up to w^1 and the private demand for labour goes down from L^0 to L^2. The increase in the wage rate also has the effect of increasing the number of workers willing to work at this higher wage rate, and the equilibrium number of workers goes up to L^1. Now, we are ready to calculate the social opportunity cost of the workers hired by the project.

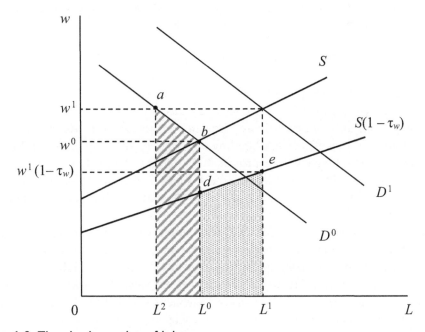

Figure 4.2 The shadow price of labour

The project needs ($L^1 - L^2$) units of labour. This quantity of labour has two components: new workers who want to work at the new equilibrium wage ($L^1 - L^0$) and workers already employed in the private sector, ($L^0 - L^2$), who shift to the project at the higher wage w^1. The opportunity cost of previously voluntarily unemployed workers – that is, ($L^1 - L^0$) – is represented by area deL^1L^0, the value of leisure lost when they accept the new jobs. Although they are paid $w_1(1 - \tau_w)(L^1 - L^0)$, their social opportunity cost is:

$$\left[\frac{1}{2}(w^0 + w^1)(1 - \tau_w)\right](L^1 - L^0).\tag{4.6}$$

The opportunity cost of those already working in the private sector ($L^0 - L^2$), who shift to the project at the higher wage w^1 are also paid $w^1(1 - \tau_w)$, but the social opportunity cost of these workers is higher, represented by area abL^0L^2, the lost value of the marginal productivity of labour in the private sector, when the amount of labour ($L^0 - L^2$) shifts to the project. They are paid $w_1(1 - \tau_w)(L^0 - L^2)$ but the social opportunity costs of these workers is:

$$\frac{1}{2}(w^0 + w^1)(L^0 - L^2).\tag{4.7}$$

This is the opportunity cost of the deviated labour when w the unit cost of labour for the firm as represented in Figure 4.2. In the case of a proportional social security contribution paid by employers (α_w) plus the existence of *ad valorem* indirect taxes (e.g., value-added tax), levied on the product market, the shadow price of the deviated labour must reflect the social value lost as a consequence of displacing labour from other productive activities, and this includes the tax revenues and any other charges lost in the process. The shadow price of labour in this later case is:

$$(1 + \theta)(1 + \alpha_w)\left[\frac{1}{2}(w^0 + w^1)(L^0 - L^2)\right].\tag{4.8}$$

When the workers of the project are involuntarily unemployed, willing to work at the current wage, the supply curve is perfectly elastic, as in Figure 4.3.

The supply has an infinite elasticity, showing that the workers are willing to work at the equilibrium wage if they are hired by the firms. At the level of demand D^0 there is involuntary unemployment. The project shifts the demand for labour D^0 to D^1. The project requires ($L^1 - L^0$) units of labour, the distance between the demand without and with the project, and this amount is supplied to the market without any change in the initial wage rate.

A useful distinction is between the reservation wage, the worker opportunity cost and the social opportunity cost. Figure 4.3 shows that the unemployed worker receives unemployment benefits equal to u, and if he accepts the job there is a proportional income tax (τ_w). Hence, as his reservation wage is w^0 (he is not willing to work for less than this wage), the worker's payment is equal to the value of leisure plus the unemployment benefits (u) plus the income tax (τ_w) he has to pay if he accepts the job.

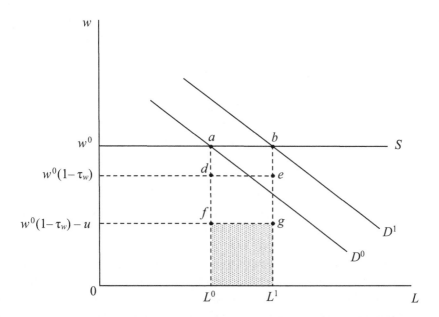

Figure 4.3 The shadow price of labour with involuntary unemployment

The individual opportunity cost is, therefore, his value of leisure plus the unemployment benefits. However, the social opportunity cost cannot include the unemployment benefits (a transfer) as a cost of the project because the real loss in resources when the individual is employed is the marginal value of leisure. The shadow price of labour is then:

$$w^0\left(1-\tau_w\right)-u, \tag{4.9}$$

and the social cost of these workers for the project is:

$$\left[w^0\left(1-\tau_w\right)-u\right]\left(L^1-L^0\right), \tag{4.10}$$

corresponding to area fgL^1L^0 in the figure. Another case showing the importance of being consistent in following one of the two approaches in the evaluation. In the case of adding the change in surpluses, the private opportunity cost is applicable, whereas it is the social opportunity cost that matters if the approach is the change in willingness to pay and resources.

For the sake of exposition, let us assume that the project's good is provided free of charge. The social opportunity cost of $(L^1 - L^0)$ in Figure 4.3 is represented by area fgL^1L^0, the value of leisure. The private opportunity cost is higher and represented by the areas deL^1L^0. Change in surpluses are the following: the consumer surplus is the total WTP, the producer surplus is negative and equal to area abL^1L^0. There is no change in worker surplus as they are paid their private opportunity cost. Finally, the taxpayer surplus increases in the income tax collected (area *abed*) and the unemployment benefit payments avoided (area *degf*). Therefore, the change in social surplus is equal to the change in *WTP* minus the area fgL^1L^0. The treatment of the opportunity cost of labour can be misleading unless the practitioner strictly follows one of the described approaches.

When there is a minimum wage regulation we also need to correct the market wage to account for the social opportunity cost of labour in the same manner as described above, by looking for what society gives up by employing the workers in the project. This can be done by distinguishing between the minimum wage and the lowest reservation wage, as no one accepting to work is paid a wage lower than the minimum wage, and hence the reservation wage of anyone employed thanks to the project is going to be higher than the lowest reservation wage. In the absence of information on the lowest reservation wage, the shadow wage could be estimated as one-half of the minimum wage (i.e., assuming the lowest reservation wage is zero).

The previous treatment of the shadow price of labour, when there is unemployment, does not consider what happens to the output that is generated by the project. If the production generated by the project is sold in a competitive market and reduces the price in this product market, it may happen that labour is reduced as a result of business closures in the private sector of the economy; but it could also be true that the product or service associated with the project is complementary to other competitive markets and therefore it encourages job creation. Determining the true shadow price in these cases is not immediate. In any case, a careful analysis of the markets closely related to the project and its potential impact on them can help the evaluator (see Johansson, 1991).

4.6 THE SHADOW PRICE OF PUBLIC FUNDS

Many projects require public funds. Sometimes, users are not charged for the service supplied, as in the case of a free-access road. Even when they pay, some projects require public funding, as is the case of a natural area with an entry fee insufficient to cover the total cost. In these and similar cases, they are partially or totally funded by taxes. The problem of tax revenue from the standpoint of efficiency is that tax collection is not a mere transfer of income between consumers, workers, producers and the government. Generally, there is an efficiency loss associated with the operation of transferring funds through taxes that leads to the question of how much the deadweight loss of the tax is.

The excess tax burden or deadweight loss of the tax is the net value of the production lost with the introduction of the tax and hence must be included as an opportunity cost of the project. Hence, the social cost of public funds (*SCF*) devoted to a project includes the tax revenue (*R*) plus the tax excess burden (*EB*):

$$SCF = R + EB. \tag{4.11}$$

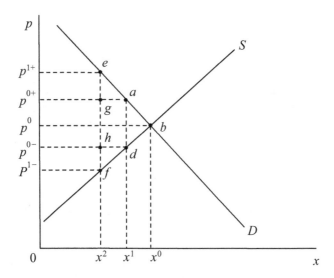

Figure 4.4 The shadow price of public funds

The excess burden of the tax will depend on what tax is raised and the magnitude of the tax, among other things such as the demand and supply elasticities. To illustrate why it is necessary to estimate the shadow price of public funds, let us assume there is only one taxed good, the economy is perfectly competitive and, in order to avoid income distribution effects, all producers and consumers are identical (see Dahlby, 2008). This market is represented in Figure 4.4.

The government charges an indirect tax (in year 0) in a market unrelated to the project. The tax is intended to finance a project whose investment costs (I_0) occur only in year 0. It produces constant annual benefits ($\bar{B}$) during each of the T years of life of the project. The real interest rate is zero and the benefits $\bar{B}$ correspond entirely to a gain in consumer surplus (assuming that nothing is charged for the good).

The net present value (NPV) of the project is equal to the difference between the flow of benefits and the investment costs:

$$NPV = -I_0 + T\bar{B}. \qquad (4.12)$$

Nevertheless, a simple look at Figure 4.4 shows that the social cost involved in the finance of the project is greater than I_0, because the effects of the introduction of the tax are not limited to an income transfer. Initially, the market is in equilibrium at b with a price p^0 and a quantity equal to x^0. The introduction of the tax changes the equilibrium of the market by raising the price paid by consumers to p^{0+} and reducing the quantity demanded to x^1. The price received by producers is p^{0-} and tax collection is represented by the area $p^{0+}adp^{0-}$, which is equal to the investment cost I_0.

The introduction of the tax has caused a reduction in the quantity from x^0 to x^1. This reduction of the quantity represents a negative effect on the economy, as the consumers were willing to pay the area abx^0x^1 for goods or services whose opportunity cost is represented by the area dbx^0x^1. The net loss of efficiency caused by no longer producing $x^0 - x^1$ equals the area abd. This extra cost of collecting the funds, the excess tax burden, must be included in the evaluation of the project.

Assuming that the area abd is, for example, 20 per cent of the tax revenue, the marginal cost, the shadow price (or shadow multiplier) of public funds is equal to 1.2, and the cost of the project is equal to $1.2I_0$. Let λ_g be the shadow price of public funds. Then we should modify equation (4.12) in order to reflect the opportunity cost of the investment:

$$NPV = -\lambda_g I_0 + T\bar{B}, \tag{4.13}$$

so we can appreciate that, to obtain an NPV greater than zero, the following must be satisfied:

$$\frac{T\bar{B}}{I_0} > \lambda_g. \tag{4.14}$$

The economic interpretation of expression (4.14) indicates that, for a project funded by taxes to be socially profitable, the social benefit obtained per unit of money invested has to be greater than the opportunity cost of the public funds.

The previous argument assumes that the project is financed entirely by taxes. A more general expression is the following:

$$NPV = -I_0\lambda_g + \sum_{t=1}^{T} \frac{CS_t + \lambda_g PS_t}{(1+i)^t}, \tag{4.15}$$

where:

CS_t: consumer surplus in year t;
PS_t: producer surplus in year t;
i: social discount rate.

Expression (4.15) shows that the shadow price of public funds should be applied to both costs and revenues. The annual net revenue reduces the need for public funding and therefore the need for taxes, so that $1 collected by charging the users in any year in the life of the project has a present value equal to $\lambda_g(1+i)^{-t}$.

The social marginal cost of public fund ($SMCF$) is obtained taking the first derivative of (4.11) with respect to R:

$$SMCF = 1 + \frac{dEB}{dR}. \tag{4.16}$$

Under the assumption of a tax introduced at the competitive equilibrium point, the social marginal (or rather incremental) cost in Figure 4.4 is equal to the excess burden (abd) divided by the tax revenue (area $p^{0+}adp^{0-}$), and so the shadow price of public funds in this case can be calculated as $\lambda_g = 1 + \frac{EB}{R}$ (1.2 in our example).

Let us assume alternatively that the competitive market represented in Figure 4.4 is in equilibrium at point a as the commodity is already taxed. Now the project under evaluation needs to increase the existing specific tax, resulting in a new market price p^{1+}. In this case it is straightforward to see how the marginal excess burden is increasing. For a similar reduction in output, the new excess burden (area $eadf$) is now higher than the initial one (area abd).

A simple inspection of Figure 4.4 shows that the marginal excess burden dEB/dR is positive and increasing with the size of the tax, so financing new projects through additional taxation must face an increase in the social marginal cost of public funds. This also implies a demanding benchmark to the number and size of public projects that pass the test of a positive NPV, as the marginal benefit of additional projects requiring financing is expected to diminish while the social marginal cost of public funds is expected to increase.

THINGS TO REMEMBER

1. The cost of a project is the net benefit lost in the next best alternative of the resources committed to that project. In other words, it is the utility lost when giving up some goods for the implementation of the project. This value is, expressed in monetary terms, the sum the individuals are willing to pay for the goods that are no longer produced.
2. The opportunity cost of an input is the net value lost in its next best alternative. The market price in the factor markets is the first candidate for the opportunity cost. There are circumstances, such as the existence of taxes, externalities or unemployment, where the market price must be adjusted to obtain the opportunity cost. This is what is called shadow pricing.
3. The shadow price of an input for the project has a lower and an upper bound depending on the source of that input. When the input comes from additional production, the opportunity cost is its social marginal cost of producing the input, its market price net of any indirect tax. When the input is deviated from the production of other goods, the opportunity cost is the total value of those goods lost.
4. Labour is an input, not an output. The opportunity cost of labour in cost–benefit analysis varies, as with many other inputs, depending on the preceding use of the input. When a worker is previously employed, the gross value of her marginal productivity can be used as the opportunity cost. With involuntary unemployment, the shadow price can be as low as the value of the worker's leisure.
5. There are many projects requiring public financing. Some projects are provided free and others have prices that are not high enough to break even. When projects are financed (partially or totally) by taxes, the distortionary effect of taxation must be considered. Tax collection is not a simple transfer between taxpayers and the government. There is a loss of economic value along the way. The deadweight loss of the tax must be included in the shadow price of public funds.

5
Discounting and decision criteria (I)

Should Americans work harder and invest more to increase industrial production? The economist's answer is, only if it makes them happier. Newscasters report economic growth as if it were a benefit with no offsetting cost. Growth does benefit individuals, because it allows them to increase their consumption in the future. The conditions that create growth impose costs on individuals, who must work harder and consume less in the present. Is this trade-off worth it? The answer depends solely on the preferences of the individuals themselves.

(Steven E. Landsburg, 1993, p. 101)

5.1 INTRODUCTION

Benefits and costs occurring in different years must be aggregated to obtain the net present value (NPV) of the project. In cost–benefit analysis, economists add the flow of benefits and costs of different kinds in a single dimension. To add units of benefits or costs corresponding to different individuals and to different time periods we require two types of weights. The first is basically for reasons of equity (see Section 2.5 in Chapter 2), and the second, considered in this chapter and the next, because the temporal dimension of benefits and costs matters.

There are many possible reasons explaining the intertemporal marginal rate of substitution, and it is useful to distinguish between time discounting and time preference. Time discounting incorporates any reason to give less importance to the future. Time preference refers to the preference for the utility in the present over delayed utility (Frederick et al., 2002).

This chapter has two parts. The first is devoted to covering the mechanics of discounting (Sections 5.2 and 5.3). Homogenization involving the arithmetic of discounting allows the comparison of the sacrifice of present consumption, implied by the decision to invest in a project, with the flow of net benefits that occurs throughout its life.

The second part is devoted to a basic discussion of the social discount rate, a key parameter for the economic evaluation of projects. The discount rate determines in many circumstances whether a project is socially worthy, because it is a sort of exchange rate between the present and the future and may be the determinant of an advantageous trade-off – that is, to renounce a certain amount of present consumption for the reward of future goods. In Section 5.4 we review the concepts of marginal rate of time prefer-ence, marginal productivity of capital and interest rate. In perfect capital markets the social discount rate is easy to determine because the three rates are equal. With distor-tions, like taxes on savings and investment returns, the interest rate is no longer equal to the marginal rate of time preference and the marginal productivity of capital, hence in Section 5.5 we discuss how to calculate the social discount rate in these conditions. Finally, in Section 5.6, we address the problem of discounting when future generations are involved.

5.2 DISCOUNTING THE FUTURE

Most projects involve costs in the present in exchange for a stream of net benefits in the future. The flows of expected benefits and costs resulting from the implementation of the project must be aggregated to obtain the NPV. This economic indicator represents in a single figure the net benefit of the project, the profitability (social or private) of the project under evaluation.

The basic decision rule in both the financial and the economic evaluation of projects is: accept the project if the NPV is positive and reject it if it is negative,[1] since in the latter case a better use of the resources is possible. A positive NPV is a necessary condition to undertake a project, but it is not sufficient, as shown in Chapter 6.

Even in the absence of uncertainty, individuals do not generally assign the same value to a monetary unit regardless of the time in which it is received. Only in cases where indi-viduals were indifferent between present consumption and future consumption could the net benefits of different periods be added unweighted. An expression for the calculus of the net present value that allows for a positive marginal rate of time preference (one unit is more highly valued in the present than in the future) is the following:

$$NPV = \sum_{t=0}^{T} \delta^t \left(B_t - C_t \right),$$ (5.1)

where:

B_t: benefits in year t;
C_t: costs in year t;
T: life of the project in years;
δ^t: discount factor.

---

[1] It should be noted that the basic rule of decision based on the NPV without further qualification requires the investment to be reversible; that is, if the annual benefits are not the expected ones the investment can be recovered; or even in the case of irreversibility, the investment decision cannot be postponed ('now or never'). If investment is partially or totally irreversible, there is uncertainty over the future net benefits, and it is possible to postpone the investment, the opportunity cost of killing the option to invest should be included in the calculus of the NPV (see chapter 6).

The common discount factor used in cost–benefit analysis is shown in expression (5.2). This is what is called exponential discounting, which gives exponentially decreasing weight to the benefits and costs occurring in the future:[2]

$$\delta^t = \frac{1}{(1+i)^t}, \tag{5.2}$$

where i is the social discount rate.

The project life is determined by the evaluating agency. It may or not coincide with the physical life, but it generally coincides with the estimated economic life, which is usually shorter than the physical life. In the case of a longer lifespan than the period chosen for evaluation we need to include the residual or salvage value. The residual value is the value of the flow of net benefits from year $T + 1$ to infinity and hence it could be positive or negative depending on the characteristics of the project. In the case, for example, of recovering costs through the sale of equipment at the end of its life, the residual value could be positive. On the contrary, when there are significant dismantling costs, the residual value could be negative.

The mechanics of discounting values generated in different time periods assumes that the individual has a stronger preference for the present than for the future. If the individual's utility depends on consumption in successive periods we assume that the individual gives more weight to the consumption that is closer to the present, so that her utility function includes a positive marginal rate of time preference that discounts the value of consumption according to its location in time.

There are two opposing forces in the utility function of individuals with regard to the discounting of consumption over time. One supports the idea of not discounting because of the diminishing marginal utility of consumption; the other goes in the opposite direction and supports discounting because of the impatience of individuals, for whatever reason. The first justifies the individual trying to spread the consumption over different time periods. The second explains that an individual values the satisfaction derived from the consumption of one unit today more than the delayed satisfaction of the consumption in one year's time.[3]

The discount factor in expression (5.2) has two fundamental characteristics: it is less than one for values of $i > 0$ and $t > 0$, and it decreases rapidly as t increases. Its implementation implies reducing the present value of benefits and costs that occur when $t > 1$ and also implies that benefits and costs far apart in time are irrelevant.

If the discount rate is, for instance, 6 per cent, the value of $100 of benefit (or cost) in year one is converted into $94 in the base year. In the fifth year, $100 is equivalent to $75 once it is discounted to the present. In 30 years, the value drops to $17, and in 100 years the present value is only 30 cents.

---

[2] All benefits and costs, and the social discount rate are expressed in real terms. For the treatment of inflation see section 2.4 in Chapter 2.

[3] In fact, it is a different moment in time: a year, a month, or any other time period (see section 5.3).

This fact has been of concern to environmental economists, who believe that exponential discounting penalizes projects whose benefits are realized in the long term (e.g., reforestation), and benefits projects with huge costs in the distant future (e.g., radioactive waste) – that is, it ignores the welfare of future generations.

As an alternative to exponential discounting, some economists have proposed using a hyperbolic discount factor, which, although it is also less than one for values of $i > 0$ and $t > 0$, its value decreases more slowly when t increases. Unlike exponential discounting, with hyperbolic discounting the present value of benefits and costs that occur in the distant future affects the profitability of the project.

It has also been argued that when there are different discount rates to reflect individual differences in intertemporal preferences, and the government takes an average of these preferences, the resulting discount rate decreases with time, tending to the lowest value of the range of rates as we move further away in time (see Section 5.6).

The time horizon of many projects can exceed 50 years (some sections of roads built by the Roman Empire are still in use). The choice of discount rate is one of the key aspects of economic evaluation as it can dramatically affect its social profitability in an accept/reject situation or change its relative profitability when choosing among different projects. When the flows of net benefits of the projects being compared have different time profiles, the discount rate may be decisive in the selection process, as we shall see below.

As noted previously, the common approach to discounting is shown in expression (5.2). This discounting procedure is generally accepted for those projects that do not involve a loss of human lives or environmental impacts, or significantly affect the welfare of future generations.

Let us see with an example the arithmetic of discounting. Project A, represented in Figure 5.1, has a duration of 11 years. Initially (base year: $t = 0$), it requires an investment of $2500. After a year[4] the project generates net benefits of $2000. From the second until the 11th year, the annual net benefits are $100. At the end of the project the residual value is zero.

Project A

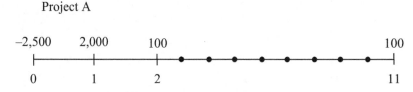

Figure 5.1 Time profile of project A (values in $)

---

[4] Between zero and one, 365 days have passed, so in fact zero and one are moments in time and the year is the interval. For simplicity we refer to the points zero, one, two, and so on in Figure 5.1 as year zero, year one, year two, and so on. Of course, the periods of time can be less than a year (see section 5.3).

According to expression (5.1) the economic profitability of project A is as follows:

$$NPV(A) = -2500 + \frac{2000}{1+i} + \sum_{t=2}^{11} \frac{100}{(1+i)^t}. \tag{5.3}$$

The profitability of the project, measured by NPV, heavily depends on the chosen discount factor. Suppose that the discount rate is 5 per cent. In this case the NPV of the project is positive ($NPV(A/i = 0.05) = 140$), so the discounted net benefits are higher than the investment costs. The value of $140 is equal to the investment less the discounted value of the benefits from years one to 11. This positive difference of $140 indicates that the project allows the remuneration of the investment at its opportunity cost, recovering the invested capital and generating a social surplus that, valued in year zero, is equal to $140.

Let us maintain the same time profile of project A and the same initial investment but change the discount rate. For example, suppose that the interest rate on this project is 10 per cent instead of 5 per cent. The result of the investment is now negative ($NPV(A/i = 0.10)) = -123$). The flow of net income represented in Figure 5.1 is now not enough to offset an investment that is now required to yield a higher return.

Figure 5.2 shows how the NPV of project A changes when the discount rate changes. In this way, at a zero interest rate, the NPV is equal to $500, which is the direct sum of the net benefits less the initial investment cost; when the interest rate is 5 per cent, the NPV is equal to $140. The NPV curve as a function of i cuts the horizontal axis at an interest rate equal to approximately 7.5 per cent. This interest rate, for which the NPV is

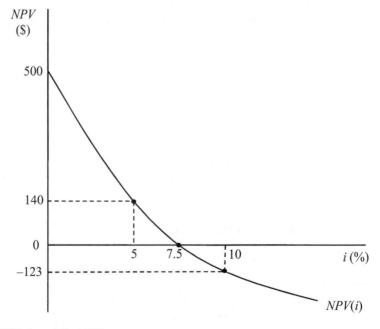

Figure 5.2 *NPV, i and the IRR*

Project B

Project C

Figure 5.3 Time profile of projects B and C (values in $)

zero, is called the internal rate of return (*IRR*) and indicates that the net benefits of the project equal their opportunity costs, valued at 7.5 per cent per year; or, equivalently, the project allows the recovery of the capital invested and its remuneration at a rate of 7.5 per cent per year.

We have seen how the *NPV* is reduced when the discount rate rises, becoming negative for interest rates higher than the *IRR*. Even when it does not change the sign of the *NPV*, applying a higher discount rate can affect the profitability of various projects with different time profiles, and change the order of preferences among such projects. Consider the case of two projects, B and C, whose temporal profiles are represented in Figure 5.3.

The economic life of both projects is 11 years. They also require the same investment costs in the base year ($2000). Projects B and C differ, however, in the profile of their annual benefits. Project B, in contrast with project C, has an important part of its benefits at the beginning of its life.

The economic returns of both projects are:

$$NPV\left(B\right) = -2000 + \frac{2000}{1+i} + \sum_{t=2}^{11} \frac{100}{\left(1+i\right)^{t}}, \tag{5.4}$$

$$NPV\left(C\right) = -2000 + \sum_{t=1}^{9} \frac{100}{\left(1+i\right)^{t}} + \frac{2000}{\left(1+i\right)^{10}} + \frac{2100}{\left(1+i\right)^{11}}. \tag{5.5}$$

It can be appreciated how the value considered for the interest rate affects the two projects unequally. Suppose that initially the interest rate is 5 per cent. Applying this discount rate, project C is preferred to project B since *NPV*(*C*/*i* = 0.05) = 1166 and *NPV*(*B*/*i* = 0.05) = 640. Both projects are socially desirable when the interest rate is 5 per cent and there are no budget constraints because they have an *NPV* greater than zero.

However, in cases where there are limited funds ($2000), project C would be preferred to project B.

What happens with a higher discount rate – for example, an interest rate of 10 per cent? The two projects are still profitable, $NPV(B/i = 0.1) = 377$ and $NPV(C/i = 0.1) = 83$, but now project B is preferable to project C. It is interesting to examine why the selection of projects changes when we change the discount rate. The rationale is that the profitability of a project depends not only on the magnitude of its benefits, but also on when they occur – that is, their location in time. Without discounting, the net benefits of project C are higher than those of B; however, they occur later in time. A high interest rate 'penalizes' these benefits, indicating that they have less present value for the individuals because they occur in the future.

The discount factor acts as a weight for the benefits and costs over the life of the project. This weight tends to zero as t increases (provided that i is greater than zero). The economic rationale is clear: if the discount rate applicable to the project rises, the later the benefit is realized, the lower its present value. Figure 5.4 shows how the ranking of two mutually exclusive projects changes when modifying the interest rates.

As Figure 5.4 shows, the profitability of a project compared with its alternative is sensitive to the interest rate. For interest rates between 0 and approximately 7.9 per cent, C is preferred to B; however, for values of $i > 0.079$, the comparative advantage of C disappears. Raising the discount rate has changed the order of preferences of two mutually exclusive projects.

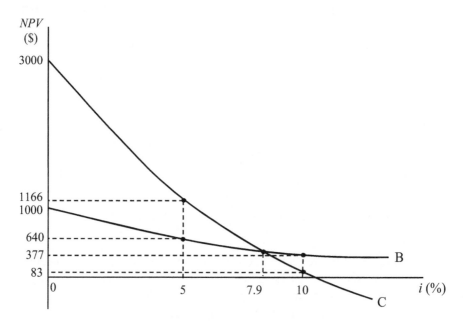

Figure 5.4 The ranking of two mutually exclusive projects

5.3 THE MECHANICS OF DISCOUNTING: SOME USEFUL FORMULAS

Cost–benefit analysis can be applied to investment projects and policies that involve effects on society for long periods of time. The evaluation of investments and regulatory measures, or any other public policy that can sensibly be quantified in economic terms, has an associated flow of benefits and costs during T years that have to be added to obtain the NPV.

Year T may not be the last year of the life of the project but its duration for evaluation purposes. The reason that T can be less than the real life of the project may be because the regulatory framework so requires, because it is pertinent to evaluate the period covered by the contract of private participation or because it is expected that, technologically, T is the maximum length that can reasonably be considered before technical obsolescence applies.

In any of the above cases it is necessary to calculate the *residual value* of the project. This value is the net present value of the benefits and costs of the project from $T + 1$ until infinity. This could mean the cost of dismantling a provisional infrastructure with no further use beyond T; or perhaps, the benefits obtained from the future use of the assets and deducting the costs of obtaining such benefits, which would include the cost of dismantling the equipment or cleaning and decontaminating the soil, and so on. Sometimes the residual value is calculated as a percentage of the investment costs, as an estimate of the remaining value of the assets, but this accounting practice seems to be quite unrelated to the concept of the remaining social value of the project (the benefits and costs beyond T).

Leaving aside the investment costs (which we assume for simplicity to correspond to the year zero) and focusing our attention on the flow of benefits and costs from year one onwards, we have:

$$\sum_{t=1}^{T} \delta^t \left(B_t - C_t \right).$$

(5.6)

Denoting $(B_t - C_t)$ as V_t in expression (5.6), where V is value, and assuming that V_t, realized at the end of each year, is positive and constant $(V_t = V)$ during the life of the project, the time profile of net benefits is shown in Figure 5.5.

The NPV is equal to:

$$\sum_{t=1}^{T} \frac{V}{(1+i)^t} = \frac{V}{(1+i)} + \frac{V}{(1+i)^2} + \ldots + \frac{V}{(1+i)^T}.$$

(5.7)

To calculate the NPV in expression (5.7), remember that this is the sum of the terms of a geometric progression, whose first term is $V/(1 + i)$ and the common ratio is $1/(1 + i)$. The sum of this finite geometric progression is equal to:

$$V\left[\frac{1 - (1+i)^{-T}}{i} \right].$$

(5.8)

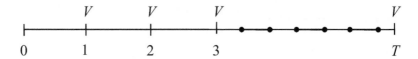

Figure 5.5 Benefits at the end of the year

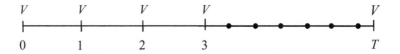

Figure 5.6 Benefits in year zero and at the end of the year

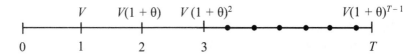

Figure 5.7 Benefits grow at a constant rate

Expression (5.8) is the general formulation for calculating the NPV of a stream of a constant value for any duration.[5] The expression in parentheses is the factor that turns a constant flow of benefits over time into a value discounted to the present. This factor increases with the duration of the project and decreases with the interest rate. When T tends to infinity, expression (5.8) is equal to V/i.

Using expression (5.8) to calculate the NPV, the example in expression (5.3) can be written as:

$$NPV(A) = -2500 + \frac{2000}{1+i} + 100 \frac{1-(1+i)^{-10}}{i} \frac{1}{1+i}. \tag{5.9}$$

If the time profile of the project includes benefits in year zero (Figure 5.6) we simply add V to expression (5.8). Calculating the sum of the progression of $T + 1$ terms we obtain expression (5.10):

$$NPV = \frac{V(1+i)}{i}\left(1 - \frac{1}{(1+i)^{T+1}}\right). \tag{5.10}$$

Expressions (5.8) and (5.10) rely on the assumption of constant annual benefits. When benefits change over time according to a constant average annual rate, both expressions should be modified. Suppose that V is a function of gross domestic product and grows at an annual rate equal to θ, so that $V_{t+1} = V_t(1 + \theta)$. Now the time profile is represented by Figure 5.7, and the equation for NPV is expression (5.11):

---

[5] Assuming benefits start in year one. This formula allows us, solving for V, to calculate the annual value that corresponds to the present value of an asset or a fixed cost that has to be annualized: $V = NPV\,((1 + i)^T i)/((1 + i)^T - 1)$.

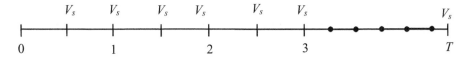

Figure 5.8 Benefits occur more than once a year

$$NPV = \frac{V}{(1+i)} + \frac{V(1+\theta)}{(1+i)^2} + ... + \frac{V(1+\theta)^{T-1}}{(1+i)^T}.$$ (5.11)

For a discrete time length, expression (5.11) is equal to:

$$NPV = V\left[\frac{1-(1+\theta)^T(1+i)^{-T}}{i-\theta}\right].$$ (5.12)

When $T \to \infty$, if $\theta < i$, $((1 + \theta/1 + i))^T \to 0$, and thus for a given V in the first period that grows at a rate θ to perpetuity:

$$NPV = \frac{V}{i-\theta}.$$ (5.13)

The benefits and costs may occur at the end of the year, quarterly or monthly, or continuously, as with the demand for a dam that supplies water without interruption or a road that saves time for a continuous flow of vehicles driving on it since opening up to T.

When benefits are produced twice a year, for example, and the annual discount rate is i, we have the time profile shown in Figure 5.8.

To discount the benefits, we need the semester interest rate i_s equivalent to the corresponding annual rate i (or, in general, the interest rate that matches the corresponding subperiod) for the discounting of the benefits, that occur every six months (or in other periods shorter than a year), called V_s:

$$(1+i_s)^s = (1+i),$$ (5.14)

where s is the number of subperiods (semesters in this case). Solving for i_s:

$$i_s = (1+i)^{\frac{1}{s}} - 1.$$ (5.15)

Given that $1 + i_s = (1 + i)^{1/s}$, the discounting for the first four semesters in Figure 5.8 is as follows:

$$NPV = \frac{V_s}{(1+i)^{0.5}} + \frac{V_s}{(1+i)} + \frac{V_s}{(1+i)^{1.5}} + \frac{V_s}{(1+i)^2},$$ (5.16)

or

$$NPV = \frac{V_s}{(1+i_s)} + \frac{V_s}{(1+i_s)^2} + \frac{V_s}{(1+i_s)^3} + \frac{V_s}{(1+i_s)^4}.$$ (5.17)

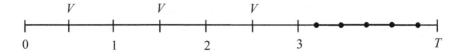

Figure 5.9 Benefits in the middle of the year

Expression (5.18) generalizes the calculus of the NPV of a stream of benefits V_s that occur in periods shorter than a year. It is obtained by replacing the number of subperiods and the subperiod interest rate obtained according to expression (5.15) in expression (5.8):

$$NPV = V_s \left[\frac{1-(1+i_s)^{-Ts}}{i_s} \right]. \tag{5.18}$$

The discount formulas obtained above are useful for constant flows of benefits and costs ($V_t = V$) or those that grow at constant rates ($\theta_t = \theta$). In practice, this is not often the case, as the annual values do not conform to a pattern that allows the direct application of the previous expressions.[6]

It is worth noting that many projects have annual benefits V that are generated in an almost continuous manner, but they are often treated as if they occur at the end of year, as in Figure 5.5. Consider the case of an airport, a dam or a sports centre whose output is produced from 1 January until 31 December. It seems obvious that if the benefits are located at the end of the year, as happens to be the case, the NPV appears to be lower (the further in time the benefits, the lower the present value).

It can be argued that if benefits and costs occur every day of the year, and should be located in an instant of the year, it is more appropriate to place them in the middle of the year than at the beginning or the end. The time profile is shown in Figure 5.9.

The formula for discounting the annual benefits located in the middle of the year, applying the annual discount rate, is as follows:

$$NPV = V \left[\frac{1-(1+i)^{-T}}{i} \right] (1+i)^{0.5}. \tag{5.19}$$

Expression (5.19) corrects the annual discount formula (5.8) with the factor $(1+i)^{0.5}$ in order to place the discounted value at time zero. Otherwise, the application of expression (5.8) would have located it at time '−0.5'. Applying expression (5.19) we would obtain the same results as applying expression (5.18) with benefits expressed per day ($V_s = V/365$) – that is, the benefits are realized daily and discounted with a daily discount rate that corresponds to the annual rate $i_s = (1+i)^{1/365} - 1$.

If the project delivers a continuous flow from the beginning of the first day of the year (health service, roads, airports, water supply, etc.), it seems reasonable in view of these results to place V in the middle of the year, which is equivalent to treating the benefits

---

[6] The NPV and IRR are available in the menu of formulas of any spreadsheet.

as if they occur daily or continuously. This may not be too important in many projects but it is worth knowing the implications of the formulas we use.

5.4 THE MARGINAL RATE OF TIME PREFERENCE AND THE MARGINAL PRODUCTIVITY OF CAPITAL

The economic analysis of the intertemporal choice that individuals make between present consumption and future consumption helps us to understand the difficulties of choosing the social discount rate. Although it may be possible for some individuals to consider present consumption (x_0) and future consumption (x_1) as perfect substitutes, it is more likely that the trade-off changes both due to time preference and the endowment of both goods that the individual has at the time of making a choice. For ordinary preferences, the higher x_0 is with respect to x_1, the more willing the individual will be to give up x_0 by an additional unit of x_1.

The compensation the individual requires in excess of a unit of future consumption for giving up a unit of consumption today is called the marginal rate of time preference (ξ). Therefore, the individual is indifferent between a unit of x_0 and $(1 + \xi)$ of x_1. However, the market compensates the individual with a return that does not necessarily coincide with ξ. The rate that indicates what the individual receives is the interest rate (i) that represents the additional amount that is obtained on a unit in the future if he gives up a unit in the present.

Both ξ and i can be negative: ξ is negative in cases where, for example, the individual has a strong preference for the future and/or has a very high initial endowment of present consumption compared with future consumption, and so is willing to give up a unit of x_0 in exchange, for example, for 0.9 units of x_1 ($\xi = -0.1$). A negative interest rate is possible if the nominal interest rate is close to the rate of inflation and there are taxes on the return of financial assets.

A third rate in the analysis of intertemporal decisions is the marginal productivity of capital or the internal rate of return on investment (r), which indicates what the individual receives if he invests one unit in productive projects. Ignoring the existence of taxes and uncertainty, if r is greater than i, investing in a project is attractive because it yields higher returns than putting the money in the bank. Assume that all the projects are ordered from the most to the least profitable. The individual will undertake all the productive investment projects that satisfy $r > i$ until in the last project he is indifferent between investing in the project and putting the money in the bank ($r = i$).

An individual who allocates his funds according to this criterion maximizes the present value of his wealth; and once the NPV is the maximum possible, he takes his consumption choices between present and future according to his marginal rate of time preference. If $\xi < i$ he will lend money to the bank and if $\xi > i$ he will borrow. In equilibrium, the three rates are equal.

The equality ($r = i = \xi$) means that the marginal rate of time preference is equal to the rate of marginal productivity of capital and the interest rate. This result shows that all the investment projects that offered higher profitability than the individual was willing to sacrifice in terms of present consumption have been carried out. This is so because the existence of a perfect capital market discourages one from investing in one's own projects with lower profitability rather than other investment projects available in the economy whose profitability is represented by the market interest rate.

Investment projects and public policies compromise public funds obtained from the private sector with the purpose of financing actions decided by the government that are expected to increase social welfare. The use of these public funds to finance projects has an opportunity cost. Assuming that these projects are funded with taxpayers' money, consumption and investment have been left without funding because the public sector has absorbed those funds. To these opportunity costs, the deadweight loss of taxes should be added (see Section 4.6).

We have seen how the interest rate, the marginal rate of time preference and the marginal productivity of capital coincide when there are no restrictions on the financial markets, no taxes and no distortions in the production or consumption that prevent the achievement of the equality of the three rates.

Figure 5.10 represents the capital market in an economy without distortions. The interest rate i is the opportunity cost of capital for the financing of projects. At i_0, the curves of demand and supply of the available funds (K) intersect. The demand curve D represents the investment options in the economy, investment opportunities with declining marginal productivity. When the interest rate falls, new projects turn out to be

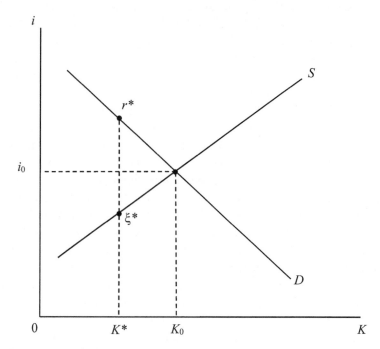

Figure 5.10 The market for available funds

profitable in the private sector because the internal rates of return of these projects are now higher than the cost of financing (interest rate).

The supply of available funds (S), the savings, increases with the interest rate, indicating that as i increases, individuals are willing to give up more units of present consumption. At the equilibrium, the interest rate i_0 is equal to the marginal rate of time preference; at interest rate level i_0 savings are equal to K_0, with no more individuals willing to give up present consumption for future consumption at this interest rate.

Let us see what happens starting from K^*, where the marginal rate of time preference (ξ^*) is less than the marginal rate of return on capital (r^*). In this case there are some projects that produce higher returns than lenders require to give up present consumption. It is socially desirable to transfer funds from lenders to investors, and this is what will happen in the capital market if there are no distortions that prevent it.

For the level of investment K_0 there is no investment project whose internal rate of return is less than the rate of time preference. Then it is not worth investing in public projects that do not achieve a return equal to i_0 (remember that there are no distortions such as externalities or taxes). If the public agency decides to invest in projects with a rate of return lower than i_0, the social welfare decreases, as present consumption will be replaced by future consumption at a suboptimal rate. It can be concluded that, under the conditions described above, the marginal rate of time preference equals the social discount rate and the interest rate.

5.5 THE SOCIAL DISCOUNT RATE AND THE RATE OF INTEREST

Figure 5.11 represents a capital market with distortions caused by taxes on savings and corporate profits. The supply curve S shifts upwards, S^* being the function that represents the interest rates required for different amounts of savings. The height of the shift is the tax, which is assumed to be constant per unit of returns on savings. Similarly, the investment demand function shifts to the left and downward in the amount of the unitary tax on profits, reflecting the fact that the internal rate of return on investment has declined for all the projects.

The new equilibrium interest rate can be equal to (as in Figure 5.11 for convenience), greater than or less than the one in a market without restrictions, depending on the elasticities of supply and demand. The amount of investment K_b is lower than K_0, because of the higher cost of borrowing and the lower returns on investment. The social discount rate in a capital market without distortions is equal to the market interest rate because $i = \xi = r$, while in the most realistic case represented in Figure 5.11, $i \neq \xi \neq r$. The question is, which of the three rates should be used as the social rate of discount?

If the project is financed with savings of the consumers, the social discount rate is i_d, which is the marginal social rate of time preference, lower than the market interest rate, as represented in Figure 5.11; on the contrary, if the project is financed with funds displaced from private investment projects, we must use the social rate of discount i_e,

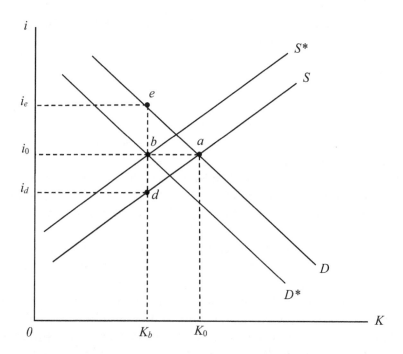

Figure 5.11 Determination of the social rate of discount

higher than the market interest rate, as this marginal rate of return on capital is what is being obtained from the displaced projects in the private sector of the economy.

It is convenient to distinguish between two different situations: first when the public sector competes with the private sector to implement a specific investment project (in this case the marginal rate of return on capital should be used as the social rate of discount); and second when we evaluate projects within the public sector, discussed below.

When the project receives funding from several sources, one way to find the social rate of discount is to find a weighted average of the marginal rate of time preference (ξ) and the marginal rate of return on capital (r). Thus the social rate of discount is equal to $\alpha r + (1 - \alpha)\xi$, where α is the proportion of funds obtained by crowding out private investment and $(1 - \alpha)$ the proportion of funds that come from the displacement of consumption. The calculus of the social discount rate as the weighted average of both rates requires information on the source of investment funds (Harberger, 1972).

The economic criticism of this approach leads to a more complicated option. The methodology proposed as an alternative to Harberger's weighted average[7] is the discounting of the flow of benefits and costs using the marginal social rate of time preference as the social discount rate, but having previously converted the flow of net benefits into a flow of consumption using the shadow price of capital. For example, if in the private sector the marginal rate of return on capital before taxes is 20 per cent and

---

[7] Bradford (1975); Little and Mirrlees (1974).

the marginal social rate of time preference is 5 per cent, in the margin, an additional investment unit is four times more valuable than a unit of consumption.

The society is investing below the optimum ($K_b < K_0$ in Figure 5.11) and hence the flow of benefits is corrected depending on its destination (consumption or investment). If funds are reinvested, they will be multiplied by the shadow price (in our example, $r/\xi = 4$) and then they will be discounted with the marginal social rate of time preference. Another way to see the logic of this procedure is as follows: if the benefits V are wholly reinvested in year t, each subsequent year we obtain rV of return in consumption, and reinvest V; so rV in perpetuity is equal to rV/ξ, which will be discounted by multiplying by $1/(1 + \xi)^t$.

This procedure is more complicated because of the information that is required on the destination of the benefits throughout the life of the project. For this reason, practitioners frequently choose more pragmatic approaches consisting of using, for example, the interest rate of long-term treasury bonds in the belief that in the private sector no investment will be undertaken with a lower marginal return.

However, we must not forget that when there are taxes on profits, marginal rates of return on investment are greater than the interest rate; and in the case of taxes on funds supplied by savers who do not displace private projects, it is possible to find very low marginal rates of time preference.

In this chapter we have seen the consequences of the social discount rate on the value of future benefits and costs and consequently on the social profitability of projects. In the evaluation of actual projects,[8] the social discount rate is usually within the 3–5 per cent range but higher values can be found like 9 per cent (6 per cent for projects that primarily generate environmental benefits) in the Asian Development Bank. These rates are considerably lower than the 6–8 per cent recommended in the recent past in the EU and the US, and it is convenient to bear in mind that these rates are risk free, so it is assumed that the flows of benefits and costs are expressed in certain equivalents. In practical terms, a reasonable course of action may be to work with the lower and upper bounds and to see the sensitivity of the project's social profitability.

5.6 INTERGENERATIONAL DISCOUNT

The conversion of future benefits and costs to present values, according to the traditional method based on the logic of compound interest, produces results in which the distant future does not count unless the discount rate is close to zero. When the future is defined within the coordinates of the private sector, 20 or 30 years is regarded as the very long term. In the evolution of species, 300 years is nothing.

Exponential discounting is appropriate for projects or policies that affect the same individuals at different time periods. Many public projects with a lifespan of 20 or 30

---

[8] See Evans (2007); Pearce and Ulph (1999); Asian Development Bank (2017); European Commission (2015); HM Treasury (2018), and other cost–benefit analysis guidelines.

years can be evaluated with the usual discount approach to the financial analysis. The problem arises when investment projects or policies that affect the stock of natural resources have a positive or negative impact on the welfare of future generations.[9] Should these costs and benefits be discounted?

Applying the method of exponential discount, the distant future becomes irrelevant for relatively low interest rates. The present value (assuming zero inflation) of benefits (or costs) of $100 million that occur within 300 years is $2.60 if discounted at 6 per cent. The benefits of preserving some species or preventing global warming are very low if they are discounted with the same discount rates as short-term actions. With the above figures, it would not be desirable to invest $3 today at a 6 per cent discount rate to avoid a loss of $100 million within 300 years.[10]

In the case of the energy policy, the choice of discount rate is critical. If we want to have alternative sources of energy available for future generations, we must devote resources to that aim in the present. The research and development costs are very high, and the expected benefits are distant in time – therefore, by applying a high discount rate it may become an unprofitable R&D policy in sustainable energies (Lind, 1982).

The same argument applies to nuclear power, which produces immediate benefits (cheap energy) but social costs that may occur hundreds of years later. In this case many find it morally unacceptable to apply a discount rate that renders negligible the costs associated with exposure to radiation that may be suffered by future generations. In contrast, an argument in favour of discounting the benefits of future generations is the possibility of per capita income continuing its past growth rate. If future generations are much wealthier than we are, to what extent is the sacrifice of the present generation justified? Nevertheless, this argument does not seem to apply to serious irreversible damages.

Another view of this issue is that discounting flows of benefits and costs of future generations is fundamentally an ethical problem, and so it might be adequate to separate the discounting of the benefits and costs that occur in different periods of time and the issue of intergenerational equity. This position suggests that the problem is not the choice of the value of the discount rate, but the state of the stock of natural resources that we must leave in the best possible condition for future generations. In this view the debate over the use of natural resources would take place in the context of sustainable development (Heal, 1997).

Criticism of exponential discounting in projects with very long-term effects is not exclusively based on ethical grounds. The empirical evidence on the preferences of individuals about the trade-off between present and future consumption shows the existence

---

[9] Although it is also argued that, in the case of discounting the benefits from the reduction of deaths and injuries, the marginal rate of time preference does not necessarily coincide with the one used for the discount of other kinds of benefits and costs.

[10] Which, on the other hand, may seem reasonable, because by saving $3 today we will have $117 million within 300 years if the interest rate is 6 per cent. The problem is that there is no guarantee of maintaining for 300 years the flow of benefits that would, within 300 years, compensate the individuals living at that date.

of a wide range of discount rates both during the lifetime of the project and for different goods and intertemporal choices. Frederick et al. (2002, p. 362) reveal five regularities: (1) gains are discounted more than losses; (2) small amounts are discounted more than large amounts; (3) greater discounting is shown to avoid delay of a good rather than to expedite its receipt; (4) in choices over sequences of outcomes, improving sequences are often preferred to declining sequences though positive time preference dictates the opposite; and (5) in choices over sequences, violations of independence are pervasive, and people seem to prefer spreading consumption over time in a way that diminishing marginal utility alone cannot explain.

Two interesting lines of work are those described below. Both are based on the preferences stated by individuals when they are interviewed about their intertemporal preferences in the long term. Both lead to the conclusion that future benefits and costs should count more in the economic evaluation of projects.

Based on the stated preferences in interviews with 3200 households with respect to the implicit discounting of deaths avoided at various future dates, Cropper et al. (1992) concluded that, although the respondents give more value to lives saved in the present than in the future, the implied discount rate in accordance with their responses is not constant. Instead of the exponential discounting, a hyperbolic discount factor fits the preferences stated by individuals subject to the dilemma between lives saved in the present and in the future. The results of the work of Cropper et al. (1992) are the following:

- A high proportion of respondents would not accept life-saving programmes in the future at the expense of giving up programmes that save lives in the present, even if the number of lives saved in the future is 50 times larger. The reason many of the respondents always preferred to save lives in the present lies in the belief that society would find other means of saving those lives in the future (hence they did not accept the alternative suggested in the survey). The other reasons are because this will protect them and their loved ones, and programmes of the future (especially those in 100 years) will not.
- The implicit discount rates obtained are significantly higher than zero, even at horizons as far as 100 years. Although individuals discounted the future, they did not do so at a constant exponential discount rate. The discount rates are much higher for short time horizons than for distant horizons, and there is considerable heterogeneity of discount rates.

Information from the survey indicates therefore that individuals use different discount rates depending on the trade-off proposed between present and future. The pattern that seems to follow the discount rate over time is that of a convex curve with a negative slope.[11]

---

[11] The answers given by respondents to the contingency of saving anonymous lives in the present or in 5, 10, 25, 50 or 100 years (for each respondent only one option was given) allow us to infer a possible implicit

Hyperbolic discounting has been criticized because it implies inconsistent intertemporal preferences as individuals change their discount rate when situated in different years, which is not the case with exponential discounting. This being true, these discount rates appear to conform to the stated preferences of individuals subjected to hypothetical choices between present and future.

Another contribution regarding the determination of the social discount rate is called gamma discount and its rationale is as follows (Weitzman, 2001): from 2000 interviews with economists from 48 different countries, and from the values of their responses on the type of discount, Weitzman obtained the distribution of discount rates, which ranged from zero to a maximum of 20 per cent. It is a gamma distribution with higher frequencies between 3 per cent and 5 per cent, and a long tail on the right with very low frequencies.

Weitzman noted the error of averaging from the distribution of individual rates to obtain the social discount rate. The correct procedure is to average discount factors. Let us see the logic. Consider a project that consists exclusively of future benefits of $100 million within 300 years. If the discount rate is 1 per cent, the present value of these benefits is equal to $5 053 449. If the discount rate is 10 per cent, the present value is practically zero ($0.00004). In addition to showing the effects of exponential discounting on future benefits, this example illustrates the effect of averaging the interest rates instead of the discount factors.

Suppose that the economy is composed of two individuals, A and B, with discount rates of 1 per cent and 10 per cent, respectively, and that the government uses, as a social discount rate, the average for discounting the benefits of $100 million in 300 years. If we apply the average rate of the two individual discount rates (5.5 per cent), the result is a present value of $10.60, which does not seem reasonable given that individual A values the $100 million as $5 million in the present and individual B gives a value close to zero. The average of these two values is $2.5 million, a figure significantly higher than the $10.60 that results from applying the average rate.

The key is that we cannot average rates but discount factors. If we calculate the implicit discount rate, which is to convert $100 million received within 300 years into $2.5 million in the present, we obtain a discount rate of 1.2 per cent, very close to 1 per cent, the minimum value of the distribution of types (Table 5.1).

Table 5.1 shows how, in the early years, the outcome of averaging the discount rates does not generate very different results compared with the average of discount factors. However, in a relatively close time horizon of 30 years, using the average of the discount factors implies doubling the benefits that result from applying an average discount rate. It can be seen how the implicit discount rate, which is the average of the present values that both individuals attach to $100 million, decreases with time, approaching the lowest value in the range of discount rates.

---

discount rate from 16.8 per cent in the lives saved in year 5, to 11.2 per cent in year 10, 7.4 per cent in year 25, 4.8 per cent in year 50 and 3.8 per cent in the year 100.

Table 5.1 Discount rates and discount factors

Year	1%	10%	Average of rates	Average of factors	Implicit rate (%)
5	95 146 569	62 092 132	76 513 435	78 619 351	4.92866
10	90 528 695	38 554 329	58 543 058	64 541 512	4.47589
20	81 954 447	14 864 363	34 272 896	48 409 405	3.69397
30	74 192 292	5 730 855	20 064 402	39 961 574	3.10473
50	60 803 882	851 855	6 876 652	30 827 869	2.38142
100	36 971 121	7 257	472 883	18 489 189	1.70231
200	13 668 638	0.5	2 236	6 834 319	1.35065
300	5 053 449	0.0	10.6	2 526 724	1.23363

Note: Present value of $100 million received at different times, discounted at 1 per cent, 10 per cent, the average of the discount rates and the average of the discount factors.

THINGS TO REMEMBER

1. Benefits and costs occur at different moments during the lifetime of the project. There are projects with a lifespan of 30 years, and others whose effects, in practical terms, can last forever. People are not indifferent with respect to when benefits and costs happen, and hence, the net benefits during the lifetime of the project should be weighted according to the individual preferences.

2. If the individuals discount the future – that is, they prefer a unit of benefit today rather than tomorrow – we need a method to homogenize the flow of benefits and costs. Exponential discounting is the common procedure to express all the future benefits and costs in present terms. The logic of compounding interest is the rationale behind exponential discounting. If $1 has a value of $(1 + i)$ next year, the present value of $1 next year equals $1/(1 + i)$, where i is the interest rate.

3. The marginal rate of time preference, the marginal productivity of capital and the interest rate are not equal unless very unlikely circumstances occur. Hence the selection of the social discount rate is difficult and controversial. The practitioner takes the discount rate as a parameter given by the government and can introduce several plausible values to see how sensitive the results are with respect to changes in the discount rate.

4. It is doubtful whether exponential discounting is appropriate for dealing with benefits and costs affecting future generations. Many argue that exponential discounting does not reflect the individual's preferences and that a declining discount rate should be used to give more weight to the future. The use of lower rates of discount for environmental impacts or life savings is already being introduced in standard cost–benefit analysis.

6
Discounting and decision criteria (II)

As an emerging literature has shown, the ability to delay an irreversible investment expenditure can profoundly affect the decision to invest. It also undermines the theoretical foundations of standard neoclassical investment models, and invalidates the net present value rule as it is usually taught to students in business school: 'Invest in a project when the present value of its expected cash flows is at least as large as its cost.' This rule – and models based on it – are incorrect when investments are irreversible and decisions to invest can be postponed.

(Robert S. Pindyck, 1991, p. 1110)

6.1 INTRODUCTION

The net present value (NPV) is the key single value indicator to measure the economic profitability of a project. Once the benefits and costs have been discounted, we need a decision criterion to accept/reject a project and compare between different projects. In Section 6.2 we discuss the most used economic indicator, the NPV, to help take those decisions. The NPV allows us to express the whole flow of benefits and costs of the project in a single figure. The internal rate of return and the benefit/cost ratio (B/C) are also discussed.

When the decision is accept/reject we are in the easiest situation we may face when evaluating a project. However, even in this straightforward situation, a positive NPV is not enough to make the decision. It may well be that postponing the investment is a superior alternative. In other cases, we must choose between different projects, all of them with a positive NPV but not comparable because of their scale or duration. On other occasions, the expected NPV is positive but waiting reveals relevant information whose value is lost when the project is implemented. In Section 6.3, we discuss the decision criteria when one must choose between mutually exclusive projects with different lifespans. Finally, in Section 6.4, when the investment decision can be postponed – that is, it is not a 'now or never' proposition – the benefits of delaying the investment are analysed.

6.2 DECISION CRITERIA: THE NET PRESENT VALUE

Accept/reject

There are several alternative ways to measure, with a single value indicator, the social profitability of a project whose benefits and costs occur in different years. The most reliable indicator is the NPV of the flow of benefits and costs (see Brealey and Myers, 1996). The NPV summarizes in a single figure the social value of the project by subtracting the costs (C) from the benefits (B) once both have been discounted with the appropriate discount rate (i). A general expression is as follows:

$$NPV = B_0 - C_0 + \frac{B_1 - C_1}{1+i} + \frac{B_2 - C_2}{(1+i)^2} + \dots + \frac{B_T - C_T}{(1+i)^T}. \tag{6.1}$$

If expression (6.1) is zero, the project's present value of benefits is equal to the present value of its costs, which would leave the decision maker indifferent between approving or rejecting the project, because implementing the project will only allow the reimbursement of the initial investment, the operating costs and the interest payment, which is what one can obtain by leaving the investment in the next best alternative. When the case is to choose between accepting or rejecting a single project we use the first decision rule: if $NPV > 0$, accept; if $NPV < 0$, reject.

The economic logic of this decision rule is based on the concept of opportunity cost. Consider an investment project of \$2487 that produces constant benefits equal to \$1000 during its three years of life. Suppose the discount rate i is the interest rate (10 per cent) at which this investment would be remunerated if it were not invested in the project. The opportunity cost of this investment expressed at the end of the third year is: $2487(1+0.1)^3$.

An initial figure of \$2487 reaches approximately \$3310 in the third year if it is lent to a financial institution. This is the opportunity cost of investing in the project, the renouncement of receiving \$3310 in the third year. Therefore, if we invest \$2487 in the project, we should expect at least \$3310 in the third year or an equivalent amount during the lifetime of the project – for example, \$1000 every year over the three years.

When we invest \$2487 in the project and gain \$3310 in the third year, the NPV is:

$$NPV = -2487 + \frac{3310}{(1+0.1)^3} = 0. \tag{6.2}$$

The NPV is approximately zero, indicating that the same payoff is obtained by lending the money to the bank or investing it in the project. The same happens if we gain \$1000 each year because:

$$NPV = -2487 + \frac{1000}{(1+0.1)} + \frac{1000}{(1+0.1)^2} + \frac{1000}{(1+0.1)^3} = 0. \tag{6.3}$$

If by investing \$2487 in the project the $NPV > 0$, the funds invested in the project generate benefits in excess of its opportunity cost, allowing not only the recovery of the invested funds plus the interest payment, but also an additional benefit.

Choosing between projects with positive *NPV*

The *NPV* rule is not only valid for the acceptance or rejection of a project, it is also an appropriate criterion with which to choose between mutually exclusive projects or to select from a group of projects within a budget constraint. In this case the objective is to choose the set of projects that maximize the *NPV*.

Table 6.1 illustrates the use of the *NPV* in contrast with the benefit/cost ratio. The *B/C* ratio is the fraction of the discounted benefits and the discounted costs, and it is frequently used as an indicator of the social profitability of projects. In Table 6.1, four projects are ranked according to their *B/C*. It can be seen how project E is the one with the highest *B/C* value (1.5) but G has the highest *NPV* value, so the *B/C* criterion provides an incorrect ranking of the projects in Table 6.1. The lowest benefit per unit of cost corresponds to project H, 0.8. One explanation of the rationale for rejecting project H is because *B/C* = 0.8 is less than unity and hence for each monetary unit invested in the project we only recover 0.8, thereby 20 per cent of the investment is lost.

The *NPV* rule would have rejected project H because it implies losses of \$240 if it is undertaken. The criterion of accepting the project with *NPV* > 0 indicates that the profitable projects are E, F and G, all of them with a *B/C* greater than 1.

Usually, there are more projects with an *NPV* > 0, or *B/C* > 1 than funds available, and public agencies are forced to choose between the set of profitable projects, a subset that simultaneously ensures the maximum social welfare and satisfies the budget constraint.

Consider that the budget constraint is \$800. In this case we choose projects E and F, and the total *NPV* is \$280. The ranking of projects by the *B/C* ratio leads to the same selection. Suppose now that the budget is extended to \$1600. In this case the projects that allow a higher overall *NPV* (\$430) are F and G; and E, the one with the higher *B/C*, is outside the subset.

An additional problem with the use of *B/C* as an indicator of project profitability is that it is sensitive to the way the benefits and costs are computed, unlike the *NPV*, which produces the same result whether the costs are defined as costs or as negative benefits.

Table 6.1 Indicators for project selection (discounted values in \$)

Project	Benefits	Costs	*NPV*	Benefits/Costs
E	300	200	100	1.50
F	780	600	180	1.30
G	1250	1000	250	1.25
H	960	1200	−240	0.80

Take, for example, project E of Table 6.1 and suppose that it is composed of two periods – the year zero, in which the investment is materialized, and the year one – and assume a 10 per cent discount rate. Consider two alternatives compatible with an *NPV* of $100:

$$NPV = -200 + \frac{330}{1+i} = 100, \tag{6.4}$$

$$NPV = -100 + \frac{330-110}{1+i} = 100. \tag{6.5}$$

In the first alternative, the ratio *B/C* is equal to 1.5, as shown in Table 6.1. In the second it depends on how we define the costs. If the costs are defined as such, the value of $110 is a discounted cost with a value of 100, and *B/C* is equal to 1.5. However, if the cost is treated as a negative benefit (e.g., an aggregation of winners and losers is equal to $220), the *B/C* would be equal to two. Note that the *NPV* is $100 in both cases.

Although there are cases in which a positive *NPV* is not a sufficient condition for the approval of a project, the *NPV* is widely considered the most reliable criterion, and the only recommendation is to avoid its mechanical use without thinking about the characteristics of the projects that we wish to compare, as we discuss in the rest of the chapter.

The internal rate of return (*IRR*)

Another indicator is the *IRR*, which consists of finding the value of *i* that makes the *NPV* equal to zero. The *IRR* is thus the highest discount rate that leaves the project on the border of profitability (see Figure 5.2 in Chapter 5). The more profitable the project, the greater the range of values of *i* with a positive *NPV*.

Going back to Figure 5.2 in Chapter 5, it can be seen how the *NPV* and the interest rate are inversely related. If we conveniently increase *i*, a value for which the *NPV* becomes zero is reached (*i** = 7.5 per cent). This is the *IRR* and the decision rule is to accept the project if *i** is higher than the interest rate, and to reject it otherwise.

The *IRR* also has some weaknesses, since there may be more than one value of *i* that makes the *NPV* equal to zero. This can happen if, during the life of the project, net benefits change the sign. Moreover, it is not always the highest *IRR* project that has the greatest *NPV*.

6.3 DECISION CRITERIA: DIFFERENT LIFESPANS

Selection between mutually exclusive projects with different lifespans

Using the *NPV* as a decision rule, the likelihood of mistakes in the selection of alternative projects diminishes; however, it is required that projects are comparable. An example will help. Table 6.2 shows two mutually exclusive projects with the purpose of saving a

Table 6.2 Selection between projects with different lifespans (monetary values in $)

Project	Lifespan (years)	I	C_t	B_t
X	50	1550	150	360
Z	25	500	250	360

Note: I: construction cost; C_t: operation and maintenance annual cost; B_t: annual benefit as a result of time savings.

natural obstacle in the construction of a road. The service provided by both alternatives is identical. Project X has a lifespan of 50 years, the cost of construction is $1550, and the operation and maintenance costs are $150 per year. Project Z has a shorter life (25 years), its construction costs are $500, and its operation and maintenance costs are $250 per year. Both projects have the same annual benefits ($360), which we assume are limited to time savings. The discount rate is 10 per cent.

There is a trade-off in these projects with the costs of construction and operation: a higher cost of construction at the beginning allows a lower level of operating and maintenance costs during the project life. Calculating the *NPV*:

$$NPV(X) = -1550 + \sum_{t=1}^{50} \frac{360 - 150}{(1+i)^t}, \tag{6.6}$$

$$NPV(Z) = -500 + \sum_{t=1}^{25} \frac{360 - 250}{(1+i)^t}. \tag{6.7}$$

With a 10 per cent discount rate the values of the *NPV* are the following:[1]

$$NPV(X) = -1550 + (9.91481)\,210 = 532.11, \tag{6.8}$$

$$NPV(Z) = -500 + (9.07704)\,110 = 498.47. \tag{6.9}$$

One might think that project X is better than project Z because its *NPV* is higher; however, the projects are not comparable because, while resolving a problem with the same degree of effectiveness, project X does so for 50 years and project Z for 25.

The comparison of the two projects requires a previous process of homogenization. Two procedures to make the projects comparable are as follows. The first is based on considering an imaginary project that consists of constructing Z twice to solve the problem for the same time interval as project X. From equation (6.9) we know that the net present value of project Z equals $498.47. An identical project Z is constructed at the beginning of

---

[1] Remember that the discounted sum (*S*) of a unit of net benefit during *T* years is $S = (1 - (1 + i)^{-T})/i$; for $i = 0.1$ and $T = 25$, $S = 9.07704$; with $T = 50$, $S = 9.91481$ (see Chapter 4).

year 26 and the flow of net benefits lasts from year 26 to year 50. The *NPV* of this identical project is \$498.47 but situated at the end of year 25 (or at the beginning of year 26), so to obtain the present value of the *NPV* in year 25 we need to divide by $(1 + i)^{25}$.

$$NPV(2Z) = 498.47 + \frac{498.47}{(1+i)^{25}}. \tag{6.10}$$

For a period of 25 years and a 10 per cent discount rate, the discount factor is equal to 0.09230, therefore:

$$NPV(2Z) = 498.47 + (0.0923)\,498.47 = 544.48. \tag{6.11}$$

This result shows that it is more profitable to choose alternative Z, which will be repeated at the end of its useful life.

The other procedure is to calculate the *equivalent annual net benefits* $(\hat{B})$, which consists of calculating the average annual benefit, which, multiplied by factor S (see footnote 1) corresponding to the lifespan and the discount rate, is equal to the *NPV* of the project:

$$NPV = S\hat{B}. \tag{6.12}$$

Solving for $(\hat{B})$, we obtain the equivalent annual net benefit:

$$\hat{B} = \frac{NPV}{S}. \tag{6.13}$$

The value of $\hat{B}$ for project X is equal to \$53.668 and for project Z is equal to \$54.916, so project Z is preferable to project X, despite having a smaller *NPV*.

6.4 OPTIMAL TIMING: WHEN POSTPONING IS PROFITABLE

A positive *NPV* indicates, in principle, that the project is socially worthy. Nevertheless, claiming that the project has a positive *NPV* in the base year does not mean that the project should be approved. When postponing a project is possible it is required to consider the optimal timing. We consider two cases depending on whether waiting reveals additional valuable information.

When additional information is not revealed by waiting

Even with a positive *NPV*, we must check whether it is more profitable to start today or to wait until next year. There may be some circumstances that make it sensible to postpone the project when this is technically feasible. Perhaps the demand is growing during its lifetime but the social benefits derived from that demand in the first year do not offset the opportunity cost of the required funds. Suppose that the project involves an initial investment equal to I and annual net benefits equal to B_t. Postponing the project by one year is profitable if:

$$\frac{iI}{1+i} + \frac{B_{T+1}}{(1+i)^{T+1}} > \frac{B_1}{1+i}. \qquad (6.14)$$

The strict inequality in (6.14) shows, on the left-hand side, the present value of the benefit of postponing the project by one year, and consists of the interest payment on the investment cost multiplied by the discount factor $(1/(1+i))$ and the discounted benefits obtained in period $T+1$ as a result of starting the project a year later. The right-hand side represents the discounted lost benefit in year one because of postponing the project.

If the benefit in the year $T+1$ is not significant we can simplify expression (6.14) to:

$$i > \frac{B_1}{I}, \qquad (6.15)$$

where B_1/I is the rate of return on investment in the first year. If the discount rate is higher than the first-year rate of return investing in the project, waiting is preferable.

When delaying the project reveals additional information

When there is uncertainty over the future net benefits, the investment is partially or totally irreversible, and it is possible to postpone the investment decision to acquire more information, the *NPV* rule can be misleading unless it includes the opportunity cost of exercising the option to invest (Dixit and Pindyck, 1994). This investment option is clear in the case of governments that have the property rights for land and natural resources and the authority to decide on the construction of projects of general interest now or later in the future.

In these circumstances, if we invest today we have renounced the value of the information that will be revealed in successive periods, including information that could change the decision to invest, which cannot be altered once the decision to invest has been taken, given the irreversibility of investment and hence the unrecoverable nature of the costs (sunk costs). If delaying the project reveals valuable information on the annual net benefits, the economic value of that information is lost when the investment is made. Under the described conditions (i.e., irreversibility, uncertainty and the possibility of delay) there is an additional opportunity cost of undertaking the investment in the present. Investing today will imply the loss of the economic value of the information revealed by waiting, and therefore it should be included as a cost. The *NPV* rule is still valid if the mentioned opportunity cost is included as a cost when calculating the *NPV*.[2]

What is the cost of losing this information by investing now? It is the amount the investor (assuming she is risk neutral) would be willing to pay for the option of

[2] See Dixit and Pindyck (1994); Pindyck (1991). Earlier contributions are: Arrow and Fisher (1974); Fisher and Hanemann (1987); Henry (1974). See also Mensink and Requate (2005).

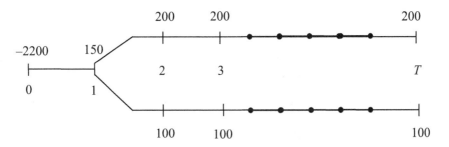

Figure 6.1 Example: a project with demand uncertainty

flexibility. We calculate the *NPV* by investing in period zero, then we calculate it again but delaying the project, and the difference is the value that is lost if we do not wait (i.e., the cost of investing now).

The above reasoning to calculate the cost of investing now can be presented as the decision between two mutually exclusive projects: one consisting of investing now, and the other delaying the investment. We only have to calculate the *NPV* of both projects and choose the one with a higher *NPV*.

An example may help us to understand the significance of considering the option of waiting as an alternative. The project represented in Figure 6.1 shows an investment in port infrastructure for trans-shipment container traffic.

The project requires an investment of $2200 in the base year. The social benefit in year one is $150. In the second year, depending on the decision of a shipping company to sign a long-term contract with the port or with a competing port, the benefit goes up to $200 or down $100 with equal probability and forever ($T \to \infty$). The decision of the shipping company is known at the beginning of year two. The social rate of discount is 5 per cent.

We face an irreversible investment, there is demand uncertainty and the investment decision may be postponed waiting for the decision of the shipping company. We assume there is no strategic action that may affect the decision of the shipping company, or other additional benefits or social costs than those already described.

The expected *NPV* (*ENPV*) of this investment project is as follows:

$$ENPV = -2200 + \frac{150}{1+i} + \sum_{t=2}^{\infty} \frac{100 \cdot (0.5) + 200 \cdot (0.5)}{(1+i)^t} = 800. \tag{6.16}$$

As indicated, once the investment has been made and after the first year (with a certain benefit of $150), the benefits in the rest of the years may increase to $200 or decrease to $100 with equal probability, depending on the decision of the shipping company.

Therefore, the *NPV* of the project if the company does not sign the contract, given that the life of the project is infinite, is:

$$NPV_{(no\ contract)} = -2200 + \frac{150}{1+i} + \sum_{t=2}^{\infty} \frac{100}{(1+i)^t} = -152. \tag{6.17}$$

Alternatively, if the shipping company signs the contract:

$$NPV_{(contract)} = -2200 + \frac{150}{1+i} + \sum_{t=2}^{\infty} \frac{200}{(1+i)^t} = 1752. \qquad (6.18)$$

These results show that the investment will lead to a loss of \$152 or a benefit of \$1752 with the same probability (i.e., 0.5). Therefore, the expected NPV is equal to $-152 \cdot (0.5) + 1752 \cdot (0.5) = 800$, a result that we had already obtained in expression (6.16). If the agent who takes the decision is risk neutral, the project is accepted.

It is worth pointing out that postponing this project by one year would not be profitable if the information revealed in year two is not considered, as the benefit of the first year is higher than the interest rate multiplied by the investment (see expression (6.15)). Therefore, even though it seems that there are no gains obtained by waiting, delaying not only implies losing the benefit of the first year and saving the opportunity cost of the money invested (reflected in the discount rate), there is also an additional benefit that comes from the valuable information revealed by waiting. When the project is delayed by one year, we lose the benefit of the first year, but we now know whether the shipping company will sign the contract or not. Therefore, we know whether the yearly benefits are \$100 or \$200 from year two onwards.

Consider an alternative project consisting of not investing in the present and waiting a year. Once the expected NPV has been calculated, compare this value with the expected NPV of investing now, and then choose the project with the highest expected NPV. If by waiting we know that the company is not going to sign the contract and therefore the annual benefit is equal to \$100, the best option is not to invest and because of this decision the negative NPV in expression (6.17) is avoided, so the NPV is in this case zero.

As this result ($NPV = 0$) can occur with equal probability to the contract being signed and the annual benefits being equal to \$200, the expected NPV of delaying is:

$$ENPV_{(delaying)} = \frac{1}{2}\left(\frac{-2200}{1+i} + \sum_{t=2}^{\infty} \frac{200}{(1+i)^t} \right) = 857. \qquad (6.19)$$

Comparing the expected NPV of investing now (\$800) with the expected NPV of postponing the investment one year (\$857), the optimal decision is to delay the project and, after waiting a year, build only if the shipping company chooses to operate in the port. The willingness to pay to maintain the option to invest is \$57, the difference between expressions (6.19) and (6.16).

It is interesting to note that the expected NPV of investing in the present is positive and therefore the project would be approved if the investment is of the 'now or never' type. Even waiting a year is not profitable when no additional information is revealed. However, if the option to wait is feasible, we may think of it as if there is another project consisting of waiting that we have to compare with the project of investing now. The optimal decision in the previous case is to wait.

Therefore, the conventional *NPV* rule is still valid if the problem is addressed as the choice between two mutually exclusive projects – one investing now, the other waiting one year – since, otherwise, the mechanical application of the *NPV* rule would lead to misleading conclusions. Using the *NPV* rule is still valid as a decision criterion provided that the cost of investing in the present includes the opportunity cost of not waiting, or that the option to wait is defined as an alternative to investing now and comparing the *NPV* of both projects.

The option value is the opportunity cost of investing now. The value of the flexibility of making the investment decision next year is the difference between the two *NPV*s (€57 in our case). In other words, the investor would be willing to pay €57 more for this flexibility. The calculus of the option value can also be addressed as the additional investment cost that the investor is willing to accept to gain flexibility of making the investment decision next year:

$$ENPV_{(delaying)} = \frac{1}{2}\left(\frac{-I}{1+i} + \sum_{t=2}^{T} \frac{200}{(1+i)^t} \right) = 800. \tag{6.20}$$

In this case, the investment cost rises to $2320, indicating that the investor is willing to pay $120 more to have the flexibility of investing in one year's time when the information is revealed than to invest 'now or never'.[3]

Finally, it should be emphasized that in the previous discussion we have assumed that the investor is risk neutral. In the case of a risk-averse investor, the comparison between investing now and waiting introduces a new element of variability in the outcome that affects the decision: by investing now, the outcome is a loss (−$152) or benefits ($1752); by waiting one year the possibilities are quite different when the project is rejected (zero benefits) or when it is accepted ($1714).[4]

THINGS TO REMEMBER

1.   The net present value of a project is the key single value economic indicator to express the social value of a project. It consists of the sum of all the discounted benefits and costs of the project. The discount rate is crucial in the calculation of the *NPV*. There are other decision criteria such as the benefit/cost ratio or the internal rate of return. The *NPV* is the most reliable, but it is only a necessary condition, as in the case of mutually exclusive projects with different lifetimes.

---

[3] Notice that the additional $120 investment cost happens to be in year one with probability 1/2. Expressed in present value the result is $57, the option value as a difference between the present values of two mutually exclusive projects consisting of investing now or postponing the decision until the next year.

[4] When the decision maker is risk averse, the utility of the expected value is higher than the expected utility. For the analysis of uncertainty in the investment projects and the public sector attitude toward risk, see Chapter 9.

2.   The calculus of the *NPV* should include the opportunity cost of the option to invest. When there is uncertainty over the future net benefits, the investment is partially or totally irreversible, and postponing reveals relevant information, the *NPV* rule can be misleading unless it includes the opportunity cost of exercising the option to invest.

3.   This option value is clear in the case of governments that have the property rights for land and natural resources and the power to decide on the construction of projects of general interest now or later in the future. Projects like large infrastructure investments are both irreversible and subject to demand uncertainty. Investing today will imply the loss of the economic value of the information revealed by waiting, and therefore it should be included as a cost. The *NPV* rule is still valid if the mentioned opportunity cost is included as a cost when calculating the *NPV*.

7
Economic valuation of non-marketed goods (I)

Only the fool confuses value with price.

(Antonio Machado)[1]

7.1 INTRODUCTION

The evaluation of positive and negative impacts of projects and public policies is particularly difficult (and controversial) when there is no market for such impacts. Sometimes the project is specifically designed to improve an environmental good or to prevent its deterioration. On other occasions the purpose is of a different nature and the environmental impact is a side-effect of the project.

For example, there are safety policies that reduce the risk of death on the job and projects that increase the recreational value of lakes and rivers by improving the water quality. In contrast, there are policies such as the promotion of industrial production (or livestock) that contribute to global warming, and projects like the construction of an airport with external effects such as noise or deterioration of the landscape.

Ignoring the negative or positive externalities of a project may hide its true opportunity cost or, equivalently, the true benefits that society obtains from its implementation. If the social profitability of the project is sensitive to the magnitude of the externality, it may even change the accept/reject decision or alter the ranking if the decision is to choose among a set of projects. The problem is how to value the benefits and costs of goods for which no quantities are exchanged in the market and no prices are available for their valuation.

Section 7.2 describes how externalities and public goods are a challenge for economic valuation. When there is no market where the good affected by the project is traded, the estimation of the willingness to pay (or accept) involves the search for alternative methods such as observed market data on some ordinary good, or the design of questionnaires that would put individuals in hypothetical situations to elicit monetary values for non-marketed goods. Measurement requires prior understanding of the key relationships behind the change in the non-marketed good and the well-being of the individuals.

---

[1] Spanish poet (1875–1939).

The monetary measures of changes in individuals' utility is addressed in Section 7.3. A change in the quantity or quality of a public good affects individual well-being, but utility is unobservable, and the economist relies on monetary measures of the change in utility. Compensating variation and equivalent variation are discussed, and their relationship with property rights and the reasons explaining why they usually diverge.

There are basically two approaches to the valuation of non-marketed goods: the first based on revealed preferences and the second through interviews with individuals, the so-called stated preferences (Chapter 8). The revealed preferences approach has two main methods, presented in Section 7.4: the travel cost and the hedonic price method. In both, the practitioner relies on a related market where the information is obtained.

7.2 THE ECONOMIC VALUATION OF NON-MARKETED GOODS

Externalities and public goods

The private cost of a good is the net benefit lost by an economic agent in the next best alternative of the resources used in the production of that good, while the social cost is the net benefit lost by society. The difference is pertinent when individuals, by consuming or producing goods, affect the welfare of other individuals outside the market transaction. In this case we say that there is an *externality*, and the private and social costs differ. Externalities can be positive or negative and can be produced by firms or consumers.

An example of positive externality is associated with a security service hired by an individual who is paying for the service while other residents are benefiting from a safer neighbourhood without paying for it. A negative externality would be caused by a company that pollutes the air and damages the health of residents affected by emissions. There may be different possibilities, and they all have in common the inexistence of (or the difficulty of finding) markets for such goods.

The marginal social cost equals the marginal private cost plus the externality. If there are no externalities or any other distortions such as taxes, the social cost of producing one unit of good equals its private cost. If the externality is negative (e.g., pollution) the social cost equals the private cost plus the extra cost that the externality generates. If the external effect is positive (e.g., a vaccine) the social cost will be lower than the private cost. The difference between social and private marginal cost (i.e., the value of the externality) is not necessarily constant and may increase or decrease with the scale of the activity.

When an individual consumes a private good, another individual cannot enjoy that good (rivalry) and the supplier can exclude the individual if he refuses to pay the price (excludability). We have argued that the production or consumption of some goods affect other individuals outside the market, but there is an extreme case of non-rivalry and non-excludability that is called a *pure public good*. If the good is non-rival and non-excludable, it cannot be produced and sold in the market. Lighthouses have been the classical textbook example.[2]

In cost–benefit analysis there are many cases of changes in the provision of a public good (such as the reduction of air pollution or the enhancement of the quality of the water of a river) that need to be evaluated, though there are no market transactions where we can obtain information on willingness to pay.

Sometimes the change in the level of the public good is not the primary target but the project produces side-effects that change that level. This is the case with public works that reduce the visibility of scenic views. Hence the social cost represented by the reduction in the pleasure of contemplating the landscape is a cost of the project. A different issue is the difficulty of sensibly expressing this cost as a number for the calculation of the net social benefit of the project.

Other important non-marketed goods in cost–benefit analysis are related to health and safety. Investment in road safety has a primary objective to reduce the number and severity of accidents. The output of this type of project is measured in the number of lives saved and injuries avoided. Other projects affect the health status of people, though this is not the primary objective of the project – for example, a power station that increases the production of electricity and reduces the quality of air. In both cases there is a change in the welfare of the affected individuals, and the challenge for the economist is to calculate the economic value of these effects, overcoming the problem of the absence of markets for these goods.

A change in the natural resources or in the probability of health risk affects consumers and producers through the market. This is the case with an increase in the quality of water in a reservoir that reduces the prices of agricultural products. In other cases, the consumer benefits directly, and not through a market transaction – for instance, when the government provides more recreational areas in a city. On other occasions, individuals are affected through a market transaction in which they do not participate as sellers or buyers, as happens in the case of noise or pollution with the annoyance and health consequences for people who are not direct users.

Moreover, when considering the owners of the production factors, the provision of a public good can increase the rent of a factor of fixed supply, as happens in the case of the restoration of a polluted natural area that increases the value of the surrounding

---

[2] The lighthouse example was questioned by Ronald Coase after reviewing the history of lighthouses and finding that they had been privately operated in England and Wales, though others argue that this only means that there are alternative mechanisms for the provision of public goods (in this case, the government allowed charges levied on ships that used nearby ports). The Global Positioning System (GPS) may be a more updated example of public good. There is probably an almost infinite number of variations, ranging from a pure public good to a strictly private one. A bridge is an example of a variation where drivers may be excluded unless they pay a fee. However, if the marginal cost of an additional user is equal to zero, the use of the bridge is non-rival and the outcome is inefficient. Then, when demand is high enough, congestion appears, and the marginal cost is positive.

private land. Finally, the taxpayers will in many cases be negatively affected, bearing the investment and maintenance costs of the improvement in environmental goods.

It is worth emphasizing here that individuals can belong to more than one group in our simplified society and hence their welfare can be affected through different channels because of their several 'identities'. The introduction of a clean air regulation can make the individual better off as a citizen who belongs to the 'rest of society' group or as the owner of the land, and worse off as a producer and as a consumer of electricity or a tenant now paying a higher rent for her house.[3]

The practical side of this argument is that the analyst needs a model before going into the quantification of benefits and costs. Adding the change in consumer surplus, producer surplus and 'rest of society' surplus can lead to double or triple counting if the change in consumer surplus has been obtained by asking individuals how much they are willing to pay for the implementation of the clean air regulation. In this case the reduction in profits of the firms affected by the stricter policy or the higher quality of the air they breathe will normally be included in their answers. The individual is not only a consumer. He can also be a shareholder and so the question this individual is asked should be clearly formulated before we make use of any resulting number. This gives us a clue as to the difficulties associated with the economic valuation of non-marketed goods based on the responses obtained by surveying individuals about their monetary valuation of changes in the natural resources, the environmental attributes or the level of risk in their lives.

The effect on welfare of a change in the non-marketed good

The understanding of the relationship between the change in the environmental good and social welfare is not restricted to its economic content. Some knowledge is required of the biological and ecological links behind the changes in the quantity and quality of the environmental and resource service flows. Freeman (2003) proposes to view the economic value of these flows as the product of three sets of functional relationships.

The first is the relationship between the human intervention and the change in the environmental good (e.g., biomass of some species for commercial or recreational use or quality of the air). Two types of human interventions are relevant here. One occurs in the market when a factory pollutes the air. The other is the government actions to regulate the commercial activities that affect the environment (e.g., internalization of externalities through Pigouvian taxes) or actions that directly focus on the protection or enhancement of the environmental good (e.g., the creation of wildlife sanctuaries).

There are two channels for the intervention on the environmental good: one is direct, such as the increase in fauna when land use is restricted through a government

---

[3] In the extreme case of a world of homogeneous agents, only the owner of the fixed factor would benefit from this regulation. See the excellent chapter 'The indifference principle' in Landsburg (1993).

regulation; the other is indirect, such as the behaviour of private agents changing with the new regulation. The reaction of the individuals and firms should be considered before predicting the final effect of the government action on the environmental good.

Once the change in the quality or quantity of the environmental good is established, a second relationship is required to know the effect on the human uses of the good. The use of the resources can happen in the market, as is the case with commercial fishing, or could be the level of quality of the resource for recreational activities (e.g., number of days of acceptable quality of the water for sports activities in a river). Again, there is a direct effect on the output (e.g., tons of fish caught and days of recreational activity) related to the change in the level (quantity or quality) of the environmental good; and an indirect effect, as the output is also affected by the use of other inputs, beside the environmental good, whose quantities vary as a response to the change in the level of the environmental good (e.g., climate change affects the crop indirectly as farmers change the use of inputs as a reaction to the new conditions of production).

The third relationship is the link between the output, or resource flow, and welfare. This consists of the economic valuation of the change in the environmental good. The final goal of the economist is not to measure the change in the number of days the river is open for recreational purposes, or some physical indicator of the pollutants in the air after any action to improve the environment. The objective is to measure the change in social welfare, and this may include two types of value: the use value and the non-use value of the change in the environmental good.

7.3 WILLINGNESS TO PAY AND WILLINGNESS TO ACCEPT

The problem with goods such as clean air, silence and scenic views is that there are no markets in which they are traded and therefore a variation in the level of atmospheric pollution, noise or visual intrusion associated with a project is difficult to measure in economic terms.

In the absence of a primary market for the valuation we should look for other related goods for which a market exists and where the economic effects of the changes in the good not directly subject to market transaction are reflected. For example, the real estate market reflects in housing prices the noise that is involved in the operation of a nearby airport or the provision of parkland. When there is no possibility of using an 'ally' market, the alternative is to ask individuals directly for the economic value of the effect on their welfare. The first case is called *revealed preferences* and the second *stated preferences*.

Starting from the indirect utility function $U = V(P, M)$ where the utility (U) of the individual depends indirectly on the prices (P) of the goods consumed and his income (M) (see Chapter 11), we incorporate a public good (Johansson, 1993) so that, according to expression (7.1), we can express the individual's utility as a function of the price vector of private goods, the level of provision, defined in terms of the quantity or quality, of public good (g) and his income:

$$V(P, g, M). \tag{7.1}$$

Suppose that a given project improves the environmental quality of the public good g. This improvement could be in air quality or noise reduction. The initial utility of the individual is represented as U^0 and the final utility, once the project has been carried out, as U^1 (the superscripts 0 and 1 indicate *without* and *with* the project, respectively):

$$U^0 = V(P^0, g^0, M^0), \tag{7.2}$$

$$U^1 = V(P^1, g^1, M^1). \tag{7.3}$$

The increase in individuals' welfare that occurs because of the enhancement in the public good is equal to $U^1 - U^0$. Ideally, the change in utility resulting from the project is what we should measure, but the utility is not observable and economists, unable to measure utility directly, rely on monetary measures of changes in utility (see Chapter 11). There are two approaches for obtaining individual valuations of changes in the non-marketed good: the willingness to pay and the willingness to accept.

One way to measure in monetary terms the utility change experienced by an individual is to ask how much money she would be willing to pay for the improvement. This is the compensating variation (CV) and, assuming that the individual responds with sincerity, she would be willing to pay an amount (CV) that would leave her indifferent with respect to the initial situation without the improvement. Expression (7.4) captures the idea of how to measure the improvement in the public good:

$$U^0 = V(P^0, g^0, M^0) = V(P^1, g^1, M^1 - CV), \tag{7.4}$$

Another way to measure the increase in an individual's utility in monetary terms is to ask the individual for the minimum amount of income that she would accept to forgo the improvement. This is the equivalent variation (EV) and, assuming that this reveals the true value, she would be willing to accept an amount that would leave her indifferent with respect to the situation she would have reached with the improvement. Expression (7.5) incorporates the application of the concept of equivalent variation to an improvement in the public good:

$$U^1 = V(P^1, g^1, M^1) = V(P^0, g^0, M^0 + EV). \tag{7.5}$$

An example will help to clarify the difference between the two concepts and their practical use. Consider the case of an individual whose hobby is fishing in a river that will be contaminated if the project of building a factory is approved. The expected fall in the quality of life of this individual must be valued for its inclusion in the evaluation of the project that involves the river pollution among its social costs. The lack of a market for the good 'clean water' creates the difficulty of valuation of this damage. If you ask the fisher how much he is willing to pay to avoid the damage, he will probably angrily answer zero and that, in any case, we should compensate him for the damage. The question is, who has the right to pollute?

Consider the case in which the factory has the right to pollute. The question of how much the individual would be willing pay to avoid the damage has another connotation to the respondent and, if he answers truthfully, the response would be, within the limits of his income, the maximum that would make him indifferent to continuing to fish in unpolluted waters.

Assume alternatively that the individual has the right to uncontaminated water. The question that would now make sense is: how much is the minimum compensation he would accept for the pollution of the river? Depending on the value that the individual gives to fishing, and the closeness of substitutes, he would require a larger or smaller amount of compensation – compensation that, in this case, would not be limited by his income, so it could be infinite.[4]

The case of the fisher shows that the measurement of external effects is not unique, and it depends on who has the property rights. Suppose, alternatively, that the individual fishes in a polluted river and that the project substantially improves the fishing conditions. If the property rights of clean water belong to the fisher, the valuation question is how much he would be willing to accept to continue with the river polluted (i.e., not to undertake the renovation project). Here, there would be no income limit to the compensation. In the case in which the factory has the right to pollute, the question is how much the fisher is willing to pay for clean water. Now the response is limited by the individual's income (Table 7.1 represents the various possibilities).

This example shows that in some questions there is a limit of income and in others there is not. Furthermore, there is no reason to expect that the amounts of income accepted or paid by individuals in their responses are equal, as the standard of living of the individual varies with the type of question, and if the marginal utility of income is not constant, the compensating and equivalent variations are different (see Chapter 11).

According to the modelling of society made in Chapter 2, a project that enhances the quality of water in a river may affect different social groups – for example, the 'rest of society' group (better environmental quality enjoyed by excursionists), 'producers' (higher profits because of cost reductions derived from higher inputs quality), 'workers' (change in wages and labour conditions), 'consumers' (through the lower prices of goods supplied by producers with lower costs) and 'taxpayers' (who finance the project and receive tax revenues).

In practice, the correct formulation of the question that induces the individual to calculate the monetary valuation of the change experienced by an environmental good is critical. If the individual is asked about willingness to pay for the environmental

---

[4] An example illustrating why infinite compensation might be needed is where there is an extremely high risk of dying. Typically, one is not prepared to take this type of risk even if the compensation goes to infinity.

Table 7.1 Methods to value the externality

	Who has the property right to clean water?	
	Fisher	Factory
Clean river to be polluted	*CV/WTA*	*EV/WTP*
Polluted river to be cleaned	*EV/WTA*	*CV/WTP*

Note: CV: compensating variation; *EV:* equivalent variation; *WTP:* willingness to pay; *WTA:* willingness to accept.

improvement, without any clarification, we will probably obtain a value that includes the individual's surplus as a consumer but also as a producer, worker and taxpayer. Unless the individual is informed that his valuation of the change in the environmental good should exclude the change in his income as a shareholder, worker or taxpayer, the sum of the surpluses of the social groups included in our model would be incorrect.[5]

We have seen that *CV* and *EV* may be different (see Chapter 11 for a more detailed explanation), but the observed disparity between willingness to pay (*WTP*) and willingness to accept (*WTA*) is larger than the income effect would explain. An empirical study (Horowitz and McConnell, 2002) concluded that there are significant disparities: the differences are minimal for private goods but the ratio *WTA/WTP* is about 10 for public goods and the explanation cannot be found in survey-related problems.

Some possible explanations of the observed differences are the following. First, substitution effects in the case of goods with hardly any substitutes available, as happens with some environmental goods. If the possibilities of substitution are limited, higher compensation will be required for a reduction in the quantity or quality of the environmental good (Hanemann, 1991). Other explanations refer to concepts like loss aversion and reference dependency, meaning that the individual gives more weight to a loss than to an identical gain (see Kahnemann and Tversky, 2000). Another explanation is based on the idea of irreversibility in the context of uncertainty (see Section 6.4 in Chapter 6). The additional cost of killing an option (when the environmental good is not kept at the present level) could be reflected in the higher compensation required for the reduction of that level (Zhao and Kling, 2001).

7.4 VALUATION THROUGH REVEALED PREFERENCES

There are two approaches to measuring the benefit of a project involving an environmental good: the measurement based on revealed preferences and one based

---

[5] For a rigorous analysis of how to express the equivalent and compensating variation when it results in questions posed to individuals, see Johansson (1993).

on stated preferences – that is, surveying individuals to seek information about their preferences.

The simplest situation occurs when the change in the non-marketed good is an input to produce a marketed good. For example, when a public project improves the quality of water used as the input for a residential water supply firm, the provision of the public good (water quality in reservoirs or underground) affects the cost function of the water supply firm because it reduces the average cost of producing drinking water. This cost reduction interacts with the demand function, affecting the utility of consumers if prices fall and the utility of the owners of production factors if their surpluses increase.

The problem of not having a market for the valuation of a public good can be illustrated with two examples of actions that affect environmental goods. The first consists of a municipal project to provide the city with a green area. The second is the construction of an airport that increases the noise in the surrounding residential area.

In both cases, the evaluator needs to know the change in the social benefit with the project: in one case the benefit of the individuals derived from the new green area; and in the other case the loss of social benefit as a result of the noise produced by the aircraft. In the second case one might think that, as we know how much it costs to soundproof a house, we could estimate the cost of noise by calculating the cost per household and multiplying by the number of houses within the noise map. Is this really the cost of noise? Possibly it is not, because exposure to noise cannot be avoided when individuals go outside or open their windows.

The problem with defensive expenditures, as well as averting behaviour (i.e., costs individuals incur in actions to avoid noise or a higher risk of illness) is that they do not measure the total value of the change in the non-marketed 'bad' (e.g., noise) but a lower bound of the willingness to pay of the individuals to avoid the loss of utility.

In both cases, green area and noise, we can try to estimate the economic value of the non-marketed good by observing the behaviour of the consumers in the market of another ordinary good – for example, the property market, or in the case of health risks, the labour market. However, this method provides information on the use value of the environmental good, but it generally overlooks the non-use value, which could be significant in many cases.

Going back to the case of the river, the fisher and the quality of water, two conditions are required to measure the social benefit of cleaning the river and improving the water quality with actual data observation in the fishing permits market. We need the good to be non-essential and with weak complementarity. The first condition means that the individual can be compensated with some level of income if fishing is prohibited; the second is that when the quantity of the good (the number of permits) is zero, the increase in water quality leaves the individual utility unaffected.

When these conditions are not satisfied, the value of the improvement of water quality cannot be estimated in the allied market, as any other non-use values will be missed in the market for fishing permits. When this is the case, we need to estimate the benefits of the environmental good through direct methods, the so-called stated preferences.

The hedonic price method

An approach based on revealed preferences is to see how noise affects the price of housing, comparing prices of houses near to the airport with others of similar characteristics but with different locations and levels of noise exposure. The starting assumption is that among a set of similar houses, individuals pay more for those that are less exposed to noise, and hence we can estimate the willingness to pay to avoid it, and infer from that price difference the implicit cost of noise for individuals.

This approximation is based on the conception of the good as a set of attributes (Lancaster, 1966). Thus, a house is described as a composite good comprising a number of rooms, size of garden, views, quality of construction, location, and so on. If we also add to this that the houses have different levels of noise exposure, we can estimate the implicit cost of noise.

The problem is that the price difference between a house exposed to noise and another house that is not exposed cannot be explained solely by this fact, because the airport also benefits the area by increasing, for example, the accessibility to the city centre with access roads or by building new subway lines that are part of the airport construction project. Moreover, those who have chosen to live near the airport may not have the same preferences as the average individual in society and hence the estimated cost of noise is not representative for most individuals. In other words, with this problem of selection bias the cost of noise will be underestimated.

Suppose the price of housing (P) is a function of the following variables:[6]

$$P = f(R, N, A, F, O), \tag{7.6}$$

where:

P: housing price;
R: number of rooms;
N: noise level;
A: access time to city centre;
F: characteristics of the area (crime rate, number and quality of schools, etc.);
O: other factors.

Once we have a representative sample of houses, we estimate the function (7.6) whose functional form is often assumed to be logarithmic:

---

[6] Two common assumptions in the hedonic price method are that the individual's utility function is weakly separable and that weak complementarity exists. The first assumption implies that the marginal rate of substitution between housing and noise level does not depend on the quantities of other goods. The second assumption is that if housing demand is zero, so is the willingness to pay to avoid noise. The value of passive use or non-use (Section 8.2, Chapter 8) of environmental quality is not captured by this method because it is not reflected in the price of housing.

$$\ln P = b_0 + b_1 \ln R + b_2 \ln N + b_3 \ln A + b_4 \ln F + b_5 \ln O. \tag{7.7}$$

First, we want to know how the price of housing varies with respect to changes in the noise level, and equation (7.7) allows us to estimate this relationship. Computing the derivative of the logarithm of price with respect to noise level, holding the other explanatory variables constant, we obtain price elasticity with respect to noise level:

$$\frac{\partial \ln P}{\partial Ln \, N} = b_2, \tag{7.8}$$

or

$$b_2 = \frac{\partial P}{\partial N} \frac{N}{P}. \tag{7.9}$$

In expression (7.9), $\partial P/\partial N$ is the change in the price of houses when the noise level changes, which is called the implicit price or the hedonic price of noise. Solving for $\partial P/\partial N$ in expression (7.9) we can obtain the value of the hedonic price of noise:

$$\frac{\partial P}{\partial N} = b_2 \frac{P}{N}. \tag{7.10}$$

As shown by expression (7.10) the price of noise depends on the parameter b_2 (which is expected to be negative), the price of housing (P) and the level of noise (N). Therefore, the hedonic price of noise is not constant unless P and N always vary in the same proportion, which is not what is known from empirical work, as the price of the private good does not have a linear relationship with the environmental quality at the observed levels.

It is worth recalling what $\partial P/\partial N$ measures. This partial derivative is the price of noise understood as how much the price of the house decreases when the noise increases in the area where the house is located. This hedonic price is therefore the net present value of the negative externality during the lifespan of the house. The externality is therefore measured by a single figure for the whole period. A note of caution on the risk of double counting is necessary, since any additional measurement of noise damage would, in general, already be accounted for in the reduction of home prices.

Problems with this method are associated with the difficulties of information on long-term damage to health, selection bias, omitted variables, sufficient variability of the observations, and so on.

The travel cost method

The travel cost method is also based on the use of an ordinary market related to the non-marketed good under evaluation. The idea is to estimate a demand function that captures what the visitors who come, for example, to a wildlife park, are willing to pay for its use. Total willingness to pay includes the admission fee, travel costs (fuel, for example), spending on equipment (fishing and climbing equipment, etc.) and time spent on the trip from their place of residence. The population is constituted by the individuals who visit the wildlife park.

This method is used to measure the benefits that individuals gain from the enjoyment of recreational activities and outdoor sports such as fishing, rowing or simply visiting the park. The further away the visitor lives, the more expensive the visit. There will be a distance for which the full (or generalized) price is so high that the demand is zero. Individuals make a different number of visits according to the distance, the closeness of substitutes, income, and so on. The researcher's task is to obtain a demand function that relates the number of visits and the generalized prices they pay by having to travel from longer distances.

Consider the case of a natural park visited by individuals from different zones increasingly distant from the park. Suppose we have identified those areas with their respective population, income, education, age, and so on. The number of visits to the park from zone i can be expressed as:

$$Q_i = f(C_i, H_i, F_i, O_i), \qquad (7.11)$$

where:

Q_i: number of visits originated in zone i;
C_i: generalized cost (or price) of travel from zone i;
H_i: population of zone i;
F_i: characteristics of the population of zone i;
O_i: other characteristics of zone i.

In expression (7.11) the generalized travel cost C_i can be expressed as:

$$C_i = cD_i + v_i T_i + P, \qquad (7.12)$$

where:

C_i: generalized cost (or price) of travel from zone I;
c: cost per kilometre;
D_i: distance from zone i;
v_i: value of time in zone i;
T_i: travel time from zone i;
P: park entry fee.

Once we have estimated an equation relating the number of visits to the explanatory variables according to expression (7.11) the results usually show that the number of visitors is lower when the generalized price increases. The next step is to assume that by raising the admission fee, the number of visits will go down according to the estimated coefficients from the sample that includes all the areas that generate trips to the park. In this way we construct a market demand function with the number of visits on the horizontal axis and the price on the vertical axis, whose points are obtained by hypothetical price rises and observing how the resulting increase in the generalized cost affects the number of visits. The maximum reservation price is the one that would make the number of visits equal to zero.

It should be emphasized that this hypothetical demand function is constructed under the assumption that the observed relationship between the number of visits and the change in the actual generalized price (given a constant admission fee) is similar to the relationship between the number of visits and hypothetical increases in the entry fee. Once we have this demand function the estimation of the surplus that individuals obtain from their visits to the park is straightforward.

The travel cost method is therefore based on the valuation of a good for which there is no market (visits to the park) through the cost of accessing it (entry ticket, travel costs, equipment, etc.). Just as with hedonic prices, the travel cost method assumes weak complementarity between the environmental good and private goods that are jointly consumed, which means that, when spending in private goods is zero, the utility derived from the environmental good is zero; so the travel cost method measures only the value of use, ignoring passive use value. The assumption implies that the value of a natural park is only related to its use. With this method, the value of the park is zero for non-visitors.

<h2>THINGS TO REMEMBER</h2>

1. The reduction of accidents or the improvement of an environmental good can be the main objectives of a project. In other cases, changes in the number of accidents and in the quality of some environmental attributes are side-effects of projects that pursue entirely different objectives. In both cases we need to measure the value of changes in the level of some non-marketed goods.

2. It is important to have some knowledge of the physical and biological relationships between the environmental impact and the final effect on individual well-being, otherwise some key elements might be overlooked, affecting the validity of the results.

3. The economic valuation when there is no market where the good is exchanged follows two basic approaches. One is based on the revealed preferences, using markets for ordinary goods related to the non-marketed good; the other consists in asking the individuals directly through surveys specially designed to elicit the their willingness to pay or accept with respect to changes in a particular non-marketed good.

4. The two main methods, based on revealed preferences, for the economic valuation of a change in the environmental good are the hedonic price and the travel cost

approaches. The estimation of the economic value through the costs associated with defensive expenditure and averting behaviour can only be considered a lower bound of the maximum willingness to pay of society to avoid the negative effect of the impact.

5. In the travel cost and hedonic price methods the analyst works with a related market where some useful information is revealed about the willingness to pay of the individuals. This approach for the economic valuation of the non-marketed good reveals information on the use value of the environmental good; hence, if the good had a non-use or passive value, the total economic value would be underestimated.

8
Economic valuation of non-marketed goods (II)

Disaster demands a response, but it is often the wrong one. That is what the experience of Sir Bernard Crossland, a safety expert who led the inquiry into a disastrous underground railway fire in London in 1987 which killed 31 people, suggests. This week Sir Bernard questioned the £300m ($450m) spent on fire-proof doors, metal escalators and suchlike on London's underground after the disaster. The money, he said, might better have been spent on putting smoke detectors in people's houses. It would have paid for one in every house in the country. House fires kill around 500 people a year, mostly in homes without smoke detectors.

(The Economist, 11 September 2003)

8.1 INTRODUCTION

When the measurement of economic changes in non-marketed goods cannot be derived from direct observation of individuals' choices, economists try to obtain this information by asking the individuals directly through carefully designed surveys to reveal the monetary value of changes in the environmental good, the safety level, or any other non-marketed good. This is particularly the case of the non-use value or passive value (willingness to pay for its existence with independence of its direct use).

There are two opposing positions with respect to measurement of the economic value of non-marketed goods, like the environment good. One rejects the possible quantification in monetary terms of changes in welfare derived from changes in the environmental good or in the probability of physical risk (having an accident); the other admits the possibility of assigning monetary values to air pollution, the preservation of wildlife or a reduction in the risk of dying.

Section 8.2 explains the concept of non-use value and the attempt to measure it through the *contingent valuation* method, a survey-based technique that creates a hypothetical market where the practitioner tries to elicit values through a questionnaire. We present the main elements of this stated preference method, when it is carefully designed to avoid the most obvious biases, as well as the position of the economists who consider that these design efforts are not sufficient to modify the hypothetical nature of the exercise.

The stated preference approach is not reduced to contingent valuation. When the non-marketed good is defined as a set of attributes, *conjoint analysis* is an alternative with which to elicit individuals' preferences. Section 8.3 describes one of the most used methodologies for the application of conjoint analysis: the so-called *choice experiments* consisting of the description of the good according to the selected attributes and levels. The respondent chooses between options that can include a price. From the trade-offs revealed by the interviewee, it is possible to estimate the monetary valuation of different attributes.

In Section 8.4 we discuss some issues concerning individual willingness to pay and social welfare. First, the treatment of altruism in cost–benefit analysis mainly concerned with the possibility of double counting if the altruistic motive is added to the purely selfish valuation. Second, the ethical problem associated with the monetary measures of some unique goods, and the impacts on future generations or human life. Third, when individual preferences may be distorted, and a conflict arises between the satisfaction of individual preferences and individual welfare.

The economic valuation of changes in physical risk is presented in Section 8.5. The value of saving an anonymous life is addressed, as well as the methods most used for its estimation. Changes in the probability of accidents can be converted into numbers of injuries and deaths, and by observing people's trade-offs between safety and other goods or, through stated preferences, it is possible to estimate the value of small changes in the level of risk.

Finally, in Section 8.6, we discuss the transfer of values obtained in other studies to avoid the costs of conducting specific surveys and its potential drawbacks.

8.2 VALUATION THROUGH STATED PREFERENCES: THE CONTINGENT VALUATION METHOD

Passive use value

The economic value of an environmental good cannot be reduced to what its direct users are willing to pay. The value of this good is higher than its valuation for the direct users (e.g., those who walk in a natural area). For environmental economists, the value of non-use (or passive use) is the value that individuals attach to environmental goods that they do not use directly, though they would be willing to pay a positive amount of money for their conservation.

The total value consists not only of the use value, bequest and option values (to have the possibility of future use). The endangered species or national parks also have intrinsic or existence value, not necessarily related to their direct or indirect use by individuals (Pearce and Turner, 1990). The passive use value of environmental goods and the various positions that may be taken against the possible monetary valuation can be illustrated by the example of a public policy consisting of declaring an area a reserve for endangered fauna or leasing the area for mining. If one opts for the natural reserve the public will not be allowed to visit it, so the social benefit is only derived from the passive use value (Carson et al., 2001).

One position regarding the possible quantification of passive use value is that this value cannot be expressed in money terms. Although non-use value should be considered in, for example, the decision to declare the area a wildlife reserve or for mining, the decision maker assisted by experts will make the choice. Alternatively, the cost–benefit analysis of the project includes the benefits that individuals gain from the passive use of the resource, and these benefits can be monetized by asking individuals their willingness to pay for the existence of the natural reserve.

The report from the National Oceanic and Atmospheric Administration on the contingent valuation method (NOAA, 1993), which is often cited as the original academic support[1] for the valuation of the non-use value of environmental goods, backed the idea of passive use of natural resources and their monetary valuation. The aim of the report was to evaluate procedures for the assessment of environmental damages resulting from oil spills into the sea.

The authors distinguish between use value and passive use value. The first can be identified and measured through the information contained in market transactions. Damage to commercial fishing and tourism are easier to estimate than damages to fishers and other sports people who visit the place in which oil spills occur, although such damage can also be estimated with somewhat more difficulty.

The losses of direct users are what is known as the use values because they are enjoyed by those who make active use of the damaged resource. Nevertheless, as stated in NOAA (1993, p. 4602), these are not the only losses associated with the environmental impact:

> ... for at least the last twenty-five years, economists have recognized the possibility that individuals who make no active use of a particular beach, river, bay, or other such natural resource might, nevertheless, derive satisfaction from its mere existence, even if they never intend to make active use of it.

This concept has been denominated as the existence value and it is the main component of what is now called non-use value or passive use value.

The limitations of methods based on revealed preferences to determine the value of a non-marketed good, especially with regard to passive use value, led economists to use surveys in which, by creating a hypothetical market, individuals were asked directly how much they are willing to pay to preserve the conservation of endangered species, to prevent a negative impact on a scenic view, to avoid an increase in health risk, and the like.

Economists have made great efforts to assess in monetary terms the damage to environmental goods, and the benefits of specific policies for the conservation and improvement of such goods. The sceptics of the methods based on surveys for the

---

[1] The report is signed by Kenneth Arrow, Robert Solow, Raul R. Portney, Edward E. Leamer, Roy Radner and Howard Schuman.

valuation of environmental goods point to the origin of the data (stated preferences), as many economists prefer data obtained by observing market behaviour.

The resistance to accepting this valuation method based on the use of stated preferences in a simulated context is justified by theoretical and practical difficulties. However, the preference for the estimates obtained by direct observation of behaviour is not shared by other social sciences (Carson et al., 2001).

The need to value the environment beyond the use value of the resource seems obvious when it comes, for example, to the valuation of damage from oil spills into the sea. It does not seem reasonable to limit the economic value of the damage to the compensation that insurance companies must pay to those directly affected. In many cases, the environmental goods are neither excludable nor rival, particularly in the case of non-use values. Many individuals would be willing to pay for the conservation of Alaska, for example, free of contamination despite not enjoying direct use.

Contingent valuation

The contingent valuation method tries to capture the non-use value of environmental goods – value that, as we have seen, is not captured by the hedonic price method or the travel cost method. In Section 7.3 in Chapter 7, we reviewed the concepts of compensating and equivalent variation and their relationship with the willingness to pay and to accept, and how the use of one or the other depends on the status quo and the allocation of property rights. In the practice of contingent valuation, the willingness to pay is generally used to make the exercise of valuation more credible. Basically, this method relies on asking individuals how much they are willing to pay for an action that prevents environmental damage or improves the existing situation.

Hanemann (1994) points out that in research the details matter, and therefore the way the survey is designed and conducted is crucial, and there is now accumulated experience and good practice to carry it out sensibly. The point is how to capture the value that the environmental good has for the individual. Two key developments have been that the individual is faced with a specific and realistic situation rather than abstractions, and that he tries to respond to closed-ended questions that simulate the context of voting in a referendum.

Since the objective is to measure the preferences of individuals, the good practice of contingent valuation avoids general questions like: 'How much would you be willing to pay to conserve the forests?' According to Hanemann (1994, p. 22) such questions are meaningless: 'what is meaningful is paying higher taxes or prices to finance particular actions by somebody to protect a particular wilderness in some particular manner'.

In this quest to simulate actual situations and to escape abstraction, Hanemann recommends avoiding a counterfactual, such as 'What would you pay not to have had the *Exxon Valdez* oil spill?' Because the accident is irreversible, it is an extremely hypothetical situation. Faced with this question, the following alternative is much more tangible: 'What would you pay for this new programme that will limit damage from any future oil spill in Prince William Sound (the place where the *Exxon Valdez* oil spill occurred)?'

The compensating variation (*CV*) or maximum willingness to pay for the project (environmental improvement in the discussion below) could be obtained from the open question that reflects expression (7.4) in Chapter 7, where *g* is an environmental good that will experience an improvement through the project. Gathering this information for all individuals we would have the monetary expression of the change in utility caused by the project.

The problem is that this open question did not lead to good results in the past and it was replaced by the closed question as in expressions (8.1), (8.2) and (8.3), where ω is a quantity asked by the interviewer that varies in different subsamples. If ω > *CV* the individual prefers the situation without the project; if ω < *CV* the individual prefers the project; and if what he is asked to pay is equal to its reservation price (ω = *CV*) he will be indifferent:[2]

$$U^0 = V\left(P^0, g^0, M^0\right) > V\left(P^1, g^1, M^1 - \omega\right), \tag{8.1}$$

$$U^0 = V\left(P^0, g^0, M^0\right) < V\left(P^1, g^1, M^1 - \omega\right), \tag{8.2}$$

$$U^0 = V\left(P^0, g^0, M^0\right) = V\left(P^1, g^1, M^1 - \omega\right). \tag{8.3}$$

Unlike the prices (*P*) of private goods, the willingness to pay of individuals is not observable. Individuals know (if one accepts that they have well-formed preferences on the good about which they are surveyed) the reservation price but the analyst does not know it. Expressions (8.1), (8.2) and (8.3) have a random component that allows them to be expressed in terms of probability and therefore to build on the responses a cumulative probability function that allows us to infer the willingness to pay for the environmental good.

To obtain an estimate of the value of ω that satisfies expression (8.3) is the objective of these surveys. Most of them contain the following (Carson et al., 2001):

- an introductory section that contextualizes the project;
- a detailed description of the good on which the interviewee must respond;
- the institutional framework where the environmental good is provided;
- the methods of payment;
- a method to obtain the individual's preferences with respect to the good;
- clarification questions that allow us to know why the individual answered some questions as he did;
- a set of questions on the characteristics of the individual, including attitudes and demographic information.

---

[2] The elicitation question to obtain ω has been presented in different formats: open-ended, bidding game, payment card, single-bounded dichotomous choice, double-bounded dichotomous choice and one-and-a-half-bounded dichotomous choice (see Pearce et al., 2006).

All the above elements require the interviewee to understand exactly what is asked and to be convinced by the information the interviewer has provided before he is asked to answer questions concerning the changes in the environmental good. The survey should be designed so that the individual believes that his responses will influence the decision-making process regarding the environmental good. For the exercise to be credible it is necessary for the method of payment to be realistic and for the respondent really to believe he will have to pay the amount stated in his answers if the project is approved.

'Hypothetical answers to hypothetical questions'

For many economists, these design efforts are insufficient to modify the hypothetical nature of the exercise. The critique of the contingent valuation method can be summarized in the sentence: 'We receive hypothetical answers to hypothetical questions'. Diamond and Hausman (1994) argue that this method of valuation is not valid for measuring the non-use value of environmental goods. Given that we have no real data on transactions in the market for environmental goods for making comparisons with the responses from respondents about hypothetical willingness to pay, we need standards for judging credibility, reliability and accuracy. The accuracy is improved by increasing the number of responses, but the credibility and the absence of significant bias are not.

Diamond and Hausman (1994, p. 63) argue that the main problem with contingent valuation is not the survey design but that this method does not measure the preferences of individuals:

> This scepticism comes from the belief that the internal consistency problems come from an absence of preferences, not a flaw in survey methodology. That is, we do not think that people generally hold views about individual environmental sites (many of which they have never heard of); or that, within the confines of the time available for survey instruments, people will focus successfully on the identification of preferences, to the exclusion of other bases for answering survey questions. This absence of preferences shows up as inconsistency in responses across surveys and implies that the survey responses are not satisfactory bases for policy.

Problems with the contingent valuation method are well known: the hypothetical bias, routed in the hypothetical nature of the survey; the strategic bias, as the individual intentionally changes its true value to affect the result; the so-called 'embedding effect', meaning that when the scope of the environmental good changes, the responses do not vary significantly; anchoring bias, meaning the influence of the first number provided to the interviewee on his response; and framing bias, which refers to the influence on the way the information and questions affect the individual's response.

The contingent valuation experts have redesigned their surveys to avoid the most obvious biases, but Diamond and Hausman put the emphasis of their criticism on the fact that the method produces answers that are not consistent with economic theory. They cite the embedding effect, as the willingness to pay values obtained in different surveys are similar regardless of the magnitude of the problem faced by the respondent.

If when asked how much individuals are willing to pay to solve a problem that kills 2000 birds, the answer is about the same as when the figure is 20 000 or 200 000 (Desvousges et al., 1993). Something worrying is happening, and it may well be explained by the absence of individual preferences with respect to the public good and the failure of the individuals to consider the implications of their answers on their budget constraints.[3]

If the responses do not measure the intensity of preferences of individuals – that is, the amount they are willing to pay for the environmental good – then what do they measure, assuming that these are not random numbers? According to Diamond and Hausman, respondents may be expressing an attitude towards the environmental good, expressed on a monetary scale, because this is what has been requested by the interviewer. Maybe they are receiving some sort of reward for their moral support for a good cause, especially when they do not actually have to pay for it. They may be making a kind of informal cost–benefit analysis on what they consider to be good for the country. They may even be expressing their reaction to the action that has occurred (discharge of oil into the sea) instead of the economic valuation of the change in the environmental good.

Faced with this criticism, Carson et al. (2001) point out that consumer sovereignty is an essential principle in economic theory and then it does not make any difference if the willingness to pay for the non-marketed good is motivated by moral satisfaction. Economic theory does not go into questioning the reasons behind the utility obtained when the individual consumes the goods he chooses. However, the motive is not irrelevant if moral satisfaction does not arise from contributing to the continued existence of an environmental good or raising its quality, for example, but to please the interviewer. The problem now is that the willingness to pay revealed does not reflect any connection to the good, but to the interaction with the interviewer. This effect is avoided by competent interviewers and careful design of the survey.

Regarding the insensitivity of responses to the size or scope of the environmental good, there is empirical evidence that supports the critical position on the irrelevance of the size or scale of the good being valued (2000, 20 000 or 200 000 birds), but also against those who argue that this is a general problem of contingent valuation. Carson et al. (2001) discuss the available evidence, holding that, besides the hypothesis of insensitivity being rejected in most studies, the identified problems are associated with poor design of the survey and how it is carried out – problems that have disappeared in contingent valuation surveys that are performed nowadays.[4]

Another problem is the information handled by the individual about the phenomenon under analysis when responding to the survey. The individual may be interested

---

[3] For a review of similar cases in surveys of willingness to pay for public goods, see Frederick and Fischhoff (1998).

[4] For a discussion of the problems with contingent valuation, see Pearce et al. (2006).

in preserving some species of birds but be unaware of key biological facts, like the relationship between population size and the probability of survival, as well as the impact of the ecological damage under evaluation with respect to the size variation in the population of that species.

According to Diamond and Hausman, these preferences based on limited information are a bad basis for environmental policy, so it would be preferable to have an expert assessment of the impact of the environmental change instead of asking the public directly. For those who believe that the economic valuation of non-marketed goods is possible and its validity depends on a serious effort of the survey design, any relevant information (like the critical population for the survival of some species) should be presented to the interviewee in order to obtain meaningful responses.

Probably part of the discreditation of the contingent valuation method is a result of work carried out by many of its proponents. There is no doubt that to devise a hypothetical market, to convince the respondent to answer honestly regarding the valuation of something not directly experienced and to obtain reliable answers is a difficult task. In the words of Hanemann, one of the most prominent economists in the theory and practice of contingent valuation:

> [It] would be misleading for me to suggest that contingent valuation surveys can be made to work well in all circumstances. I am sure situations could exist where a contingent valuation researcher might be unable to devise a plausible scenario for the item of interest. Nor would I wish to argue that all contingent valuation surveys are of high quality. The method, though simple in its directness, is in fact difficult to implement without falling into various types of design problems that require effort, skill and imagination to resolve. Each particular study needs to be scrutinized carefully. But the same is true of any empirical study.
>
> While I believe in the feasibility of using contingent valuation to measure people's value for the environment, I do not mean to advocate a narrow benefit–cost analysis for all environmental policy decisions, nor to suggest that everything can or should be quantified. There will be cases where the information is inadequate, the uncertainties too great, or the consequences too profound or too complex to be reduced to a single number. (Hanemann, 1994, p. 38)

8.3 CONJOINT ANALYSIS

The conceptual basis of conjoint analysis rests on the modelling of the demand of a good as the demand of a given bundle of attributes (Lancaster, 1966). Any good can be contemplated as a set of characteristics (e.g., a car consists of a given engine, accessories, size, safety devices, design and price). The consumer's preferences are defined over the set of attributes and it is possible to estimate the values of the characteristics by asking the individual to choose between different alternatives consisting of bundles containing different levels of the attributes (for example, in one option, the attribute 'spaciousness' is higher but speed is lower; in another, speed and price are higher and so on).

This valuation method has been widely used in marketing and in transport economics. Public transport has been analysed using this approach (Domenich and McFadden, 1975). The utility of public transport users increases when travel time, waiting time, access and egress time, and price are reduced, and increases with service quality, so conjoint analysis offers the practitioner the possibility of estimating how much the individuals value the different characteristics of the service and therefore to allow the economic evaluation of different actions to improve public transport.

There are different methodologies for the practical application of conjoint analysis (choice experiments, contingent ranking, contingent rating and paired comparison) but the basics consist of the description of the good according to the selected characteristics and the levels of these characteristics. The individual is asked to rank, rate or choose several options (differentiated by their characteristics and levels). Choosing or ranking are considered better than rating because respondents are not forced to translate the intensity of their preferences into numbers. The advantage of this approach is that by including price or cost in the options, the trade-offs stated by the respondents allow us to estimate the monetary valuation of different attributes.

Pearce et al. (2006) provide an example of conjoint analysis applied to the clean-up of the River Thames. The objective is to evaluate several investment options to reduce the amount of storm water (sewage litter) entering the river and degrading water quality. The investment costs are known and so we need the economic valuation of improving this non-marketed good. This good is defined as the reduction of sewage overflow entering the river and its attributes are as follows: decreased visual disamenity, fewer days when exposure to the river water is a health risk, and fewer fish deaths.

The respondent must choose between the different options, where the level of attributes varies, including the clean-up cost. The utility of individual i is assumed to be a linear function of the attributes (and its levels) in the j different alternatives the respondent is presented with and some unobserved factors:

$$U_{ij} = b_1 (sewage)_{ij} + b_2 (health)_{ij} + b_3 (fish)_{ij} + b_4 (cost)_{ij} + e_{ij}, \qquad (8.4)$$

where *sewage* is the proportion of sewage litter in the river; *health* is the number of days per year when water sports are not advisable because of increased health risk (minor illness); *fish* is the number of significant fish deaths per year; *cost* is the cost of an option (for the respondent). The coefficients b_1, b_2, b_3, b_4 are unknown parameters, and e_{ij} is an error term to account for unobservable characteristics.

The estimated coefficients in equation (8.4) are negative, as an increase of any part of this attribute reduces the respondent's utility.[5] Each coefficient shows the weight an average household places on the corresponding attribute. This is the marginal utility

---

[5] For a complete description of the study see EFTEC (2003).

with respect to an attribute – for example, b_1 is the change in total utility with respect to a small change in the proportion of sewage litter in the river.

The ratio of one coefficient to another measures the marginal rate of substitution between two characteristics. In this study the estimated coefficients are $b_1 = -0.035$; $b_2 = -0.007$; $b_3 = -0.029$; $b_4 = -0.019$. The ratio b_3/b_2, for example, indicates that the average household values the fish-kills roughly four times as bad as the increase in exposure to minor health risks.

From equation (8.4) it is possible to obtain an average measure of the willingness to pay of the households in the sample.[6] The ratio of any coefficient with respect to the cost coefficient indicates the willingness to pay to reduce the value of the corresponding variable. In this study the average household is willing to pay b_1/b_4 for a reduction of the attribute *sewage*, and the value of this ratio is £1.84; b_2/b_4 for a reduction of the exposure to risk represented by the attribute *health* (£0.37); and b_3/b_4 for a reduction in the fish deaths represented by the attribute *fish* (£1.53).

From these implicit prices of the changes in the attributes it is possible to calculate the total benefits of an investment project that reduces the storm water (sewage litter) entering the river. Taking the status quo as the base case characterized by the physical value for each attribute without the project, once we know the expected physical values with the project, the total willingness to pay of the average household to eliminate storm water overflows is:

$$WTP = 1.84\Delta sewage + 0.37\Delta health + 1.53\Delta fish, \tag{8.5}$$

where *WTP* is the average willingness to pay of each household. Multiplying this value by the number of households in the Thames Water area we obtain an estimation of the total willingness to pay per year.

It has been argued that this method is superior to contingent valuation as it is possible to estimate the values of the main characteristics of the environmental good under evaluation. In addition, respondents (in choice and rank modelling) do not have to put a monetary value on their preferences, and the number is obtained through the information revealed in the trade-offs when choosing between options where a cost variable has been included.

Although conjoint analysis can be considered a better option when the environmental good is complex and has multiple attributes, it is true that this complexity creates problems of validity and reliability common to any stated preference method. The cognitive difficulties of the respondent facing choices between bundles with several attributes and several levels for each attribute create problems of design and interpretation (see Adamowicz et al., 1998; Pearce et al., 2006).

---

[6] 1214 Thames Water customers.

8.4 INDIVIDUAL PREFERENCES AND SOCIAL WELFARE

Altruism and non-use value

It is argued that individuals are willing to pay to increase the welfare of others besides themselves and, therefore, that the altruistic motive should be added to the purely selfish valuation. If so, the value of preserving the environment would be higher than the valuation that overlooks altruism. The characteristics of the environmental goods favour the individual being willing to pay more for their conservation if she cares about the welfare of others.

Although the results in stated preferences-based surveys suggest that people are willing to pay in excess of their private values, it is important to consider the nature of these altruistic feelings to answer the question on whether the additional willingness to pay of individual i, because of concern with respect to individual j, should be included in cost–benefit analysis.

With non-paternalistic altruism, the utility function of individual i includes the utility of individual j as an argument. This means that individual i cares about the well-being of j but the consumption bundles of j are irrelevant for i. In the case of paternalistic altruism, the consumption of the good by individual j, is an argument in the utility function of individual i.

It is considered that when the altruism is non-paternalistic, the altruistic feeling is irrelevant to cost–benefit analysis. The following example (Bergstrom, 2006) serves to illustrate that it is easy to make a significant bias in the valuation if the right question is not formulated. Suppose A and B are a couple who maintain separate budgets and are wondering whether to rent a larger apartment with two extra rooms. One room will be exclusively used as a study by A and the other exclusively as a playroom for B. A is willing to pay $100 for the study and, as she loves B, she would pay $50 more to see B happy with his playroom (which A will never use). Similarly, B is willing to pay $100 for his playroom and, as he loves A, he would pay $50 more for A to have her study (which B will never use).

The additional rent for the new apartment is $250, which will be divided equally. Should they rent it? If the altruistic willingness to pay is included, the answer is yes (300 > 250) and if it is excluded, the answer is no (200 < 250). What is the correct answer?

Consider the case where the apartment is rented based on the inclusion of the willingness to pay for the welfare of the other in addition to one's own welfare. Once the apartment is rented, individual A is worse off because she values the change at $100 and has to pay $125 (half the additional rent). However, as she cares about B, she reviews the status of her partner and notes that he is also worse off (he paid $125 for something that brings a satisfaction of $100). They were wrong to rent the larger apartment.

The paradox of this result is solved by considering that if the benefits are included, the costs should also be included. Each of the individuals is better off if the other has a good that makes the other happy, but they are also worse off if their partner must pay a higher rent. The problem is solved in practice by including the costs in the question, or directly excluding altruism. Both alternatives lead to the same result.

It is argued that the willingness to pay of the individuals who care for the well-being of others (e.g., their safety, the consumption of environmental goods) should be included in cost–benefit analysis when the altruism is paternalistic. Then, the nature of these preferences is as important as the intensity of the altruistic preferences. For example, in the case of projects saving lives, it is important to consider how the value of a statistical life has been estimated. Jones-Lee (1992) has shown that with pure paternalism, the value of a statistical life increases significantly (10–40 per cent larger in the case of the UK) than the value for a society of purely self-interested individuals.

Moral principles and economic valuation

The economic valuation of environmental impacts has also been criticized on ethical or moral principles, with the basic position that the passive use value cannot be measured in monetary terms. Within the passive use value is the existence value. Using willingness to pay – for example, to determine that a species persists – is unreasonable from this ethical position. Abortion is moral or immoral and it is still one thing or the other regardless of the amounts that individuals are willing to pay to allow or prohibit it.

Assuming that the problems of design and implementation of the survey have been solved, contingent valuation has limitations that, although common to the neoclassical measurement of the value of goods, should not be ignored because of the impact they have on the valuation of unique environmental goods. The first is the acceptance that the willingness to pay is the value of the goods to society, taking into account that the willingness to pay not only reflects the preferences of the individuals interviewed but also their income. The second limitation is that the preferences of future generations do not count. Only the preferences of the present generation with respect to itself and to future generations matter, which in terms of the environmental goods legacy to new generations, creates an ethical problem.

Distorted preferences

There is another problem that particularly affects the environment and health evaluation: the distinction between the satisfaction of individual preferences and individual welfare. Adler and Posner (2001) call attention to the uninformed preferences, distinguishing between instrumental, intrinsic, adaptive, and objectively bad. Instrumental preferences are changed by providing information – for example, refusal to drink water with fluoride because the individual believes that fluoridation causes cancer. The intrinsic preferences change too, but not because there is an error in the individual's beliefs but because the individual does not have enough information when asked and such information changes their preferences – for example, the willingness to pay for an art project is low because the individual does not know the aesthetic qualities of the project.

The adaptive and the objectively bad preferences create an obvious conflict with the principle of consumer sovereignty. The individual lives in miserable conditions and her preferences have adapted to this situation of precariousness and loss of self-esteem so that, according to those adaptive preferences, she negatively values, for example, an improvement in her environment because her misfortune and social resentment make her believe that the improvement is bad for her.

The objectively bad preferences also violate the principle of consumer sovereignty. If society accepts that there is no social benefit from children smoking, it could give zero value to the loss of profits of the tobacco industry if a project reduces the number of children who smoke.

In any case, these are extreme examples and circumstances that do not affect most projects, but with regard to environmental impacts such as global warming it can be useful to consider the previous arguments about the sometimes complex relationship between individual preferences and social welfare.

8.5 THE VALUE OF LIFE

There are projects and regulations devoted to saving lives, while other public initiatives, regulations or investment projects, pursuing different goals, involve an increase or decrease in injuries and deaths, either in the construction phase or during the lifetime of those actions.

The title of this section may seem immoral; one should hasten to make clear that we are not talking about the life of an individual. The value of life of a real individual is not under discussion. In general, one could say that human life generally has an infinite value when it comes to one's own life; this is also so if we are asked to value the lives of our loved ones, and even, in extreme circumstances, many people risk their lives to save a stranger. Apparently, nor does society set limits to saving the life of any given individual. A mountaineer in danger of death will receive all kinds of assistance from the government to rescue him, and rescue efforts will not be stopped because they have reached a certain level of spending.

This section is not about that moral and philosophical questions. On the contrary, it is quite pragmatic and, given that individuals trade income and safety in their everyday lives, the government should, in principle, consider the values obtained from these actual trade-offs to inform public policy in this area.

Economists argue that the scarcity of resources makes choices unavoidable and those choices also affect safety. Let us think for a moment what would happen to the number of fatal accidents if it were forbidden to drive at more than 30 km per hour. It is more than likely that the number of deaths in road accidents would be reduced drastically. However, if we ask individuals if they would accept this prohibition in exchange for a reduction in the number of accidents and deaths, in which they or their families have a low but certain probability of being involved, almost certainly a majority would answer no. The reason: the higher cost of transport, with all the inconveniences and economic losses associated with such a reduction in the speed limit.

The above example is deliberately extreme and qualitative, but it serves to illustrate that individuals trade comfort, speed and income for physical risk, sometimes uninformed, but at many other times aware of the risk they bear in exchange for other goods. When one accepts this implicit trade-off, we enter the realm of the economic valuation of life. The meaning of this concept is as follows: to the extent that society accepts risks that could be reduced by giving up other public and private goods, it is interesting to see how much individuals are willing to pay, or to accept, for these types of transactions. The term 'value of life' acquires a less dramatic and more practical dimension, because what is at stake is not really the value of life in the strict sense but how much individuals are willing to forgo other goods in exchange for living with higher levels of safety.

We will see that what is valued in cost–benefit analysis is the increase or decrease in the likelihood of events that can result in injuries or deaths. We are not referring to extreme situations but to changes in the probability of death or injury associated with undertaking an activity, like building a bridge or driving a vehicle. The role of economics in this context is that resources are scarce and the need to choose among alternative uses also counts in decisions that include the good safety, respecting the preferences of individuals as long as there are no problems of information, bounded rationality or seriously distorted preferences (see Adler and Posner, 2001; Sunstein, 2014).

Suppose we are considering building a dam and among its costs we face a 1/10 000 probability that one anonymous life is lost during the lifetime of the project. Should the dam be built? If the value of life were infinite, this project would never be carried out. In practice, it is likely that if the social benefits in terms of electricity production, for example, sufficiently outweigh the costs of constructing, maintaining and operating the dam, the project will be carried out. If one takes the extreme position of not giving a specific value to the anonymous life that will be lost, it is likely that we will be giving it a zero value (or the monetary costs of legal compensation) in the economic evaluation of the project. It seems that the idea of exploring the value society gives to the loss of anonymous lives deserves some further consideration.

The value of a statistical life

It is not the value of life, nor the so-called value of a statistical life (VSL) that is really at stake. It is an average willingness to pay for, or accept, small and specific changes in the probability of death. It is worth making a distinction between the trade-off faced by a single individual and the VSL. In the former case we have a single individual who is willing to pay a certain amount to reduce the risk of death given his particular context of income, health status, safety level, risk aversion and the like; in the latter case we have a cohort of individuals. The value of the single individual is simply the marginal rate of substitution between risk and income. The VSL is the average of the marginal rate of substitution between risk and income in the cohort. This value is in fact an average willingness to pay to change a concrete probability of death (e.g., 1/10 000) within a population with income differences, among others.

Consider the case of an individual willing to pay $100 to reduce a death risk of 1/100 000. Dividing the willingness to pay by the probability, we get an implicit value of life of $10 million. Another way to express this is to consider that we have a population of 100 000 individuals commuting from A to B; they are identical and aware that one of them will die in a car accident during the year. If a representative individual is willing to pay a maximum of $100 to finance a project that will eliminate that risk, we have a maximum total willingness to pay of $10 million to avoid this anonymous (or statistical) death.

To look a bit further at the meaning of this $10 million and its limitation let us consider the following expression of the expected utility of being dead or alive:

$$E(U) = (1 - \pi)U(M,1) + \pi U(M,0), \tag{8.6}$$

where we have two possible states: dead denoted by 0 and alive denoted by 1, with associated probabilities of π and $1 - \pi$, respectively. When the individual is alive with a level of income M her utility is $U(M, 1)$ and when she is dead the utility is $U(M, 0)$, which could be zero or positive.

Let us ask the individual about the maximum willingness to pay (v) to reduce risk of death at the actual level π. The maximum amount of money that we could take from the individual would make her indifferent between the expected utility in expression (8.6) and the certain utility of being alive but with a lower income $(M - v)$:

$$U(M - v, 1) = (1 - \pi)U(M,1) + \pi U(M,0). \tag{8.7}$$

Expression (8.7) shows that the individual is indifferent between an expected utility with some associated risk of death and a certain level of utility without that risk but with lower income. The key point is to see how v responds to small changes of π. This is the trade-off to be quantified $(\delta v/\delta \pi)$. In the previous example the change in v was $100 when the risk of death π was increased by 1/100 000. Therefore, the 'value of life', equal to $10 million in our example, is obtained with the derivative $\delta v/\delta \pi$.

Assuming no problems of information, bounded rationality or distorted preferences, let us suppose that we have estimated the VSL in a population and that this value is equal to $10 million.[7] There are several qualifications to make before using this value for the economic evaluation of projects and policies (Sunstein, 2014).

The first is to clarify that, when the estimation of the willingness to pay is made, the 'value of life' as expressed by $\delta v/\delta \pi$, is not independent of the level of risk and income of the population, and the change in the current risk level, when the estimation of the willingness to pay is made. Hence, to say that the value of a statistical life is $10 million is meaningless without linking the willingness to pay to the values where the estimates

---

[7] The median US labour market estimates are in the $9–11 million range (Viscusi, 2018).

come from. For example, one could not expect to obtain the same figure of $10 million if the change in probability of death were 1/100 000 instead of 1/10 000, and so on. This would require a willingness to pay $100 to eliminate a risk of 1/100 000 and $1000 to eliminate a risk of 1/10 000. This seems unlikely, as one would not expect the willingness to pay to reduce statistical risk to be linear.

The second is that a unique VSL is incompatible with heterogeneous individuals and different types of risks. The willingness to pay is different for different people because individuals differ in their attitude towards risk. The willingness to pay is sensitive to the background risk (π in expressions (8.6) and (8.7)) and heterogeneity in preferences, age and income. Moreover, people show different degrees of risk aversion to different events, like the risk of cancer or food contamination or a plane crash. Hence, there is not a single VSL and there is evidence that older people have a lower VSL, that the willingness to pay to avoid cancer deaths is higher than for unanticipated deaths and that, unsurprisingly, rich people have a higher VSL than poor people.

Although, different VSLs should be used for different individuals and types of risk, the use of a single value within a country is the common practice. One could consider that this is equitable, but it depends on who pays to reduce the risk. The use of different VSLs for rich and poor people only reflect their differences in willingness to pay in the trade-off between risk and income.

Given an income distribution, and in the absence of lack of information, bounded rationality, and distorted preferences, the individual VSL should be respected even when income differences are the cause of the disparities in willingness to pay:

> A uniform VSL has some of the same characteristics as a policy that requires people to buy Volvos. In principle, the government should force exchanges only on terms that people find acceptable, at least if it is genuinely concerned with their welfare. That principle is the correct conception of risk equity. Note, once again, that the argument for using willingness to pay does not imply satisfaction with the existing distribution of wealth. The problem with forced exchanges is that they do nothing to alter existing distributions. In fact, they make poor people worse off, requiring them to use their limited resources for something they do not want to buy. (Sunstein, 2014, p. 117)

Nevertheless, when the individuals do not pay for the reduction of risk, as in the case of donations to poor countries, the use of a single VSL is harmless. Nonetheless, full individuation is not possible in practice and for some goods is not useful. It is practically impossible to know the VSL of every individual. It is not very helpful in the case of many projects and regulations that deliver public goods like the reduction in air pollution. In these cases, excludability is not feasible, and hence once the good is provided for some individual, the benefits accrue to the rest of the population.

Finally, it is worth stressing that the context of the theory and estimation of the VSL is for statistically small risks. We are not dealing with people's rights like access to drinkable water nor with catastrophic risks.

A related concept with significant policy implications is the value of a statistical life year (VSLY). Is the value of saving an anonymous life independent of the expected number of years of that life? If the answer is no, and an average VSL applies to the whole population, the VSL of younger people is higher than that of older people. This issue is quite controversial and in empirical terms is not clear whether the willingness to pay of older people for additional life years could be lower or higher if they face higher health risks and have savings to spend on health.

The question is far from solved if we look to the equity dimension of the problem. If for equity reasons a unique VSL is applied to anyone, disregarding their age, the VSLY will be higher for older individuals. If equity is understood as the same VSLY for both, the value of reducing the risk of death decreases with age. 'The alternatives of either using a uniform VSL or a constant VSLY per year of life expectancy give diametrically opposed estimates of how differences in life expectancy should be treated, even though both are purportedly equitable' (Viscusi, 2018, p. 5).

The discussion about the VSL for different people (e.g., level of income) applies equally to people of different ages if, facing the trade-off between a change in the probability of death and income, similar individuals in all other aspects are willing to pay a different amount depending on their age.

The value of a statistical life is also estimated through survey-based techniques such as the contingent valuation method and through choice experiments (see Sections 8.2 and 8.3). The problems associated with the values obtained by surveys in which individuals are asked for their willingness to pay for or accept changes in safety levels are the same as those previously described in the valuation of environmental goods.

The revealed preference approach has also been followed to estimate the value of a statistical life. The *compensating wage differential* is a method based on the identification of contexts in which the individual trades off income against changes in the probability of death or injury. Before dealing with method, however, we explain the *human capital* approach based on lost earnings because of the death of the individual, which is used for determining compensation in wrongful death settlements.

Human capital

The human capital or cost of death approach is a valuation method used to estimate the VSL based on the estimation of the present value of the expected future earnings of the victim, given her life expectancy and expected income. In legal disputes, for establishing death compensations in lawsuits, it is common to employ the discounted value of future earnings. A lawyer would argue that the death of a highly qualified professional should be compensated to the value of a sum equivalent to the wages that she had earned during her life.

The value of the discounted earnings (DE) lost as a result of a death is the discounted flow of annual wages of the victim for the rest of the years that she would have lived if the accident had not happened. Suppose we are estimating the value of the earnings lost because of a project in 2020 that causes the death of an individual in that year. One way to calculate it is shown in expression (8.8) where w is the wage in each year and π is the probability in the base year that the individual is still alive in a given year (denoted by the superscript). In expression (8.9) the length of the series does not matter if we do not exclude the years in which π is significantly different from zero:

$$DE = w_{2020}\pi_{2020}^{2020} + \frac{w_{2021}\pi_{2020}^{2021}}{(1+i)} + \ldots + \frac{w_{2200}\pi_{2020}^{2200}}{(1+i)^{180}}. \tag{8.8}$$

In general:

$$DE = \sum_{t=t_0}^{\infty} w_t \pi_{t_0}^{t} \, (1+i)^{-(t-t_0)}, \tag{8.9}$$

where t_0 is the base year.

The weakness of this method of valuation is that it makes a wrong use of the labour market information. The value of earnings lost represents the marginal product of the worker to the employer; it is the economic value for the firm but not for the employee, and does not measure the willingness to pay of the individual for small changes in the probability of death. Furthermore, taking the argument to the extreme, it could be argued that the death of a pensioner, or a permanently unemployed individual, does not imply any social loss.

Compensating wage differential

This method is based on revealed preferences and it is also based on labour market information. If we had information for a sufficiently large number of individuals exposed to different levels of risk that they are aware of, and with different wage premiums to compensate for taking such risks, an estimate of the value of a statistical life could be obtained.

In practice, and from a representative sample of the workforce, this method tries to determine the relationship between the wage gap in different professions with different known probabilities of death, but the required assumptions that workers voluntarily choose those professions and that they are fully aware of the probabilities of losing their lives are not always realistic.

The estimation of a simple model as in expression (8.10) would yield b_1, and so it is possible to estimate the VSL by isolating the coefficient b_1 from the the effects of other variables such as sex, experience, age and a set of relevant elements of utility or disutility of the job:

$$Annual\ wage = b_0 + b_1\ risk\ of\ death\ in\ the\ year\ + \sum_{i=2}^{n} b_i\ other\ relevant\ variables + e, \tag{8.10}$$

where e is an error term to account for the influence of unobserved variables.

This approach based on labour market data results in higher VSL values than with the stated preference approach. In the case of the US labour market, the VSL estimates are in the \$9–11 million range:

Drawing on a sample of stated preference studies, the OECD, for example, recommends a baseline VSL of $3.6 million, with a VSL range of $1.8 million to $5.5 million … The benefit transfer approach that I recommend is to use the US VSL figures as the baseline and to adjust these differences downward based on the income elasticity of the VSL. The baseline VSL figure I will use is $10 million. Income elasticity estimates for the USA are usually in the range 0.5–0.6, but international income elasticity estimates are just above 1.0, which I will use as the income elasticity estimate for my calculations. (Viscusi, 2018, p. 4)

A key question with respect to the values obtained in the labour market is whether these values of a statistical life can be extrapolated to the rest of the population. This value transfer from the labour market is difficult to justify, to say the least. The value of a statistical life obtained in the labour market derives from individuals with different characteristics with respect to the average citizen, particularly concerning their attitude toward risk.

In general, the VSL estimated through b_1 should be taken as a lower bound when extrapolated to the whole population. Moreover, there is not an implicit single value of life even for the same individual. The wage compensation that individual A requires depends on this actual level of safety in the labour market. It may well be that b_1 has been estimated in relatively safe conditions because of strict labour regulations, which means that the compensation that the worker requires is influenced by the 'high' safety level in which he is located. Had the same worker negotiated the compensation situated at a lower level of safety, he would have required a higher wage; that is, the marginal rate of substitution between income and safety has changed with the level of safety.

Furthermore, it is assumed that the worker is a well-informed individual who clearly perceives the probabilities of death in the different jobs being offered, and that he negotiates on an equal footing with the employer when setting his wage. In the real world, these conditions are easily violated. A worker born in a mining area with high unemployment may have no other job alternatives and therefore the risk premium received is not the result of a free negotiation. The consequence of this fact is the underestimation of the VSL.

As the objective is to extrapolate the VSL obtained in the labour market to the rest of the population, one should be aware of the highly probable case of a downward bias in the valuation of a statistical life –for example, when this value is used in the evaluation of projects involving deaths from pollution, road accidents and other reasons that have nothing to do with the labour market where the value was estimated. Imagine the case of two different individuals: worker A and individual B, who is more risk averse than A. Both A and B are willing to accept higher risks if they are compensated with income; however, the compensation required by B is higher than that required by A. If one accepts that individuals who accept hazardous jobs have, at equivalent levels of risk, a risk attitude less conservative than the rest of the population, the compensation for A underestimates what B would require.

Another potential problem is the risk of double counting when the value of a statistical life obtained in the labour market is used for the valuation of deaths that occur among workers represented by the sample. If workers have been compensated by raising their wages in free negotiations and are fully informed of the consequences of the risks assumed, it is double counting include separately the cost of accidents by multiplying the VSL by the number of estimated deaths resulting from the implementation of the project.

To conclude, it should be emphasized that what is looked for in cost–benefit analysis is that the small changes in the probability of death, resulting from the implementation of a project, receive adequate treatment in the calculation of the social profitability of implementing those projects. Maintaining a radical position against that valuation can simply imply that the lives lost, or deaths avoided, receive a value of zero. Economists do not try to calculate 'the value of life' in a literal sense, but to approximate the implicit value of society on another inescapable trade-off – how much of the scarce resources the individuals are willing to sacrifice to reduce risk in their lives and therefore to reduce the number of injured and dead.

8.6 BENEFITS TRANSFER

A practical problem in the economic valuation of non-marketed goods concerns the transferability of the results. In practice, given the impossibility of performing specific studies in the evaluation of some projects, practitioners often resort to the use of values obtained in other studies (and other contexts). The popularity of this procedure requires understanding what we are doing when transferring values from other contexts and settings.

The main difficulty with respect to the transfer of values of environmental impacts of existing studies is that such values have been obtained in specific contexts that may be hardly comparable to the reality of the project. It is very important to know exactly what the interviewee was asked when we received her monetary valuation of a given impact. A clear example of the risk of transferring values without prior consideration about how the information was obtained is the following:

Suppose a person in one study is asked for his willingness to pay (WTP) for a Jaguar, in a second study for his WTP for a Mercedes-Benz, and in a third study for his WTP for a Volvo. Obviously, one cannot sum these three unconditional amounts of money and interpret the result as the person's total WTP for cars. Either we must proceed sequentially ..., i.e. ask for the WTP for a car conditional on what has already been spent on cars in previous questions, or ask for the total WTP for cars. Unfortunately, using existing valuation data in a cost–benefit analysis is often equivalent to the former approach in the sense that the investigator adds unconditional WTPs collected from different studies. The outcome of such a study is difficult to interpret at best. (Johansson, 1993, pp. 78–9)

As noted by Johansson, the transfer of values from other existing studies to another project is often equivalent to the initial questions about the willingness to pay for each car, in the sense that we are adding willingness to pay that has not been conveniently conditioned.

The intuition of the previous example is that if we add unconditional willingness to pay from different studies, we may be overestimating the economic value of an environmental good. However, the opposite may also occur and we can underestimate a negative environmental impact by adding valuations from studies in a different context.

The mentioned undervaluation can be illustrated with a project involving the purchase of an expensive protection system that prevents oil spills on a coastline that has many beaches. If we add the willingness to pay to protect each separate beach, we will be underestimating the value that users attach to the elimination of the risk of contamination.

The reason for the underestimation is that, by adding willingness to pay to keep each beach clean, an individual knows she has any of the other beaches as substitutes and therefore her monetary valuation of the beach she visits will be less than if you ask her how much she is willing to pay to preserve the current state of the beach conditional on the other beaches also being contaminated. To calculate the total willingness to pay we would have to proceed as in the example of cars, resulting in this case in a greater willingness to pay for preserving the beaches, given that we have conditioned the question on the fact that the other beaches have also been contaminated.

It is common practice to use values from other studies when budget constraints do not allow us to conduct a specific survey, or perhaps as a first step before a proper estimation of the local values is carried out. In any case, it is advisable to avoid a mechanical transfer of values from other contexts without a previous correction according to some characteristics of the population on-site, such as per capita income.

Sometimes a statistical analysis of several studies (meta-analysis) can help, relating the average willingness to pay for a non-marketed good to a set of economic and demographic variables. In this case it is possible to improve the process compared with the unadjusted transfer of values that ignores key differences between the site where the value comes from and the context where the value is transferred.

THINGS TO REMEMBER

1. The stated preference approach tries to elicit users' values through survey-based methods. Contingent valuation is a technique consisting of the construction of a hypothetical market in which the respondents reveal their willingness to pay for changes in non-marketed goods, such as changes in the quality of the environment or in the probability of health risk.

2. Conjoint analysis is an alternative to contingent valuation as the respondent only has to choose between options and indirectly reveal his willingness to pay for the attributes of the non-marketed good. Conjoint analysis is particularly appropriate when the good has multiple attributes, but this also has its drawbacks in terms of

the increased complexity of the exercise and its corresponding cognitive difficulties for the interviewee.

3. The stated preferences method is an alternative to the revealed preference approach when it is not possible to observe users' behaviour in a related market. This is the case for the non-use value, or passive value, of environmental goods, which requires the construction of hypothetical situations and whose results are very sensitive to the design of the survey. Some critics argue that the main problem is not accuracy but credibility, the fact that the responses obtained in these surveys do not measure the intensity of preferences. Important research efforts have been made to improve the methods and avoid the most obvious biases.

4. Changes in physical risk, such as the reduction of the probability of severe injury or death, are the objective of some projects. Practitioners conducting cost–benefit analysis of regulatory proposals and projects that prevent, or increase, the number and seriousness of accidents, need to assign an economic value to these effects. It is not the value of an anonymous life that is really valued. It is an average willingness to pay for small and specific changes in the probability of death.

5. A common practice in cost–benefit analysis is to transfer values obtained in other studies to avoid the costs of conducting specific surveys. It is important to emphasize the fact that the values of a statistical life or environmental impacts of existing studies are context specific and perhaps cannot be easily generalized or transferred to other contexts or settings. A prerequisite to the transferability of values is to know exactly what the interviewee was asked and under which circumstances when she provided her monetary valuation of a given impact.

9
Uncertainty and risk analysis

Nothing is more soothing or more persuasive than the computer screen, with its imposing arrays of numbers, glowing colors, and elegantly structured graphs. As we stare at the passing show, we become so absorbed that we tend to forget that the computer only answers questions; it does not ask them. Whenever we ignore that truth, the computer supports us in our conceptual errors. Those who live only by the numbers may find that the computer has simply replaced the oracles to whom people resorted in ancient times for guidance in risk management and decision-making.

(Peter L. Bernstein, 1996, p. 336)

9.1 INTRODUCTION

The future is uncertain, and uncertainty means variability in the outcome associated with a given action. It is impossible to live without risk. Driving to work or purchasing financial assets, for example, are actions associated with the risk of having an accident or losing income. Individuals who want to reduce risk in their lives can do so to some extent by insuring themselves and thus reducing the variability of the possible outcomes, and to some extent by avoiding exposure to risk. In both cases individuals pay to reduce the risk to more bearable levels.

An individual whose hobby is mountain climbing can reduce the risk of death by reducing the difficulty of the challenges, or simply by leaving this risky sport. In exchange, the individual would have to pay a price in terms of the resulting loss of utility. Similarly, buying insurance can reduce the risk of a severe loss of income if the house burns down. The price to pay in this case is the annual insurance premium.

It is common to distinguish between risk and uncertainty. The decision under risk would be one in which the individual knows the true probabilities assigned to individual events – for example, the probability of obtaining two when throwing a dice is one in six (if the game is repeated a sufficiently high number of times, we obtain two approximately 16.67 per cent of the time). On the contrary, under uncertainty, we do not have an objective set of probabilities associated with the different possible cases – for example, when predicting the next technological breakthrough in energy.

However, decision makers live in a world of uncertainty where their degree of belief concerning the different possible relevant cases under consideration can be subject to hard or soft probabilities. This subjective probability concept applies equally to tossing a fair coin or a coin that could also have two tails or two heads. In both cases one has to work with the same probability function – one-half for each state (heads or tails) – though in the case of a previously tested coin we are working with hard (objective) probabilities (Hirshleifer and Riley, 1992).

This distinction is useful to characterize two types of actions the practitioner faces under uncertainty: terminal action and informational action. In a situation of terminal action, it does not matter whether the individual knows a priori the number of heads on the coin to be tossed. On the contrary, in a context of informational action, the investor might be interested in spending money to obtain some information on the type of coin he is going to toss.

The decision maker must choose which action is more adequate in project appraisal depending on the circumstances. He must evaluate the project with subjective probabilities associated with different possible states but can sometimes improve confidence in the future possible outcomes by investing money and effort to acquire additional information on the true probabilities associated with the different states of nature (for example, investing in demand forecasts or designing contracts to increase the probability of selecting an efficient constructor and therefore reducing the project costs).

The perceived risk is dependent on the analysis of the so-called a priori information, the expert opinion and the judgement of the analyst who interprets all the information at hand. In a public tender for granting the concession of a road there will probably be different traffic forecasts; one cannot assert ex ante that one is better than another because different bidders assign different probabilities to the various contingencies that can be considered to determine the volume of traffic.[1]

Section 9.2 outlines the approach to risk in the private sector. Private investors decide which projects to undertake, taking into consideration the risk involved. In principle, a risky project is less attractive unless the higher returns compensate for the likelihood of losing money if the circumstances are unfavourable. Investors require higher rates of return for riskier projects as compensation for assuming the probability of a loss.

When an entrepreneur assesses the purchase of a financial asset, which consists of an initial payment of $1000 in year zero in exchange for $1100 in year one, she is comparing a certain present amount with some other certain amount in the future. The asset has a safe yield of 10 per cent. Suppose, though, that the entrepreneur also has the option to invest $1000 in a business from which, depending on the economic cycle, she would gain

---

[1] When several competitors in a public tender have a different view on the auction that has a 'common value' (e.g., the stock of crude oil in an oil reservoir), it is said that the winner may suffer the 'winner's curse' and incur losses. The explanation is that if the value of the object is unique and common to all (unlike a piece of art, for example), the bidder making an offer above the others may have interpreted the information in an optimistic way and overstated the value of the auctioned object.

$1600 if the economy is 'doing well' and just recovering the $1000 if the economy 'goes wrong', with a probability of 0.5 for both outcomes.

Given the two contingencies and associated probabilities, the expected value equals $1300 (i.e., the return is $0 or $600 with equal probability). However, if the investor is risk averse, she does not consider the expected value as certain. It may well be that the individual decides to buy the asset where a $100 return can be obtained with certainty, as opposed to the asset that offers an expected yield of $300. The explanation is that in the risky asset she can obtain $0 or $600 with equal probability, but never $300, in contrast with the certain $100 in the first option. If she is indifferent between both assets, her certainty equivalent of an expected profit of $300 is $100.

The idea of a certainty equivalent lower than the expected value is like the discount of future risky benefits at a higher rate than the interest rate. The only reason for a risk-averse investor to accept a risky business is that the expected return, once discounted with a higher rate (it includes a risk premium), is positive. A key issue we address in Section 9.3 is whether the public sector should act in the same way as the private sector by calculating expected values with a higher discount that includes a risk premium, or whether it should behave differently.

Complete certainty does not exist; therefore, investment projects or public policies that have lasting effects require predictions of their impacts and estimations of their magnitude. The uncertainty associated with the benefits and costs of a project indicates that the results rest on a range of values and their associated probabilities, rather than on deterministic values. Sections 9.4 and 9.5 cover the fundamentals of risk analysis, a tool that, instead of using deterministic values, introduces ranges of feasible values of key variables and their probabilities of occurrence. Risk analysis provides useful information to enhance decision making.

9.2 RISK IN A PRIVATE PROJECT

When undertaking a project with a 30-year lifespan whose annual net benefits depend on various contingencies such as rainy or dry weather, or the economy growing at 2 or 3 per cent, part of the project's success will inevitably depend on our luck; however, the results are not always random. As Bernstein (1996) points out, there is a difference between gambling and those games in which skill influences the outcome. The same principles apply to roulette, dice or slot machines, but something else is required to explain the results in poker or betting on horses. It could be that the newcomer wins a round, but when the game is repeated many times, eventually the professional wins.

When the results simply obey a random probability distribution, those individuals disliking the variability of results (even if this variability is associated with higher returns) would happily accept a fixed amount in exchange for the expected payoff of the game. In this context of risk aversion, the concept of certainty equivalent is very useful for the valuation of project benefits subject to variability.

The amount of money that produces the same utility as the expected utility of playing the game is called the certainty equivalent. This amount leaves the individual indifferent between playing and not playing – for example, in a game that consists of tossing a coin and winning a million if it is heads and zero if it is tails. The certainty equivalent is the minimum amount of money (e.g., $100 000) we must offer to leave the individual indifferent between accepting this amount and not playing, or rejecting it and playing (see Chapter 11).

An individual deciding whether to invest in a project needs to estimate its net present value (NPV), to check whether it is greater than or equal to zero and so to satisfy the following condition:

$$\sum_{t=1}^{T} \frac{(p_t x_t - C_t)}{(1+i)^t} \geq I_0, \tag{9.1}$$

where I_0 is the investment cost (realized in year zero for simplicity), p_t the price, C_t the annual cost and x_t the quantity during the T years of the project, and i denotes the discount rate.

Expression (9.1) represents an investment project in which there are no fixed costs other than the investment cost in year zero. We must estimate the costs of initial investment (oil drilling, launching a new product, building a dam, etc.) and predict the benefits and costs over the T-years horizon of the project. If T is sufficiently high, it can be virtually assured that the values finally taken by the main variables, such as input and output prices, will differ from those initially predicted.

Let us consider the case of a private project involving the construction of a complex of 150 apartments for rent in a tourist resort. The cost of construction is budgeted at $13 000 and the annual net profit over the lifetime of the project ($T = 15$) depends on the number of rooms occupied (x), the rent per apartment and year (p) and annual maintenance and operation costs (C). We are facing a risky investment. The revenues and costs of construction and operation of the apartments can vary for several reasons, including changes in the domestic and the global economy (effect on costs), changes in the economy of countries of origin of tourists (effect on demand) and variation in the prices of competitors (effect on demand).

To incorporate into the analysis the uncertainty that faces an entrepreneur who is evaluating whether to invest in the project, assume that the annual demand only takes two values: high, which means a maximum occupation ($x = 150$), and low ($x = 125$). Both states are equally likely, and we initially assume that once a value is observed, high or low, in the first year, it will remain for the rest of the coming years. The annual operating cost is $400 regardless of occupancy rates, and the rent per apartment and year is $10.

The expected net present value ($ENPV$) of the project can be expressed as:

$$ENPV = -13\,000 + \frac{(0.5 \times 1100 + 0.5 \times 850)}{1+i} + \ldots + \frac{(0.5 \times 1100 + 0.5 \times 850)}{(1+i)^{15}}. \tag{9.2}$$

Assuming for simplicity that the real interest rate is zero, *ENPV* is equal to:

$$ENPV = -13000 + (975 \times 15) = 1625. \tag{9.3}$$

To understand how uncertainty affects the project, let us think about what a profit of $1625 means. This value is not an actual return; it is an expected return, in the sense of mathematical expectation – that is, the value to which the benefit tends if this project is repeated to infinity. The real return that the investor receives from the project is either a $3500 gain if the demand is high or a $250 loss if the demand is low. These are the real values the investor will receive: $3500 or –$250.

If it were possible to have full insurance at zero cost, the fair premium equals $1875 (the difference between the result with high demand and the expected value). This is a fully comprehensive insurance that guarantees the expected value of $1625 in any of the contingencies: high or low demand. With this comprehensive insurance, the variability of the results disappears, and a risk-averse investor will buy the insurance to guarantee the expected value. It is worth emphasizing that, once insured, he will not incur losses, but neither will he get the maximum benefits. A risk-loving entrepreneur would reject the offer of the insurance company for the opportunity to win $3500.

In Figure 9.1 we can see the profits with low demand (–$250), the profits with high demand ($3500), the expected value ($1625) and two new values ($1250 and $200) explained below.

In the initial situation, without insurance, let us suppose now that a tour operator offers the investor the following contract: full occupancy rent of the apartments is ensured during the 15 years in exchange for a payment below the 'free market rent'. The guaranteed price per apartment will be $9 for the 150 apartments regardless of how many are occupied (the entrepreneur is not allowed to rent the unoccupied ones). The demand may still be high or low, but now, in any event, the entrepreneur receives a fixed payment of $1250, located in Figure 9.1 on the left of the expected value:

$$NPV = -13000 + (950 \times 15) = 1250. \tag{9.4}$$

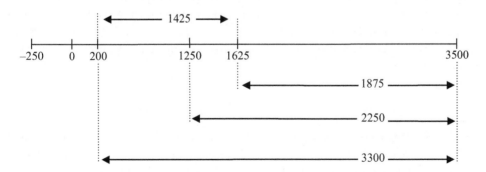

Figure 9.1 Profits under uncertainty

Would the entrepreneur accept this offer? We cannot answer this question without knowing his attitude toward risk; however, a simple observation of reality shows that many individuals accept similar offers every day. They would be willing to accept a smaller but certain amount (e.g., $1250) by giving up a higher expected value ($1625). There is a safe value (certainty equivalent) lower than the expected value for which the entrepreneurs are indifferent between accepting this safe value or playing the game consisting of a potential gain of $3500 and a potential loss of $250 – that is, they are risk averse. The offer of the tour operator is like fully comprehensive insurance where the entrepreneur pays a $2250 premium in exchange for having a safe profit of $1250.

Suppose now that the certainty equivalent of the entrepreneur is $200, as represented in Figure 9.1 – that is, he is indifferent between receiving $200 of safe benefits against the possibility of winning $3500 or losing $250 with equal probability. This means that, although the expected value of the investment is $1625, the variability associated with this expected value (profit of $3500 or loss of $250) represents a cost to the individual of $1425, which makes him indifferent between the safe profit of $200 and the expected value of $1625.

This is equivalent to saying that the entrepreneur is indifferent between paying a premium of $3300 in order to ensure the maximum profit of $3500 or investing without insurance. As the tour operator is offering a better contract – asking for less ($2250) than the entrepreneur is willing to pay ($3300) – the entrepreneur will accept the offer.

From the arguments above, we conclude that a risk-averse private investor does not use the expected value of annual net profits to calculate the NPV, but the certainty equivalent corresponding to the expected value of each year – certainty equivalents that will be smaller than the annual expected values, with a difference increasing with the degree of the investor's risk aversion.

Instead of assigning certainty equivalents corresponding to the expected values of annual net benefits, the treatment of risk in private projects is sometimes based on raising the interest rate that is used to discount the expected annual net benefits – that is, introducing a risk premium, which is added to the interest rate.

While increasing the interest rate reduces the profitability of the project, this approach is not the same as using certainty equivalents. Adding a constant risk premium to the interest rate implicitly assumes that uncertainty grows exponentially with time and this may well not be the case; sometimes the risk is higher during the first years of the project, or may not reflect the risk attitude of individuals.[2] It is therefore better to work with the certainty equivalents of benefits and costs and discount the flows with the risk-free discount rate.

---

[2] $1 in year one, using a 5 per cent discount rate, has a value of $0.952 in year zero, and in years 10 and 15 the values are $0.614 and $0.481, respectively. By adding a 3 per cent risk premium the present values are, respectively (inside brackets, the reduction of the value with respect to the situation without risk): 0.926 (−2.7 per cent); 0.463 (−24.6 per cent); 0.315 (−34.5 per cent).

9.3 RISK IN THE PUBLIC SECTOR

There are economic reasons that support a different treatment of risk when projects are evaluated in the public sector. We have seen that, for a private investor who is risk averse, there is a safe level of profitability (the certainty equivalent) lower than the expected value, which leaves the investor indifferent between the risky project and a risk-free return.

For the private entrepreneur it makes sense to discount the profits at a more demanding rate, because the risk is a real cost for a risk-averse investor. In Figure 9.1, the expected profitability of the project is $1625, but the certainty equivalent is $200. The difference ($1425) is the subjective cost of risk. This cost is a real cost to society, since the benefits and costs are measured by what individuals are willing to pay for goods and services and what the individuals are willing to pay to avoid the risk. In Figure 9.1 the entrepreneur accepts the offer because the tour operator asks for a lower price than the one the entrepreneur is willing to pay for the risk transfer to a third party.

Should the public sector maximize the NPV of the net expected social benefits of investment projects and public policies? Or should it maximize the NPV of the net social benefits adjusted for risk?

The theorem by Arrow and Lind (1970) supports the theoretical foundation to discard the risk approach in public sector projects. Previous justifications about whether the public sector should make use of risk premiums, as the private sector does, are the following:

*   The public sector should use the same risk-adjusted discount rate as the private sector because, if the public sector uses a risk-free discount rate while the private sector introduces a risk premium, there will be a misallocation of resources by overinvestment in the public sector.
*   The public sector should ignore uncertainty and act as if it were indifferent to risk. Project evaluation should be performed with the expected values and a risk-free discount rate. Given that many similar and independent projects are carried out, the results will tend to the expected value. This can be interpreted as if the public sector is insuring itself by paying for the losses in adverse situations with the gains in favourable ones.

In contrast with the second argument, Arrow and Lind's theorem is not based on the diversification of risk (by investing in a large number of projects the return will tend to the expected value) but it is based on the idea of risk spreading, as the difference between the expected value and the certainty equivalent tends to zero when the losses of the project are spread among a large number of participants (taxpayers), and then the cost of risk tends to zero.

It is true that, unless the individuals are risk neutral or risk lovers, the expected net present value overestimates what those individuals are willing to pay. The social cost of risk will depend on the preferences of the individuals who enjoy the benefits and pay the costs, and the relative importance of these costs and benefits with respect to their wealth. Another assumption in the Arrow–Lind theorem is that the project risk is uncorrelated with the other resources of the taxpayers.

What Arrow and Lind's theorem shows for the economic evaluation of projects is the following. Suppose a world in which the government charges the beneficiaries their willingness to pay, and the final net benefits, either positive or negative, are equally distributed among the taxpayers. If the impact of the project on their income is very small, the social cost of risk tends to zero and the public sector should only look to the expected value and not the variance.[3]

In the real world, costs and benefits are not always distributed in that way. Too often the government assumes the investment costs of the project and the individuals receive the benefits (and some other costs such as environmental impacts, accidents, etc.), whose magnitude can be, for some of them, equivalent to a significant proportion of their income. If the effect of a project is concentrated in a group of individuals, some adjustments must be made to reflect their preferences, which means using the certainty equivalents instead of the expected values.

An additional difficulty emerges because of the aggregated nature of the data used in the evaluation of projects. Given that costs and benefits are frequently aggregated they may hide different effects on different groups of individuals. Moreover, aggregated social benefits may include benefits for some and costs for others. In this case, the adjustment to account for risk is more complicated. If, as in many public projects, the investment and operating costs are borne by taxpayers and the benefits (and other costs) are borne by groups of individuals, the investment and operating costs should be discounted with the risk-free discount rate and the benefits (and other costs) to individuals should be adjusted downward (upward) according to the uncertainty they are associated with and attitude toward risk of those affected.

Johansson and Kriström (2009) warn of the use of certainty equivalents when there are other costs that could be easily ignored. Consider the following proposed project. A hydropower plant was asked to reduce its production by 3.7 gigawatt hours (GWh) annually. The benefits of this project are environmental and recreational. A web-based contingent valuation study was undertaken among people living along the river. A referendum-style willingness-to-pay question was asked and in total the residents were willing to pay around $2.6 million, expressed as a present value.

The Nordic (Nord Pool) spot market for electricity is illustrated in Figure 9.2. There are different production technologies, each assumed to have constant marginal costs. Hydropower and wind power have very low marginal costs. Nuclear power is intermediate and fossil-fired plants have the highest marginal costs. The market price is $50 000 per GWh. There are more alternatives available and demand fluctuates over time, implying that the figure provides a highly simplified picture of the market.

[3] When the conditions of the Arrow–Lind theorem are satisfied, the private sector should also use a free-risk discount rate. The reason the private sector adds a risk premium to the discount rate is due to the existence of market inefficiencies (Bazelon and Smetters, 1999).

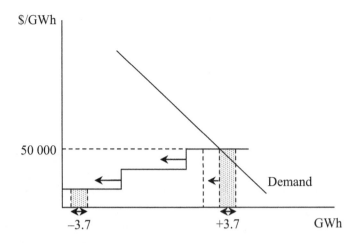

Figure 9.2 The spot market for electricity with different technologies

The owner of the hydropower plant seems willing to accept a once-and-for-all payment – that is, a certainty equivalent of $2.6 million in exchange for reducing annual electricity production by 3.7 GWh. This is a type of certainty equivalent because the alternative is associated with price uncertainty and the firm uses a much higher discount rate (> 7 per cent) than society (3 per cent in this case). So, it seems as if a deal is possible. The local residents – or the taxpayers – could pay for the loss of profits. And indeed, nobody can prevent two parties making such a deal. Still, the question is whether the project is socially profitable.

The social cost is the cost of replacing 3.7 GWh annually. In terms of Figure 9.2, the 'supply ladder' shifts to the left by 3.7 GWh. The annual cost of replacing almost cost-free hydropower by fossil-based electricity with a marginal cost of $50000 per GWh is 50000 × 3.7 = $185000. If the social discount rate is 3 per cent, then the present value cost is around $6 million. According to this analysis the proposed project is highly unprofitable for society.

From the point of view of society, we must crowd out consumption worth $185000 annually in order to release resources that can produce the replacement power. The present value of this cost is $6 million if the discount rate is 3 per cent. So, in addition to the $2.6 million that is supposed to be paid for the project, an additional $3.4 million ($6 − $2.6) of consumption must be sacrificed. The resources needed to produce the replacement power have an alternative use. In addition, we replace 'clean' hydropower with 'dirty' fossil-based electricity so there is an externality involved too. In any case, even if one involved party (taxpayers or local residents) can pay another party (the firm), there may be other effects that should be accounted for in a cost–benefit analysis. Financial or distributional effects may hide the true benefits and costs of a project.

The lesson from this project is that we need to include all the costs and the affected agents in cost–benefit analysis. The conclusion in Johansson and Kriström (2009) is equivalent to saying that we respect the private preferences (certainty equivalents of the hydropower firm and the residents) and then include any other costs, like the cost of the replacement electricity at a higher social cost. Hence, we maintain the individual preferences (using their willingness to pay/willingness to accept that include the cost of risk), and then use the risk-free social discount rate.

9.4 RISK ANALYSIS

In the previous section and under some restrictive conditions (the Arrow–Lind theorem), the government should look to the expected value and not the variance. The spread of any losses among many taxpayers was the main justification for the risk neutrality of the government. In practice, however, governments exhibit risk aversion. Politicians and civil servants are individuals who may bear the costs of an ex post negative result even if the decision to approve the project was optimal ex ante. The cost–benefit analysis should include information regarding the variability of results and not only the expected value.

In the economic evaluation of projects, the use of deterministic values is not uncommon – that is, choosing unique values for quantities and prices, that come from the best available information and are treated as if they were to be realized in the future. The social profitability of a project, however, is in fact an expected value that gives a false sense of precision.

The calculation of the *NPV* under the assumption that variables are deterministic overlooks the fact that the analyst is working with his expected values, unnecessarily restricting the analysis of the social profitability of projects. The uncertainty surrounding demand and costs recommends the inclusion of random variables that provides the analyst with a range of net present values and their corresponding associated probabilities.

Let us consider the available options to acquire more information on the risk associated with the project under evaluation. Before we describe what risk analysis involves, let us briefly examine the rationale of *sensitivity* analysis.

Sensitivity analysis

Sensitivity analysis consists of changing the value of one variable and checking how this affects the outcome of the project. When several variables are modified simultaneously, we use scenarios.

Returning to the case analysed in Section 9.2, 150 apartments are built for which full occupation is expected. The discount rate is zero. The social benefit of the project is $3500, so, if the decision is to approve or reject, the apartment complex project is approved.

Let us see the sensitivity of the *NPV* of this project to alternative changes of x and C. For example, when the demand is for 125 apartments, the profits are −$250, and when the costs are equal to $600, the profits are $500. Therefore, the analyst knows that when the occupancy rate falls and only 125 apartments are occupied, the result is a loss of $250. The selection of 125 apartments is ad hoc based on the a priori belief that this value is the worst situation the investor thinks possible.

An option within the sensitivity analysis is to calculate the *threshold values* of the relevant variables, to check how much the selected variable can be modified until the *NPV* is zero. The threshold or switching value is often presented in relative terms as the percentage change in the target variable that makes the net benefits of the project equal to zero. For example, in the case of the construction costs, the maximum increase before the *NPV* becomes negative is 26.9 per cent, the reduction in price is 15.6 per cent, and the increase in annual costs 58.3 per cent.

The rationale of scenarios is not substantially different from sensitivity analysis. Instead of modifying a single variable and holding the others fixed, in scenario analysis we look to the combined effect of changes in some selected variables, changes corresponding to different possible scenarios. For example, we can change three variables altogether (construction costs, annual operating costs and demand). The scenarios are called, for example, 'optimistic' (high demand and low cost), 'expected' (average values for costs and demand) and 'pessimistic' (high costs and low demand).

The sensitivity analysis and the use of scenarios have the advantage of revealing the degree of robustness of the results obtained by the change in the value of a variable or a set of them, and comparing the results with those obtained in the deterministic analysis. In our example, when demand falls by 16 per cent from the initial value of 150 rented apartments, the project loses money. This simple sensitivity analysis indicates that, before undertaking the project, we should put greater effort into obtaining a more reliable forecast of demand.

Once the usefulness of sensitivity analysis and scenarios is acknowledged, we should be aware of their limitations because of the use of reference values instead of a range of values and the likelihood of the *NPV* being positive or negative, given these other values within the feasible range. The use of single values does not imply an objective system. By choosing values of individual variables, the interrelationship between them are ignored. The randomness of many of the events that affect the project will result in a joint realization of the values of variables that does not need to conform to a rigid choice of scenarios.

Risk analysis

The alternative cannot be based on the addition of more variables to the sensitivity analysis as the number of possible combinations multiplies, providing too much information of little practical use to the decision taker. The alternative to the sensitivity analysis and scenarios consists of analysing the impact of the variables on the *NPV* of the project in a more systematic way. This is called risk analysis. The following is a description of the method using the previous example.

In sensitivity analysis the demand could take the value of 150 apartments in the best case and 125 in the worst case. An alternative to the previous approach is to work with probability distributions, allowing all possible values between 125 and 150. This

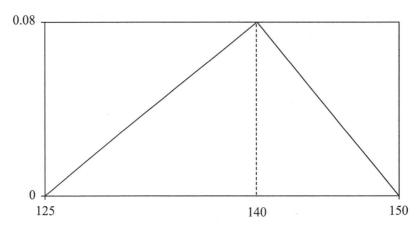

Figure 9.3 Triangular probability distribution

introduces more realism into the assessment. The main point is that in the sensitivity analysis we fix the demand value to 150 or 125 but we do not use our beliefs in the likelihood of any of these values or any other possible value in the range. If, given the available information, it is estimated, for example, that the most likely value is 140, the minimum is 125 and the maximum 150, we could use a triangular distribution function like that shown in Figure 9.3.

Risk analysis seeks to make the most of the available information. If some information is available on the a priori reasonable range over which the relevant variables are expected to fall, it is preferable to use all the values, weighted by the probability of occurrence. Any software for risk analysis will quickly carry out a very high number of iterations, each one computing a value for the *NPV*. This is because the software will randomly select a number of apartments occupied according to the information provided by the triangular distribution in Figure 9.3, or any other, previously selected. The most frequently chosen values with this probability distribution are 140 and those close to this value.

Instead of computing a single *NPV* and then performing sensitivity analysis with two or three values of demand to see how the profit changes, now we can have a very high number of different *NPV*s, which were obtained with random demand values within the 125–150 range and their assigned probabilities of occurrence in the selected probability distribution function. The risk analysis is based on the following four stages.[4]

1 Modelling the project
This stage is common to any financial or cost–benefit analysis, either deterministic or stochastic (incorporating uncertainty). It consists of constructing a model that captures

---

[4] The description of the required stages to account for risk using Monte Carlo simulations is based on Savvides (1994).

the behaviour of costs and benefits over time to predict the *NPV* of the project according to the values taken by the variables.

In the case of the apartment complex project, the model is simple. It has four variables – construction costs, operating costs, the number of apartments occupied and the price – and the last three can take different values over the 15 years of the project life.

In general, the decision on the variables of the project depends on its characteristics. Suppose a contract was signed with the construction firm fixing the price and the construction deadline. The contract includes a clause providing for an automatic review of the price if labour costs change during the years of construction. If labour costs are expected to vary and they are a significant part of total costs, wages should be a random variable of the model.

2 Selection of risk variables

Of all the variables that determine the profitability of the project, one should choose only those that, besides being likely to change, if they do change, the results of the project are significantly modified. Therefore the variables that meet one of the following two conditions could be excluded: (1) they have a high impact if they change, but it is unlikely that they do; or (2) they are likely to change, but if they do, their impact is insignificant.

The reason to reduce the number of variables included in the risk analysis as much as possible is that when more variables are included, the more difficult it is to establish correlations between them and the more likely it is that the results will be inconsistent when random simulations are generated. Furthermore, by reducing the number of variables, we can focus our effort on the behaviour and the interactions of the selected variables.

3 Probability distributions for the variables

Under conditions of uncertainty, as in our example, it is difficult to determine the value of the variables of the model. Knowing the exact occupancy rate during the next 15 years is virtually impossible; however, we may be able to determine the likely percentage range for occupied apartments in the 15 years. If, given the situation and characteristics of the complex, with information based on past experience and expert opinion, we predict that the occupancy rate will be between 70 and 90 per cent, for example, we are in a better position than the situation where we use only two values.

Once we have the minimum and maximum values, we must decide which probability distribution is the most appropriate. The choice of the range and type of probability function is indeed a prediction of the future that is based on data from the past and also on our subjective view of what we think the future will be like.[5]

---

[5] Bernstein (1996) emphasizes that the stories related in his book, are marked throughout by a persistent tension between those who assert that the best decisions are based on quantifications and numbers, determined by the patterns of the past, and those who base their decisions on more subjective degrees of belief about the uncertain future, and points out this is a controversy that has never been resolved.

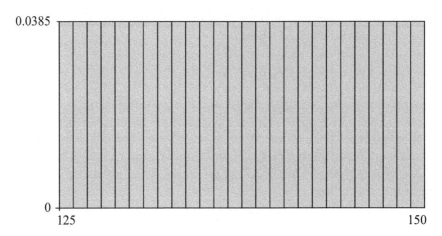

Figure 9.4 Probability distribution of the demand

Suppose that in the case of the apartments, the statistical information on occupation rates in recent decades and the information gathered through interviews with experts do not provide any reasonable belief that one particular value within the feasible range is more likely than the rest. We only know the minimum (125) and the maximum (150). In this case the uniform probability distribution (Figure 9.4) is the one that reflects our a priori beliefs.

Given this probability distribution, it does not seem reasonable to perform the risk analysis with two or three values, as in the sensitivity analysis or with scenarios. The discrete uniform probability distribution of Figure 9.4 shows 26 equally likely values. Given this expected demand pattern, the available information on the extreme values helps to build the probability function that is used to perform simulations. In many cases, given the nature of the project, it may be that one must choose a probability distribution knowing only the most likely value and having a rough idea of the changes on both sides of the mean.

For example, it may be that we expect the demand quantity for a service to be around a mean value of 100 and a standard deviation of 5, with the probability distribution approximately symmetrical. In this case a normal distribution is appropriate. In general, the symmetric distributions should be used when the value of the variable ultimately depends on opposing forces of a similar weight, while the asymmetric distributions reflect situations where there is rigidity on one side of the distribution (e.g., if it is expected that the price of land is within a range in which higher values are more likely).

In many cases, a uniform distribution (i.e., an equal probability assigned to each value) as represented in Figure 9.4 may be appropriate if there is no evidence that supports assigning a greater weight to any of the values within the range formed by the minimum and maximum. The uniform distribution is therefore the baseline, the one compatible with the lowest level of information.

4 Correlated variables

Risk analysis is based on a computer program in which the specified model to calculate the NPV is run many times, taking in each iteration the fixed value of deterministic variables and randomly drawing a value for the risk variables according to the selected probability distributions. At the end of the process, the program yields a range of NPVs with their respective probabilities.

In the computation process, the program draws a value for each risk variable regardless of the value chosen for the others, a procedure that can lead to inconsistent results since, if some variables are correlated, this relationship should be included in the program to avoid inconsistent outcomes. If airport delay depends on the 'flights per hour/ airport capacity' ratio, it makes no sense that the program can choose a high waiting time value and simultaneously a low value for the ratio. The procedure to prevent the program from generating inconsistent results is to create a correlation matrix in which the relationship between one variable and the others is reflected.

9.5 INTERPRETING THE RESULTS OF RISK ANALYSIS

The model of our apartment example is as simple as the following:

$$NPV = -I_0 + \sum_{t=1}^{15} (p_t x_t - C_t). \tag{9.5}$$

Risk analysis uses the previously selected deterministic variables. In our example, I_0 is always equal to \$13 000, p_t is equal to \$10 and C_t is equal to \$400. These three variables are not subject to variability and any time we run the program, an NPV is generated with these predetermined values. The risk variable is x_t. The probability distribution for the risk variable is represented in Figure 9.4, a uniform distribution with a minimum at 125 and a maximum at 150. We assign the same probability to any of the 26 possible values that can take the variable demand each year.

Once the software has generated a high enough number of iterations, the results can be displayed as a probability distribution function, which represents the probability distribution associated with the NPV of the project, and it will allow us to calculate the probability of the NPV being above or below a certain value or within a range of values.

The NPV of the project is now not a single number that receives a greater or lower significance depending on the risk aversion of the decision maker. With the risk analysis we have a probability distribution of the NPV of the project that contributes to a more informed decision. Obviously, the risk of the project is exactly the same as the simple analysis of expected values, the sensitivity test or the use of scenarios but the risk of making a wrong decision diminishes after a well-conducted risk analysis.

Recall that in our example of the investment in apartments, the project evaluation based on the expected value of the benefits and an annual demand given by either 125 or

150 rented apartments with equal probability, results in an expected profit of $1625 (see Figure 9.1). If the demand takes the highest value, the benefits are equal to $3500, while if it takes the lowest value, the project results in losses of $250.

Suppose, alternatively, that the value the demand takes in a year does not determine the demand in the following years. Under this assumption we must make the draw from the random variable x_t for each of the 15 years of the project. The NPV obtained in each iteration will be the result of drawing one value of x_t within the 26 possible ones for each of the 15 years. This process is routinely repeated by the computer thousands, or hundreds of thousands, of times. We must emphasize that the risk analysis not only provides NPV values but also their probability of occurrence.

Figure 9.5 shows the probability distribution of the benefits corresponding to 100 000 iterations of the model – it depicts 100 000 NPV values obtained by randomly drawing 100 000 values for the demand for each of the 15 years. The mean NPV is $1625, which coincides with that obtained with the expected value of demand (see Figure 9.1). This does not add any value to what we already know. Nevertheless, the distribution of the net present values provides new valuable information. If our assumption on the demand's behaviour is correct, we now know that a negative NPV is unlikely. Why? Because negative NPV values require that low demand values are drawn for many years, which is certainly improbable.

The probability distribution of profits represented in Figure 9.5 shows that a negative result is almost impossible, since the minimum value is $420 and the maximum is $2880, with an expected value of $1625 and a standard deviation of $291. Nevertheless, we know that there are demand values that generate losses. When the demand is for 125 apartments, the loss is $250, and as Figure 9.4 shows, the value 125 is as likely as any other. The paradox is solved when one recalls that for a negative profit of $250 the demand must take the lowest value (125) during the 15 years.[6]

What the risk analysis shows, after repeating the calculation of the NPV a sufficiently high number of times, is the impossibility of such a negative result. The variable demand takes the value 125 in a given year 3.85 per cent of the time, but the number of drawings that are made is 15, and in these 15 subsequent and independent extractions the value 125 must be realized. The trend is toward the mean, and this is what Figure 9.5 represents.

The cumulative probability distribution represented in Figure 9.6 is another way to show that this is not a risky project because there is no case where the returns are less than $420. Figure 9.7 shows the curve fitted to the histogram of Figure 9.5. The adjusted density shows that, for example, 99 per cent of the potential net present values are in the range of positive profits (890; 2360), with virtually zero probability of having negative results.

Should we rule out the possibility of losses in this project? In practical terms, the answer is affirmative if the model we have used to represent the investment in apartments is suitable and replicates the behaviour of the variables. Risk analysis software

---

[6] The probability of this event is $(0.0385)^{15} = 6.05 \times 10^{-22}$.

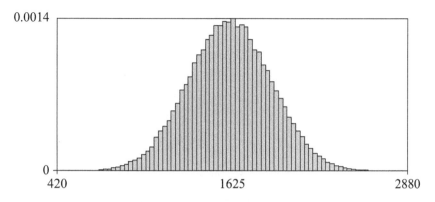

Figure 9.5 Histogram of the probability distribution of the *NPV* (one uniform probability distribution of demand for each year of the project)

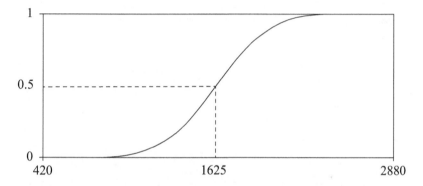

Figure 9.6 Cumulative probability distribution of the *NPV* (one uniform probability distribution of demand for each year of the project)

works with the inputs it receives from the analyst but cannot distinguish between a model that simulates actual behaviour from another that does not.

The key assumption regarding the risk variable in our example is that the demand is random each year, regardless of what happened in the previous year, and also that the number of occupied apartments will never be less than 125 out of the 150 to be constructed, any value being equally probable, including the minimum and maximum.

To illustrate the importance of the assumptions of the model, suppose now that the demand is random only in the first year within the same limits of 125 and 150, and once a value of *x* has been drawn for the first year, it remains constant during the following years. If this assumption fairly represents the real world we are trying to model, the results change dramatically. Although the mean is the same ($1625), the minimum and maximum *NPV* values change (−$250 and $3500) with a standard deviation of $1125 ($291 in the previous case).

The drastic change in the results is represented in Figures 9.8 and 9.9, which show two

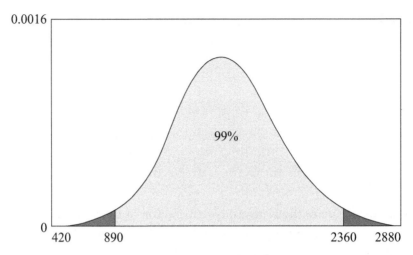

Figure 9.7 Probability density function of the *NPV* (one uniform probability distribution of demand for each year of the project)

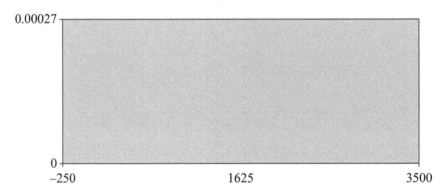

Figure 9.8 Probability density function of the *NPV* (one uniform distribution of demand for the whole lifetime of the project)

fundamental differences with respect to the previous outcome. First, the project presents the possibility of higher returns (an *NPV* of $3500 is as likely as the mean) and, second, it increases the variability of the results (including the possibility of losses − $250 is as likely as any other within the range).

As expected, the same data lead to different results depending on the assumptions on demand behaviour. From the previous simple case we can appreciate the importance of the effort to develop a consistent model that reflects the real behaviour of the variables as closely as possible, since the consequences of incorrectly modelling such behaviour might have a decisive impact on the evaluation results. This modelling allows the decision maker to work with possible results and their respective probabilities, but its relevance depends on how well the model represents the real world.

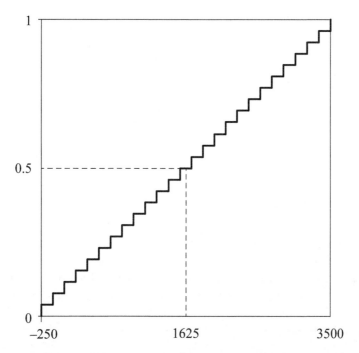

Figure 9.9 Cumulative probability distribution of the *NPV* (one uniform distribution of demand for the whole lifetime of the project)

Decision criteria under uncertainty

Sometimes the previous analysis is enough to take a decision on the desirability of a project; in other cases, nothing can be concluded with a single decision rule, especially when comparing projects or when a budget constraint is binding.

Accept or reject a project

If the decision is to accept or reject a project and the probability distribution of the social *NPV* does not show any positive value, the criterion is the same as in the case of an evaluation with deterministic variables in which the *NPV* is negative – reject the project.

When all the values of the probability distribution of the *NPV* are positive, the criterion is, in principle, to accept the project (we ignore here optimal timing). The ultimate acceptance of the project also requires the financial result to be positive, because if the financial *NPV* is negative, or if there is a high probability of negative results, the decision will depend on the budgetary constraint.

When the expected value of the social *NPV* is positive and the financial result is acceptable, the project should be approved if the decision maker is risk neutral. However, unlike the situation with deterministic values, we now know the probability of the occurrence of negative results (10 per cent in Figure 9.10) and therefore we have

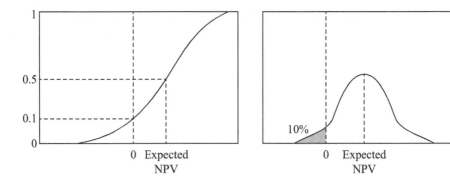

Figure 9.10 Accept/reject

additional information with which to make a decision that will also depend on the existence of budget constraints and the attitude towards risk aversion of those who take the decision. Examining other pricing policies, capacity size, level of service, and so on, may be a way to improve the balance between the project's social and financial profitability, provided that the foreseeable worsening of the social *NPV* does not go beyond acceptable levels.

Choice between projects

The basic criterion for choosing between two alternative projects, A and B, is to select the project whose probability density function shows a clear superiority over the other. In Figure 9.11, the corresponding probability distributions do not intersect, and one project is clearly superior to the other. It should be remembered that even in this favourable situation it is necessary to check, in the case of budget constraints, that the financial result is positive (or has a satisfactorily high probability of being positive).

It may occur that the cumulative density distributions of the two projects do not intersect but the density functions do, as in Figure 9.12. In this case the choice may heavily depend on the financial results. In Figure 9.12, project B is preferable to project A

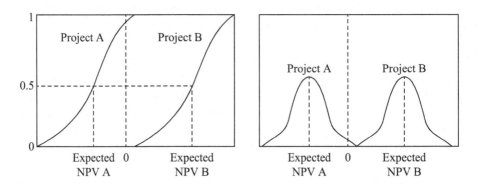

Figure 9.11 Density functions do not intersect

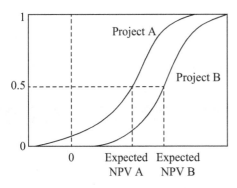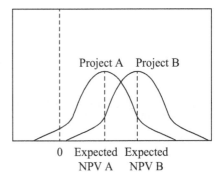

Figure 9.12 Density functions intersect

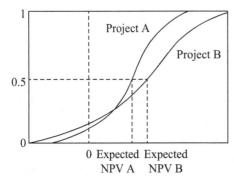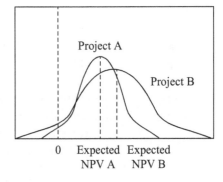

Figure 9.13 Cumulative density functions intersect

because it has a higher expected value and furthermore there are no negative values in the probability density function; however, if the financial results matter, it may be that A is preferable to B if A has a positive financial result and B a negative one.

Let us see the case of two projects whose cumulative density functions intersect. The decision on which project is selected depends, as in the previous cases, on the social *NPV*, the financial result and the level of risk.

A first criterion for choosing between the two projects represented in Figure 9.13 is to check which project has a higher expected social *NPV*. As Figure 9.13 shows, project B has a higher expected *NPV* than project A. If the financial *NPV* is positive in both projects, project B is preferred unless the wider range and cumulative probabilities of negative values in project B and the risk aversion of the public agency taking the decision make project A more attractive (a smaller but less risky expected *NPV*).

When the financial *NPV* of project A is positive and that of project B is negative, it would be preferable to choose A in the presence of a budget constraint. If in addition the risk associated with project A is smaller, as in Figure 9.13, project A would be more favourable.

When the financial NPV is negative for both projects and there are budget constraints, the best option is to look at how the social NPV is affected by changes in the price level, in the capacity design, in the quality of service, and so on. There is a trade-off between a reduction in the social NPV and the improvement in financial performance.

THINGS TO REMEMBER

1. Uncertainty is common to any project, so the economic evaluation of projects must deal with the variability of results. For risk-averse individuals the expected value overlooks the cost of risk. People are willing to accept a lower amount than the expected value if by doing so they avoid the variability of the results.

2. According to the Arrow–Lind theorem, the public sector should decide by looking at the expected values and not the variance. The rationale of this position is based on the idea of risk spreading, as the difference between the expected value and the certainty equivalent tends to zero when the results of a project are divided among a large number of participants (taxpayers), so that the cost of risk also tends to zero. Nevertheless, in the case of costs borne by specific groups of individuals, the certainty equivalent is still the right approach.

3. Although the public sector can be considered as risk neutral and bases its decisions on expected values, the information obtained through risk analysis is helpful. Information on the probability of good and bad results gives the decision maker a more complete picture of the project's expected performance and its consequences.

4. A decision of the accept/reject type or a selection between projects can rarely be exclusively based on the social NPV. The financial NPV may be useful for making the final decision. Usually, the decision maker faces a trade-off consisting of ceding some social surplus in exchange for financial viability.

5. The best software available for risk analysis does not guarantee that the prediction is reliable. The practitioner needs a model that represents the main characteristics and relationships of the project. The selection of the range and the probability distribution of the key random variables, as well as the correlation among them, will generate a more complete picture of the social value of the project. The decision maker will not only have the expected value of the NPV but all the possible values of the NPV and their probabilities. If the model does not represent the real world, the result of the risk analysis is useless and provides a false sense of accuracy.

10
Applications

I think we must take it for granted that our estimates of future costs and benefits (particularly the latter) are inevitably subject to a wide margin of error, in the face of which it makes little sense to focus on subtleties aimed at discriminating accurately between investments that might have an expected yield of 10.5 per cent and those that would yield only 10 per cent per annum. As the first order of business we want to be able to distinguish the 10 per cent investments from those yielding 5 or 15 per cent, while looking forward hopefully to the day when we have so well solved the many problems of project evaluation that we can seriously face up to trying to distinguish 10 per cent yields from those of 9 or 11 per cent.

(Arnold C. Harberger [1964] 1972, p. 1)

10.1 INTRODUCTION

This is a chapter on applications of the methodology derived previously. In this book we have approached cost–benefit analysis as a set of reasonable shortcuts in the search for the social profitability of projects in a wide sense. There are many possible candidates for a cost–benefit analysis.

The economic evaluation of transport infrastructure is the subject of Sections 10.2 and 10.3. Investment in high-speed rail infrastructure is costly, irreversible and subject to cost and demand uncertainty. The cost–benefit analysis of railways is similar to any other transport infrastructure, like highways, ports or airports. Time savings, increase in quality, reduction in congestion and the willingness to pay of generated demand are usually the main benefits.

A controversial policy is the change of ownership of public firms, either understood as the sale of public assets or, as is widely applied around the world, as concession contracts through which the public sector concedes the provision of public services to the private sector for a predetermined period of time, according to the conditions established in the contract agreement. Section 10.4 presents a basic model, which is easy to apply to the privatization of public firms, and Section 10.5 provides an application to a water supply concession contract. The analytical framework is applicable to the evaluation of price or quality regulation.

The content of Section 10.6 – the importance of incentives – is not really an application, but it is critical for the application of cost–benefit analysis. This is a topic that has not received sufficient attention in the economic evaluation of projects, though it is essential to the success of cost–benefit analysis as a tool for informed decision making. When the objective functions of social agents are overlooked, there is a high risk of losing the role of cost–benefit analysis as an instrument to help in decision making. This gives the institutional and contract design a crucial role in the success of this economic tool.

Ex ante evaluation may become an empty bureaucratic procedure unless we understand the institutional context and the conflicting objective functions of the agents involved. Understanding the different levels of government usually involved in major projects and policies, as well as the implications of a menu of contracts for private participation, is a fundamental step if we want to avoid the conversion of cost–benefit analysis into a useless administrative formality instead of an economic tool for rational decision taking.

10.2 INVESTMENT PROJECTS: ECONOMIC EVALUATION OF INFRASTRUCTURE

Investment in high-speed rail (HSR) has won the support of its direct users, who value its high quality and speed; of governments, who see it as an instrument for territorial integration, the reduction of pollution and road and airport congestion; of railway authorities, for whom it has been a pathway to renewal, in a context of railways' declining market share in the distribution of traffic between modes of transport; and, finally, of the industrial firms producing railway equipment.

The introduction of the technology known as HSR, consisting of infrastructure and rolling stock that allows the movement of passenger trains at 350 km/hour, has led to a revival of rail transport. This technology competes with road and air transport over distances of 400–600 km, in which it is usually the main mode of transport. For short-distance trips, the private vehicle recovers some ground, and for long-distance travel, air becomes the hegemonic mode of transport.

The fundamental problem of HSR is not technological, but economic: the cost of HSR infrastructure is high, sunk and associated with strong indivisibilities (the size of the infrastructure is virtually the same for a line regardless of the volume of existing demand). In corridors with low traffic density, the average cost per passenger is very high, which makes financial stability unfeasible.

Population density and the competitiveness of alternative transport modes largely determine the financial and social viability of the investment in HSR, as its infrastructure costs are well above those of the conventional network, and its use is associated with very pronounced decreasing average costs. In this section we present a simple model for assessing HSR investment. Regardless of market shares and the political rhetoric about its role in territorial integration, and its impact on the environment and on regional development, we expect to answer the following question: is society willing to pay for the social cost of HSR?[1]

Cost-benefit analysis of high-speed rail investment: a basic framework

Although the effects of building HSR infrastructure are many, the first direct effect is the reduction of travel time (while simultaneously increasing the quality of travel). Moreover, there are other potential benefits such as the reduction of pollution, and of road and airport congestion, when the deviated demand is significant and prices are not equal to marginal social cost in the alternative modes.

In cases where the saturation of the conventional rail network requires expansion of capacity, the construction of a new high-speed line must be evaluated as an alternative to the improvement and extension of the conventional network, with the additional benefit of releasing capacity. Obviously, the additional capacity has value when the demand exceeds the existing capacity on the route. In these circumstances the additional capacity can be valuable not only because it can absorb the growth of traffic between cities served by the high-speed railway but also because it releases capacity on existing lines to meet other traffic, such as commuter services or freight.

The generated traffic is a direct benefit of these projects, which is generally valued as half the benefits of existing users according to the 'rule of a half' (see Chapter 2). However, there is debate over whether this generated traffic involves greater economic benefits that are not captured in conventional cost–benefit analysis. Leisure travel and business trips can benefit the destination, though it is crucial to distinguish whether it is a genuine expansion of economic activity or a simple relocation of jobs and previous economic activity.

The debate on these issues focuses on whether these changes are additional economic activity or a simple relocation of the pre-existing activity. In addition, many indirect benefits are associated with investment in transport infrastructure in general and not exclusively in HSR, so even if they increase the social return on the investment in transport, they do not necessarily place HSR in a better position over other options for transport investment. Moreover, in undistorted competitive markets, the net benefit of marginal change is zero.

Regarding spatial effects, high-speed lines tend to favour central locations, so that if the aim is to regenerate the central cities, HSR investment could be beneficial. However, if the depressed areas are on the periphery, the effect can be negative. The HSR could also allow the expansion of markets and the exploitation of economies of scale, reducing the impact of imperfect competition and encouraging the location of jobs in major urban centres, where there are external benefits of agglomeration (Graham, 2007). Any

---

[1] For a more detailed analysis see de Rus (2008, 2009, 2011) and de Rus and Nombela (2007).

of these effects are very likely to be present in the case of service industries (Bonnafous, 1987).[2]

Based on the gravity models, Graham and Melo (2011) estimated the potential agglomeration benefits for high-speed rail in the UK, through changes in flows resulting from travel time savings. They estimated an upper bound of 0.19 per cent and a lower bound of 0.02 per cent of UK's gross domestic product, concluding that 'even in the best-case scenario for improvement in long-distance travel times and market share of classic and high-speed rail, the potential order of magnitude of the agglomeration benefits is expected to be small' (p. 23).

The environmental impact of investment in HSR takes several forms. One is the reduction in air and road traffic. In such cases its contribution to reducing the negative externalities of these modes of transport could be positive, though we must not forget that it requires a significant deviation of passengers from these modes. Moreover, the use of capacity should be high enough to offset the pollution associated with the construction of the infrastructure and the production of electric power for the operation of trains, as well as noise pollution. Rail infrastructure also has a negative environmental impact such as the barrier effect as well as the land taken for service roads needed for construction and subsequent maintenance and operation. The net balance of these effects depends on the value of the affected areas, the number of people affected, the benefits of the diverted traffic, and so on (Nash, 2009).

The assessment of the social profitability of HSR needs to consider this public intervention as an investment in fixed infrastructure and specialized rolling stock, as well as maintenance and operating costs like energy, materials and labour, some of them fixed and others dependent on the volume of demand. This investment generates a flow of benefits over the life of the infrastructure.

The costs of building the railway infrastructure and the subsequent maintenance and operation costs can be expressed in a simplified form as follows:

$$TC = I_0 + \sum_{t=1}^{T} \frac{\left(C(x_t) + C_t\right)}{(1+i)^t}, \tag{10.1}$$

where:

TC: total costs;
I_0: investment costs in year 0;
$C(x_t)$: annual operating costs dependent on x_t;
x_t: passenger-trips in year t;
C_t: annual fixed costs of maintenance and operation in year t;
T: project life;
i: social discount rate.

For simplicity we assume here that the benefits of HSR investment are limited to time savings. Indirect effects and the net benefit of environmental impacts are considered insignificant.

---

[2] See Chapter 3.

The investment in HSR would be socially profitable if its benefits outweigh its costs, requiring expression (10.2) to be greater than zero:

$$NPV = -I_0 + \sum_{t=1}^{T} \frac{\left(B\left(x_1\right) - C\left(x_1\right)\right)\left(1+\theta\right)^{t-1} - C_t}{\left(1+i\right)^t}, \tag{10.2}$$

where $B(x_1)$ and $C(x_1)$ are the benefits and costs of year 1 and θ is the annual growth rate of annual net benefits.

Given the indivisibilities affecting high-speed infrastructure, the values of I_0 and C_t are not very sensitive to the volume of demand (for a given line length). The higher the values of these parameters, the harder it is to reach a positive net present value (*NPV*). This also applies to the variable cost, although this cost depends on the demand volume. The key is therefore the benefits that, for a given T, depend on the number of users during the life of the project. The level of demand (the initial volume and its growth rate) appears as a key factor for satisfying the condition of social profitability in expression (10.2).

The importance of demand can be illustrated by Figure 10.1, which represents the function of the average cost (*AC*) and marginal cost (*MC*) of a high-speed train, whose total cost function is $C = K + cx$, where K is the annualized fixed cost, c is the marginal cost per passenger-trip and x the number of passenger-trips per year (constant over the life of the project). The figure shows two demand curves: the D_1 curve for a country of low population density, and D_2, corresponding to a country with high population density (assume both have the same level of income per capita).

Assuming that the price is equal to the marginal cost, the revenues are lower than the total costs in both countries, requiring public funding to ensure financial stability. In the cases shown in Figure 10.1, the fixed costs are not covered. However, the cost–benefit analysis of both projects reveals very different social profitability.

In the case of a high-demand country (D_2), the revenues $cgx_2 0$ only cover the variable

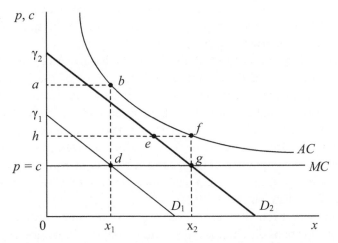

Figure 10.1 Demand, costs and social benefits of high-speed rail

costs and losses are represented by the area $hfgc$, representing the annual fixed cost; however, the willingness to pay of individuals exceeds the cost of the train: the area $\gamma_2 g x_2 0$, which is the total value of the HSR to the individuals (assuming that there are no indirect effects or externalities, or any other distortions), allows the variable costs $cgx_2 0$ to be covered. The resulting consumer surplus $\gamma_2 gc$ (which we might call the willingness to pay for capacity) exceeds the cost of that capacity $hfgc$ since $\gamma_2 eh$ is greater than efg. The economic result is positive despite the financial result being negative. In this case, the HSR infrastructure increases social welfare.

In the case of the low-demand country (D_1), the financial result is negative and equal to the area $abdc$; however, unlike in the high-demand country (D_2), the inclusion of the consumer surplus as a benefit of the project does not allow positive results. The willingness to pay for capacity in this country $(\gamma_1 dc)$ is less than the cost of capacity $(abdc)$. The economic evaluation shows an annual social loss equivalent to the area $abd\gamma_1$, so the conclusion is that the country with demand D_1 should not build the high-speed infrastructure.

It is worth recalling here the assumptions on which the conclusions regarding the desirability of building the infrastructure rest. The first is that there are no other relevant effects; the second is that there are no budgetary constraints that would increase the opportunity cost of public funds required and therefore would reduce the social returns; the third is that we are evaluating a project in isolation and the decision is of the 'accept/reject' type; the fourth is that postponing the project is unprofitable and hence an $NPV > 0$ is a sufficient condition to approve the project; the fifth is that efficiency is the only decision criterion.

10.3 COST–BENEFIT ANALYSIS OF HIGH-SPEED RAIL: AN ILLUSTRATION

Let us consider an investment project in a new HSR line of 500 km as a substitute for the previous conventional train line. This line would be built in a corridor where conventional rail, road and air transport are in operation. The lifespan of the project is 40 years. There are no intermediate stations.

The investment costs amount to $10 billion for the base year of the project (year 0); the residual value is zero, and the average avoidable cost of the high-speed train is divided into fixed maintenance costs ($150 000 per km and year) and variable costs ($30 per passenger-trip). The ticket price of the high-speed train is set at $55. The average costs of the conventional train, car and plane are also constant at $36, $50 and $90, respectively, and in all three cases the price is equal to the average cost. The rest of the economy is perfectly competitive. The generalized price of travel for each transport mode is given by $g_i = p_i + v_i t_i$ (i = train, car and air). The travel times t_i for each mode and time values v_i are listed in Table 10.1.

The time values in Table 10.1 grow every year by the same proportion as income growth. The social rate of discount is 5 per cent and all the values are expressed in real terms.

Table 10.1 Travel time and value of time (line length: 500 km)

	High-speed train	Conventional train	Car	Air
Total travel time (in decimal terms)	2.67	6.67	5.30	2.58
Value of time ($) (in year $t = 1$)	–	10	10	20

There is uncertainty about the volume of demand for the project; hence, for illustrative purposes, we consider two scenarios for predicting future demand. The first scenario is pessimistic, with an annual volume of 5 million passenger-trips for the first year of the project, while the second scenario is optimistic, with a volume of 15 million passenger-trips for the initial year. We assume an elasticity of demand of 1.2 with respect to income and an income growth rate of 2 per cent.

In Chapter 2 we discussed two equivalent approaches for conducting cost–benefit analysis: the first, adding the changes in the surplus of the social agents; the second, adding the change in willingness to pay and the change in resources – that is, time savings, the benefits of the generated traffic, and the change in costs. We assume that no other benefits or costs exist.

Change in social surplus

Following the first procedure we should add the surpluses of the social agents. First, the user gains in terms of generalized price (money plus time), calculated separately for each group of users of other modes of transport that shifts to the high-speed train. The introduction of HSR implies changes in the generalized price by mode, as reflected in Table 10.2.

From this information we can evaluate the benefits for the users of the high-speed train. Previously, we had to distinguish between the passenger-trips for the conventional train (whose consumer surplus is obtained as the difference in generalized prices given

Table 10.2 Changes in the generalized prices of existing and diverted passengers (first year)

	Generalized price in the original mode (1)	Generalized price in HSR (2)	Change (1) – (2)
Conventional train	$36 + 6.67 \times 10 = 102.7$	$55 + 2.67 \times 10 = 81.7$	21.0
Car	$50 + 5.30 \times 10 = 103$	$55 + 2.67 \times 10 = 81.7$	21.3
Air	$90 + 2.58 \times 20 = 141.6$	$55 + 2.67 \times 20 = 108.4$	33.2

Table 10.3 First year users' benefits (low demand) (values in $)

	Existent and deviated demand	Generated demand	Total benefits
Conventional train	2 500 000 × 21 = 52 500 000	0.5 × 720 000 × 21 = 7 560 000	60 060 000
Car	0.5 × 500 000 × 21.3 = 5 325 000	0.5 × 140 000 × 21.3 = 1 491 000	6 816 000
Air	0.5 × 1 000 000 × 33.2 = 16 600 000	0.5 × 140 000 × 33.2 = 2 324 000	18 924 000
TOTAL	74 425 000	11 375 000	85 800 000

the closure of the conventional train) from those deviated from other modes of trans-port (car and air) and the generated demand. For both deviated and generated demand, the increase in consumer surplus obtained with the introduction of HSR is equal to the triangle bounded by the demand curve and the price and quantities differences. The benefits are calculated as half the difference in the generalized prices, with and without the project, multiplied by the generated passenger-trips.

Table 10.3 shows, for the low-demand scenario (5 million passenger-trips), the incoming users from different modes and the generated traffic (the same proportions are assumed for the case of high demand) and the benefits that these users obtain in the first year.

In the first year of the project the costs and benefits are:

consumer surplus (conventional train, deviated and generated demand): 85 800 000;
revenue: 55 × 5 000 000 = 275 000 000;
operating costs (fixed): 75 000 000;
operating costs (variable): 30 × 5 000 000 = 150 000 000.

The results obtained for the whole project in both demand scenarios are as shown in Table 10.4.

Changes in willingness to pay and resources

The second approach to calculating the NPV of the project is to focus on the changes in the willingness to pay and the resources, ignoring transfers. Figure 10.2 shows, for the case of the conventional train in the low-demand scenario, the benefits of time savings for existing users (the diagonal striped areas) and the cost saving derived from the closure of the conventional train (the area with black shading).

In Figure 10.2, the benefits of generated trips are represented by the dotted light-shaded areas. It can be seen how, for this generated traffic, the benefits are obtained by

Table 10.4 Social and financial benefits of high-speed rail (millions of $, discounted values)

	Low demand q = 5 000 000	High demand q = 15 000 000
Change in consumer surplus	3318	9953
Conventional train	2287	6861
Car	196	588
Air	395	1.186
Generated	440	1319
Revenue	6697	20 092
Operating costs (fixed)	−1287	−1287
Operating costs (variable)	−3653	−10 959
Infrastructure costs	−10 000	−10 000
Social *NPV*	−4 925	7799
Financial *NPV*	−8 243	−2154

Note: Project life = 40 years; income growth rate = 2 per cent; discount rate = 5 per cent; income elasticity of demand = 1.2; income elasticity of travel time = 1; p = 55.

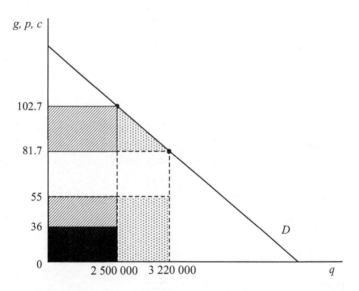

Figure 10.2 Benefits of the high-speed train (conventional train users)

calculating the willingness to pay for the new trips (the area under the demand function in the segment of the 720 000 generated trips) minus the total value of the time spent on such trips.

The operating costs of the HSR are not represented in the figure and must be deducted to obtain the benefit of the existing, deviated and generated traffic).

The calculations for road and air transport are like those followed for the generated demand in the figure. Note that the area with black shading includes the cost saving in road and air. Finally, one should subtract the investment cost of the project to obtain the social NPV. The results obtained using this alternative approach are shown in Table 10.5. As we can see, the social NPV is equal in both approaches.

The conclusion to be drawn from this evaluation is that the project is not socially worthy in the low-demand scenario since both the social NPV and the financial NPV are negative. By contrast, in the high-demand scenario, the result of the social NPV is positive, although the financial NPV remains negative. Even with high demand, this project would not be financially profitable as its revenues do not cover its costs, so that it could not be operated by the private sector without subsidy. Nevertheless, from a social point of view, and placed in a context without budget constraint, the benefits

Table 10.5 Social benefits of high-speed rail (millions of $, discounted values)

	Low demand q = 5 000 000	High demand q = 15 000 000
Time savings	3243	9730
Conventional train	3444	10 331
Car	257	771
Air	−457	−1372
Benefits of generated trips	1779	5337
Cost savings	4993	14 978
Conventional train	2192	6576
Car	609	1.827
Air	2192	6576
Operating costs (fixed)	−1287	−1287
Operating costs (variable)	−3653	−10 959
Infrastructure costs	−10 000	−10 000
Social NPV	−4925	7799
Financial NPV	−8243	−2154

Note: Project life = 40 years; income growth rate = 2 per cent; discount rate = 5 per cent; income elasticity of demand = 1.2; income elasticity of travel time = 1; $p = 55$; low demand (first year) = 5 000 000; high demand (first year) = 15 000 000.

from time and cost savings and generated demand outweigh the costs of constructing and operating the project.

10.4 POLICY EVALUATION: COST-BENEFIT ANALYSIS OF PRIVATIZATION

The economic evaluation of a privatization policy has three key elements: first, the existence of cost differences between the public and the private sector; second, the type of market where the company operates and the ability to exercise monopoly power; and third, the sale price.

Even assuming that the privatization policy yields net benefits for society, these benefits may not be fairly distributed. It may be that producers are better off with privatization, but consumers and workers are worse off. Therefore, to assess a privatization project in practice, the practitioner should make a detailed assessment of winners and losers. This will be necessary in order to design the compensation mechanisms, for reasons of equity and political acceptability.

In this section and the next we present a basic model and an application to assess whether society wins or loses with the privatization of a public firm. The privatization model can equally be applied to the evaluation of privatization in the strict sense or a concession contract. It can also be extended to the evaluation of price and quality regulation.

Social benefits of privatization and sale price

Often, the success of privatization has been associated with the sale price achieved. It is possible that the emphasis on the financial aspects of privatization has made us forget that in the sale of public assets, unlike a transaction between private agents, it is necessary to know what happens after the exchange – for example, a high sale price for the public company may simply be reflecting the net present value of monopoly profits expected by the buyer of the company.

Let us consider, as a starting point, the case of the public firm represented in Figure 10.3, and the evaluation of the project consisting of its privatization.[3]

The public company charges a price p_g and produces at the unit cost c_g; its annual profit is therefore equal to $(p_g - c_g)\, x_g$, equivalent to the area $p_g abc_g$ in Figure 10.3. When the company is public the variables are identified by the subscript g and when it passes into private hands by the subscript p.

How much is the maximum a private entrepreneur would be willing to pay for the public company represented in Figure 10.3 if there is no change in either the price $(p_p = p_g)$ or the cost $(c_p = c_g)$? Assuming that the lifespan of the firm is T years, and the rate

---

[3] The basic model in this section draws on the excellent work by Jones et al. (1990).

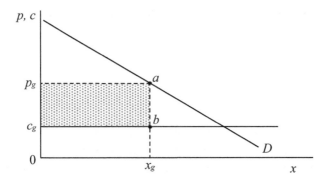

Figure 10.3 Privatization without a change in either price or cost

of discount is zero for both the public and the private sector, the private value of the company in private hands (V) can be expressed as:

$$V_{pp} = T\left(p_p - c_p\right)x_p. \tag{10.3}$$

If the entrepreneur pays V_{pp} for the firm, the public sector gains the discounted benefits generated by the company in private hands during his lifetime T. If we call Z the price paid by the entrepreneur to the government for the privatization, the highest possible value of Z is V_{pp}.

It should be recalled here that, unless money has a higher value in the hands of the government than in private hands, Z is a mere transfer of income and therefore the government would be indifferent to the value of Z. Hence we assume that the value of money in public hands (λ_g) is higher than the value of money in private hands (λ_p), λ_p having a value equal to unity, and ($\lambda_g - \lambda_p$) is the additional value of a dollar when it passes from private to public hands.[4]

Returning to Figure 10.3, for the social surplus to increase with the privatization, the following condition should hold:

$$\lambda_g Z - \lambda_p Z - \lambda_g T\pi_g + \lambda_p T\pi_p > 0, \tag{10.4}$$

where π_g and π_p are the benefits before and after the privatization (i.e., in public and private hands, respectively).

---

[4] The justification for $\lambda_g > \lambda_p$ is that when the government obtains funds through taxes it imposes an additional burden (deadweight loss of the tax) on the economy and therefore it implicitly gives more value to money in its hands than in the hands of the private sector. Therefore, if with the privatization of the public firm the government obtains funds without distorting the economy, the shadow price of these funds should reflect the additional benefit of avoiding the distortion of raising the same revenue through taxes (see Section 4.6 in Chapter 4).

Expression (10.4) shows the changes that occur with the sale of the public company, valued with the shadow multipliers of private and public funds. It can be seen how Z is received by the government and paid for by the private buyer. Also, the government loses the annual profit obtained before the sale (π_g) and, by moving the company to the private sector, the buyer obtains π_p. Since we have assumed in Figure 10.3 that the price and the cost do not change, we know that $\pi_g = \pi_p = \pi$, and (10.4) can be expressed as:

$$\left(\lambda_g - \lambda_p\right)\left(Z - T\pi\right) > 0, \tag{10.5}$$

the necessary condition to increase the social surplus that cannot be met, since Z cannot be greater than $V_{pp} = T\pi$.

Given the situation represented in Figure 10.3, if the government manages to sell the company at the highest price the buyer is willing to pay, privatization does not change the social surplus. If the entrepreneur pays a price below $T\pi$ society loses from the privatization.

Suppose now that, as shown in Figure 10.4, the private firm is more efficient than the public enterprise $(c_p < c_g)$ and the price does not change (hence, $x_p = x_g$). By privatizing, the producer surplus increases by $(c_g - c_p)x_p$ each year and therefore the private value of the company in private hands (V_{pp}) increases by T times this amount. The increase in V_{pp} may or may not be translated into an increase in Z, depending on the procedure chosen for the sale. What seems clear is that $T(c_g - c_p)\, x_p$ (T times the area $c_g bdc_p$) is the efficiency gain resulting from privatization.

To assess the change in social surplus from the sale of public companies, we can use the following expressions:

$$\Delta SS = V_{sp} - V_{sg} + \left(\lambda_g - \lambda_p\right)Z, \tag{10.6}$$

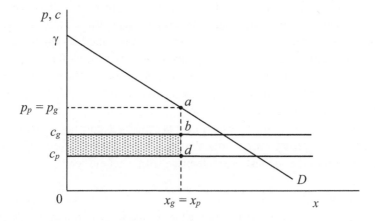

Figure 10.4 Privatization with cost reduction

$$V_{sp} = T\left(S_p + \lambda_p \pi_p\right), \tag{10.7}$$

$$V_{sg} = T\left(S_g + \lambda_g \pi_g\right), \tag{10.8}$$

where:

ΔSS: change in social surplus;
V_{sp}: social value of the firm in private hands;
V_{sg}: social value of the firm in public hands;
S_p: consumer surplus when the firm is private;
S_g: consumer surplus when the firm is public.

Expression (10.6) presents the change in social surplus as the difference between the social value of the company in private hands and the social value of the company in public hands plus a proportion of the sale price. We cannot forget that the sale price is a transfer of income between the private buyer and the government (taxpayers) and, unless the money in the hands of government is assigned a higher weight, the sale price does not affect welfare.

Substituting expressions (10.7) and (10.8) into (10.6), considering that as the price is kept constant, $S_g = S_p = S$ (area $\gamma a p_g$) and assuming that the firm is sold for the maximum value that the buyer is willing to pay ($Z = V_{pp} = T\pi_p$), we obtain the social benefits of privatization, in terms of surpluses:

$$\Delta SS = T\left(S + \lambda_p \pi_p - S - \lambda_g \pi_g\right) + \left(\lambda_g - \lambda_p\right)T\pi_p. \tag{10.9}$$

Simplifying expression (10.9) we obtain the maximum social value that can be obtained from privatization:

$$\Delta SS = T\lambda_g\left(\pi_p - \pi_g\right). \tag{10.10}$$

The expression in brackets in (10.10) is equal to $c_g bdc_p$ in Figure 10.4. The maximum potential social value of privatization is obtained when the efficiency gain achieved $\pi_p - \pi_g$ is multiplied by the T years of the project, multiplied by the shadow price of money in government hands. If the sale procedure fails to transfer efficiency gains to the government, the social surplus will be smaller despite the annual efficiency gain remaining $c_g bdc_p$. The area $\gamma a p_g$ does not appear in equation (10.10) because there is no change in the consumer surplus.

The government has two objectives with privatization according to expression (10.6): to sell the public enterprise to the bidder that generates the maximum increase in social surplus, and to obtain the highest possible price from this bidder.[5]

---

[5] Sticking to the four most common types of auctions (English, Dutch, sealed auction and Vickrey auction) the first objective can be achieved with the English and Vickrey auctions, but the second is not guaranteed by any of the four, and therefore we can expect that, in general, Z is less than V_{pp}, especially when, as happens

Previously, we assumed that the price did not change after privatization and therefore the consumer surplus remained constant ($S_g = S_p = S$). We now abandon this assumption and consider the general case in which prices, costs and quantities change after privatization, the discount rate is positive, and the privatized company returns some of its profits to the government as taxes.

The social values of the company in the public sector and in the private sector are, respectively:

$$V_{sg} = \sum_{t=0}^{T} \frac{1}{(1+i)^t} \left[S_g(t) + \lambda_g \pi_g(t) \right], \tag{10.11}$$

$$V_{sp} = \sum_{t=0}^{T} \frac{1}{(1+i)^t} \left[S_p(t) + \lambda_p \pi_p(t) + \left(\lambda_g - \lambda_p \right) Y(t) \right], \tag{10.12}$$

where:

$Y(t)$: post-privatization taxes;
i: social discount rate (we assume it equals the interest rate).

The change in social surplus is obtained by substituting expressions (10.11) and (10.12) into (10.6):

$$\Delta SS = \sum_{t=0}^{T} \frac{1}{(1+i)^t} [S_p(t) + \lambda_p \pi_p(t) + (\lambda_g - \lambda_p) Y(t) - S_g(t) - \lambda_g \pi_g(t)] + (\lambda_g - \lambda_p) Z. \tag{10.13}$$

Operating in expression (10.13), and adding and subtracting $\lambda_g \pi_p$, we obtain:

$$\Delta SS = \sum_{t=0}^{T} \frac{1}{(1+i)^t} \left[S_p(t) - S_g(t) + \lambda_g (\pi_p(t) - \pi_g(t)) \right]$$
$$- (\lambda_g - \lambda_p) \left[\sum_{t=0}^{T} \frac{1}{(1+i)^t} (\pi_p(t) - Y(t)) - Z \right]. \tag{10.14}$$

It is quite difficult for the government to make the buyer pay a price Z that is equal to the maximum that the buyer is willing to pay – that is, the private value of the company in private hands (V_{pp}). This value is equal to:

$$V_{pp} = \sum_{t=0}^{T} \frac{1}{(1+i)^t} \left(\pi_p(t) - Y(t) \right). \tag{10.15}$$

Substituting (10.15) into (10.14) and expressing the differences in surpluses and profits as Δ, we have an operational expression to calculate the social benefits of privatization:

$$\Delta SS = \sum_{t=0}^{T} \frac{1}{(1+i)^t} \left[\Delta S(t) + \lambda_g \Delta \pi(t) \right] - \left(\lambda_g - \lambda_p \right) \left(V_{pp} - Z \right). \tag{10.16}$$

to be the case, the number of bidders is not very high in a privatization process. For an analysis of auctions see Klemperer (1999).

To obtain an increase in social surplus privatizing the public company, expression (10.16) must be greater than zero. The economic interpretation of expression (10.16) is as follows: for the typical case $\lambda_g > \lambda_p$, and assuming that the government sells the company at the maximum price the buyer is willing to pay ($Z = V_{pp}$), the social benefit of the privatization equals the value of the sum of the change in consumer and producer surpluses, the latter multiplied by the shadow multiplier of money in government hands.

Let us examine expression (10.16) more closely. For a given discount rate and assuming (for simplicity) that, after the sale, both the cost and the price are lower, the maximum social benefit to be derived from privatization is in the expression in brackets: the increase in consumer surplus and the change in profits by reducing costs (this last benefit is fully transferred to the government, and so it appears multiplied by λ_g when the price of the sale equals the maximum willingness to pay of the buyer). When the sale price Z is less than the willingness to pay for the firm (V_{pp}), the social benefit decreases relative to the maximum included in brackets, in proportion to the deviation that occurs ($V_{pp} - Z$) and the shadow multiplier of public funds.

Welfare effects of price regulations

Another issue that affects the results is the pricing policy post-privatization. When the company operates as a monopoly its price tends to be regulated. If the firm is awarded to a private entrepreneur under concession, it is usual to introduce procedures for the regulation of prices. The potential efficiency gains from privatization become social benefits when they reach consumers through lower prices or higher quality, or they become a benefit of the private firm, or go to the government as the result of a well-designed sale.

If we set a price equal to the marginal cost ($p_p = c_p$), where $c_p < c_g$, the efficiency gains increase with the increase in the quantity sold, with the consumers as beneficiaries of the privatization and, unless the shadow price of public funds is sufficiently high and the elasticity of demand sufficiently low, welfare is improved in relation to the situation where the price is unchanged.

The previous argument introduces an implicit assumption that is not credible. First, if the buyer knows that the price is going to be equal to the marginal cost, why buy the company? Moreover, why should the entrepreneur try to reduce costs if the regulator sets a price equal to the actual cost?

A price regulation scheme that prevents this problem of incentives is to introduce a maximum price (price cap) – for example $p_p = \kappa p_g$, where κ is less than one and higher than the expected proportion of the reduction in the unit cost. Now the cost of the private firm does not appear in the regulatory mechanism, and the company has, in principle, incentives to lower costs because the price is fixed (κp_g), and therefore, if the company manages to reduce the cost below the regulated price, it will increase its profit.[6]

---

[6] For an analysis of the design of concession contracts and price regulation see Guasch (2004). The importance of these issues in cost–benefit analysis is crucial, since the actual social *NPV* arising from the implementation of projects is largely affected by regulatory mechanisms (see Section 10.6).

A combination of price regulation schemes based on incentives, with an auction design that maximizes the revenue from the sale of the company, is the way to maximize the social surplus if the market is not competitive. The privatization of services like water supply, electricity or public transport are a good examples.

10.5 COST-BENEFIT ANALYSIS OF THE CONCESSION OF A RESIDENTIAL WATER SUPPLY

In this section we evaluate a policy of privatizing (through a concession contract) the water supply in a medium-sized city. The aim is to show how the theoretical framework of the preceding sections can be applied to real data on costs and prices in an actual market. The methodology is equally applicable to any other public service.

To calculate the increase in social surplus we need to compute the expression (10.16). This requires information about the values of λ_g, λ_p and V_{pp} and about the water demand. We will make the following simplifying assumptions:

1. The shadow price of money in public and private hands is equal to one: $\lambda_g = \lambda_p = 1$. This assumption eliminates the last term of expression (10.16), which could also be achieved by assuming that the winning bidder pays the maximum ($Z = V_{pp}$). The assumption $\lambda_g = \lambda_p = 1$ has the additional advantage of implying equal weights for changes in consumer surplus and profits in expression (10.16).
2. The water demand is linear and therefore we can apply the 'rule of a half' to calculate the consumer surplus. Using this assumption, the changes in consumer surplus and profits are:

$$\Delta S(t) = \frac{1}{2}\left(p_g(t) - p_p(t)\right)\left(x_g(t) + x_p(t)\right). \tag{10.17}$$

$$\Delta \pi(t) = \left(p_p(t) - c_p(t)\right)x_p(t). \tag{10.18}$$

3. The average cost is lower when the firm is in private hands ($c_p < c_g$).
4. Consumer surplus and profits change over time at a grow rate of θ:

$$x(t+1) = x(t)(1+\theta). \tag{10.19}$$

5. There are no subsidies. The public company covers costs ($p_g = c_g$), while regulated private companies are allowed to set $p_p = kc_p$, where $k \geq 1$ is determined by the regulator. This assumption is imposed to abstract the problem discussed here – the evaluation of the increase in welfare through a change of ownership – from considerations of optimal pricing and optimal subsidies, plus the problem of asymmetric information.

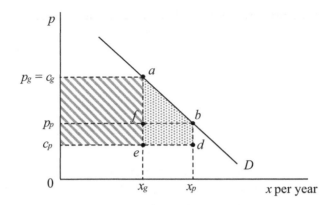

Figure 10.5 Privatization of a residential water supply

The fifth assumption allows us to determine the price levels p_g and p_p required to evaluate ΔSS. Relaxing this assumption would imply making additional assumptions about the level of subsidy.

The five assumptions we have made allow us to simplify expression (10.16) to:

$$\Delta SS = \sum_{t=0}^{T} \frac{1}{(1+i)^t} \left[\frac{1}{2} \left(p_g - kc_p \right) \left(x_g(t) + x_p(t) \right) + (k-1) c_p x_p(t) \right], \qquad (10.20)$$

where $(k-1) \geq 0$ is the mark-up (the margin of the price over the cost) that the regulated private firm is allowed to set.

Graphically, if D is the linear function of water demand represented in Figure 10.5, the terms in brackets in expression (10.20) represent the value of the area $p_g abdc_p$. The area $p_g abp_p$ is the change obtained in consumer surplus, while $p_p bdc_p$ represents the profits of the company in the case $k > 1$.

To evaluate the change in welfare obtained through privatization, using expression (10.20) the only new values needed are p_g, c_p, x_p, and k. We know that p_g and x_g are the observed values of the price (equal to the marginal cost in this case) and the production level of the public enterprise.

Table 10.6 shows the basic data of the projects consisting of privatizing the public water supply firm. The concession will last 30 years, the benefits are produced at the end of each year and the terminal value is zero. The social rate of discount and the interest rate are equal to 5 per cent. The public company sells 300 000 m³ of water per year at a price (equal to the marginal cost) of $2. The private company will be allowed a mark-up of 10 per cent over its private marginal cost (c_p). Although the reduction in the post-privatization cost is unknown, we assume a range with a maximum of 50 per cent and a minimum of zero, and with 20 per cent as the most likely value.

We need to predict the demand post-privatization. There is evidence on residential water demand elasticities (see the meta-analysis by Espey et al., 1997; also see Dalhuisen et al., 2003). Based on this evidence, and after the elimination of outliers and the less

Table 10.6 Basic data for the evaluation of the water concession project

T	30
i	5%
x_g	300 000
Price elasticity of demand	Triangular probability distribution[a] (−0.7; −0.4; −0.2)
Income elasticity of demand	Uniform probability distribution[b] (0.25; 0.5)
$P_g = c_g$	2
P_p	$1.1\ c_p$
c_p	Triangular probability distribution (1; 1.6; 2). This implies a range for cost reduction (%) of 0–50, with 20% as the most likely value
Income growth rate	Uniform probability distribution (0.01; 0.03) (each year)

Notes:
a. Triangular probability distribution (min., most likely, max.).
b. Uniform probability distribution (min., max.).

likely values, we use a triangular probability distribution with a minimum price elasticity of demand value of −0.7 and a maximum value of −0.2, with −0.4 as the most likely value.

The income grows during the concession period. The annual rate of growth is represented by a uniform probability distribution with a minimum value of 1 per cent and a maximum of 3 per cent. We also assume that the income elasticity of demand is within the range 0.25–0.5 but we do not know anything about the likelihood of any value, so we also use a uniform probability distribution.

Then we have four random variables in the evaluation: two for the demand elasticities, one for the post-privatization cost reduction and one for the annual growth of income. There is an important difference between the last one and the other three. When calculating the *NPV*, the computer program, according to our model, draws one value from the probability distribution of the income growth rate for each year of the 30 years of the concession period. Hence, for any *NPV* value there are 30 independent drawings from the income growth rate probability distribution. This implicitly assumes that the annual growth rate is uncorrelated with previous annual rates.

On the contrary, the other three probability distributions reflect evaluation uncertainty. This means that we do not know the exact values of some parameters, so we tell the program to choose only one value of each probability distribution and keep this value fixed for the *T* years in any iteration. The program will choose another value in the next iteration.

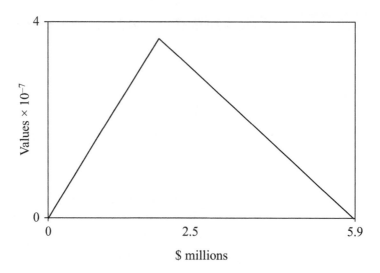

Figure 10.6 Social *NPV*

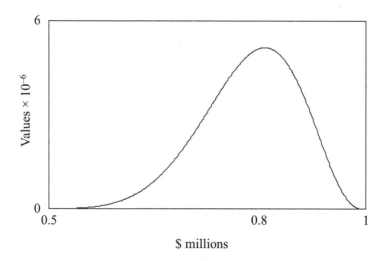

Figure 10.7 Financial *NPV*

Figures 10.6 and 10.7 represent the social and financial probability distributions for the *NPV*. Both probability distributions support the approval of the policy. The ranges of likely social and financial net present values are positive, and the expected values are $2.5 million and $0.8 million for the social and financial *NPV* respectively.

Nevertheless, the probability distribution of the consumer surplus represented in Figure 10.8 shows that although the expected value is $1.7 million there is an 8.3 per cent probability of a negative consumer surplus of between $1 million and zero. The reason for

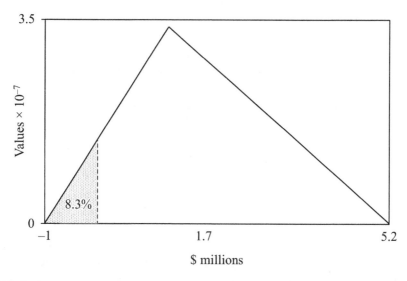

Figure 10.8 Consumer surplus

this segment of negative values for the consumers rests on the possibility of a 10 per cent mark-up combined with a cost reduction that ranges between 0 and 50 per cent. Any 10 per cent increase in price with insufficient cost reduction can produce an increase in price for the consumer, which in terms of the social NPV is partially compensated for by an increase in producer surplus. The deadweight loss of efficiency is generally compensated for, in this particular case, by the gain in efficiency thanks to the cost reduction.

One lesson from this case study is that by working exclusively with expected values we miss some valuable information. Risk analysis provides the decision maker with a broader picture of what is expected. Another lesson is that too much aggregation hides useful information. In this case, the probability distribution of consumer surplus shows that consumers may be losers in this privatization with an 8.3 per cent probability. This may be considered tolerable. Perhaps the regulator could contemplate the introduction of a price cap equal to the existing price before privatization.

10.6 INSTITUTIONAL DESIGN, CONTRACTS AND ECONOMIC EVALUATION

The development of any project involving initial investment costs and maintenance and operating costs in subsequent years requires an estimate of those costs in accordance with the criteria that have been developed in previous chapters. A positive net social benefit in the ex ante cost–benefit analysis does not guarantee the realization of this benefit during the life of the project. Unfortunately, it is common to find some projects that should not have been built according to their ex post benefits and costs.[7]

The explanation for the discrepancy between expected and actual values in the case of infrastructure lies partly in the nature of the engineering works. The fact that the expected benefits do not materialize according to the ex ante cost–benefit analysis is explained by contemplating the characteristics of the activity being evaluated. Transport energy and water infrastructures have a long life (over 30 years), have few alternative uses, are very expensive and the actual demand tends to deviate from that predicted for such long periods of time.

External shocks caused, for example, by the decline of economic activity, or a reduction in the population of the region where the infrastructure was built, significantly affect the demand of electricity, the highway or the company that supplies water – and thus the social benefit of the project. It might also happen that costs in the construction phase and subsequent maintenance and operation phases experience changes because of unexpected increases in the prices and quantities of the inputs (energy, labour, etc.) required for the normal operation of infrastructures.

These mismatches between predictions and reality are common and unavoidable during the economic life of a project. Little can be done beyond improving forecasting techniques and to a certain extent with risk analysis. However, the prediction errors are not the only explanation for the differences between ex ante and ex post economic profitability. The institutional design, and the type of contracts used for the construction and operation may change the behaviour of economic agents affecting the level of effort to minimize costs or the selection of the appropriate technology.

Now we discuss, first, the consequences of the existence of different levels of government with conflicting objectives; and second, the design of contracts for private participation. The understanding of these issues for cost–benefit analysis is paramount in a context of asymmetric information and demand and cost uncertainty.

Two levels of government and their effects on the selection of projects

The construction of a major infrastructure project is an expensive task. It is an investment that gathers the following characteristics: lumpy, irreversible and costly. The decision to invest public funds in the construction of a dam or a road is subject to cost and, particularly, demand uncertainty. The irreversibility of the decision makes the economic appraisal of the project quite relevant. Hence it is sensible to examine how the institutional design affects the final choice in the allocation of public funds to these types of projects.

---

[7] A major infrastructure project was the Channel Tunnel. It runs under the English Channel, linking Britain to the European continent and is 50 km long. An evaluation concludes: 'The cost benefit appraisal of the Channel Tunnel reveals that overall the British economy would have been better off if the Tunnel had never been constructed, as the total resource cost has been greater than the benefits generated' (Anguera, 2006, p. 314).

National and supranational governments support the implementation of key infrastructure with public funds. To understand the effects of this public support in the investment decision it is useful to distinguish two levels in the process of decision making and funding of major infrastructure projects. The first relates to the institutional design, in which supranational and national governments (or national and regional governments) agree on the projects to be financed. The second is related to the selection of contracts for the construction and operation of the infrastructure. This level includes the relationship between the national (or regional government) beneficiary of the project with the operator(s) responsible for the construction and operation of the project.[8]

There are two extreme cases in the menu of contracts: the *cost plus* and the *fixed price*. In the first case the agency responsible pays the full cost of the project and in the second case it pays an ex ante fixed amount. This characterization of contracts can be applied to funding, price regulation, construction contracts, and so on.

The problem with the cost-plus financing mechanism is that the public funds that a national government obtains from the supranational agency, or the regional government obtains from the national government, increase with the total investment costs and decrease with the net revenues. Hence this financing mechanism penalizes the internalization of externalities, leads to excessive demand and biases the capacity size and the choice of technology.

Let us suppose that a country facing a problem of capacity in the transport network is considering mutually exclusive projects, including the construction of a new high-speed rail line that can apply for financial support from a supranational planner that maximizes social welfare. The country is governed by a politician who must decide the main characteristics of the project (say, high-speed rail or an upgraded conventional train), make a cost–benefit analysis and report it to the supranational planner in order to receive funds for the construction of the infrastructure.

The effects of this type of co-financing system in which a supranational agency pays for the infrastructure and the national government decides on the type of project to be financed, can be modelled in the following way (de Rus and Socorro, 2010). Suppose only two periods. During the first period the new rail infrastructure is constructed. During the second period the citizens of the country use it. The real construction costs are paid by the supranational agency. We know that actual costs do not necessarily coincide with the minimum investment cost. To minimize construction costs requires the politician to make an effort, which is a cost for her.

It is not uncommon for national governments to be better informed than the supranational agency about the transport problem and the set of alternatives available and therefore about the minimum investment cost required to solve the problem. For this reason, we assume that the supranational planner cannot observe (or verify) either the minimum investment cost or the effort exerted by the politician in order to be efficient. Moreover, the national government must decide the price to be charged for the use of

---

[8] This second level has been widely analysed in the economic literature (Bajari and Tadelis, 2001; Guasch, 2004; Laffont and Tirole, 1993; Olsen and Osmundsen, 2005).

the new infrastructure and consequently the number of users. There are also operating and maintenance costs, which are privately known, and in many cases different technologies and/or capacity sizes with significant cost differences.[9]

Once we abandon the idea of perfect information and assume that the utility function of the politician (the national government) depends on her own private utility (only obtained if the politician is governing the country), we can go further in explaining some of the evidence concerning national government decisions on expensive infrastructure and suboptimal pricing.[10] The higher the welfare of voters in the second period, the higher the probability of re-election. The welfare of voters in the second period is the sum of their net benefits.

In a world of perfect information, the supranational agency maximizes social welfare, forcing the national government to exert the maximum level of effort and so minimizing project costs and introducing marginal social cost pricing. In the real world, efforts and marginal costs are not observable and the behaviour of the national government will respond to the incentives of the financing mechanism.

With the present financing mechanism (as well as with any other cost-plus financing system) it is costly to be efficient. Governments have no incentives to minimize investment costs or to introduce optimal pricing. There is a bias in favour of expensive latest-technology mega-projects, and the pricing will depart from user pays or polluter pays principles as the higher the price for the use of the new national infrastructure, the lower the consumer surplus of voters and the lower the probability of re-election. As a consequence the politician will choose the maximum number of users and will not charge for the external costs.

The evidence supports these conclusions. It is remarkable that national and regional governments have promoted the construction of expensive projects with a demand too low to pass a strict cost–benefit analysis. Forecasting error is not an explanation and strategic misrepresentation has been detected worldwide. Many projects show overcapacity, the use of an excessive and expensive technology given the problem to be solved, cost overruns and, in general, renegotiations that eventually allow the modification of the contract conditions, extending the construction periods, increasing costs and prices and hence breaking the basic rules of public procurement.

These disappointing results are not completely unexpected. As we have already discussed, national governments are in general better informed than supranational planners about the costs and benefits of the infrastructure projects to be constructed in

---

[9] Cost overruns are common in large infrastructure projects and it has been demonstrated that the deviation is not only explained by unforeseen events (Flyvbjerg et al., 2003).

[10] The implementation of the user pays and the polluter pays principles and the reduction of public expenditure has significant political costs (Sobel, 1998). Becker (1983), Downs (1957) and Niskanen (1971) have often assumed that legislators attempt to maximize electoral support. Even if re-election may not be the primary factor motivating their legislative behaviour, it is still true that legislators react in predictable ways to the electoral costs and benefits of their choices. Thus, legislators will favour actions that increase the probability of re-election over decisions that lower it (Robinson and Torvik, 2005; Sobel, 1998).

their own regions, and they do not necessarily share the same objectives. Governments may have incentives to manipulate project evaluation to gain more funds from the supranational planner. In a context of asymmetric information and different objectives, the relationship between national governments and supranational planners cannot be modelled in a conventional cost–benefit analysis framework.

In this context, cost–benefit analysis lacks its original power as a tool for decision making. The existence of information asymmetries and conflicting interests requires a different approach in which incentives are explicitly accounted for. A fixed-price financing mechanism may provide the necessary incentives to reduce costs and charge the socially optimal price. Moreover, with a 'fixed-price' type of financing mechanism, cost–benefit analysis is a very useful tool for governments to allocate the supranational funds in the most efficient way.

The fixed-price mechanism in this context is an ex ante *fixed quantity* of external funding unrelated to costs and revenue. The idea of a fixed quantity financing mechanism is to make national governments (in the case of supranational funding) or regional governments (in the case of national funding) responsible for insufficient revenues and cost inefficiencies as they receive a fixed amount of funding and are the residual claimants for effort. The incentive to introduce optimal pricing is now high as the costs of inefficient pricing are also borne by the politician.

It is worth emphasizing that by giving national (regional) governments an ex ante fixed amount of funds, the supranational agency (national government) loses its influence over the selection of projects. If supranational (national) governments want to establish infrastructure investment priorities, an intermediate solution is to substitute the cost-plus funding method by an alternative financing scheme based on an ex ante fixed-quantity funding linked to generic objectives such as investing in 'accessibility' or 'minimizing the total social cost of the water supply' in particular areas, a mechanism that should be dissociated in any case from costs and revenues and the selection of any specific technology. The risk of building a socially unprofitable infrastructure would be dissociated from the public funding mechanism as the selection of the more expensive (and maybe inappropriate) project will now have a completely different opportunity cost for the national (regional) governments.[11]

Contracts, incentives and risk allocation

Private participation for the construction and operation of infrastructure is usually arranged through fixed-term concession contracts. The purpose of the concession system is first the selection of the most efficient concessionaire among those presented to the public tender; and second, obtaining the greatest social benefit possible over the life of the infrastructure, while allowing the concessionaire to cover costs. To achieve both objectives, the selection system and the subsequent regulation should consider the problems of demand and cost information that characterize the activities under concession.

---

[11] As is common with fixed-price contracts, quality regulation may be required.

The fixed-term concession contract is in theory a fixed-price contract but it is a kind of cost-plus in practice, given the widely extended use of renegotiation of this type of contract all over the world (Guasch, 2004). The design of fixed-term contracts allocates the demand risk to the concessionaire and this creates problems concerning the selection of the most efficient bidders and the minimization of operating costs during the life of the concession.

Let us consider the case of an infrastructure with construction costs I_0 and maintenance and annual operation costs C_t, independent of the number of users x_t. In the fixed-term concession system the concession is awarded to the bidder who proposes to charge the lowest price,[12] having previously announced the concession period T. Cost coverage requires that the discounted value of the net revenue equals the investment cost:

$$I_0 = \sum_{t=1}^{T} \frac{1}{(1+i)^t} (p_t x_t - C_t).$$
(10.21)

One version of the fixed-term contract is to fix, ex ante, the concession period and the price to be charged, and let the bidders compete in offering a canon, that is a concessionary fee, to the public agency. With perfect information on demand, the maximum canon that a bidder will offer equals the present value of expected benefits over the life of the concession.[13]

All the existing types of fixed-term concession contract[14] share the problem of uncertainty of demand, so it is usual to introduce clauses to guarantee minimum revenue, and contract renegotiations are common throughout the life of the concession. This kind of cost-plus contract has effects on the incentives to minimize costs and on the realization of ex ante social benefit; hence it should be considered in the cost–benefit analysis of projects.

Assuming for simplicity that the discount rate is zero and that p_t, x_t and C_t are constants in expression (10.21), during the life of the concession (T), for an entrepreneur to be willing to participate in the competition he should expect that the revenue stream would at least cover the total costs:

$$pxT \geq I + CT.$$
(10.22)

If the annual revenues px are greater than the annual costs C, we can determine the value of T that will allow the concessionaire to cover its total costs:

---

[12] In practice, a multicriteria tender is commonly used, with several variables, among which the price is included.

[13] To simplify the exposition, we assume that bidders bid their reservation prices – that is, they present their offers with the most that they are willing to pay, so they earn normal profits.

[14] Another method is to set the price and award the concession to the bidder who requests the shortest concession period. This case is a variation of the fixed-term concession contract since once the public tender finishes, the concession period is as fixed as in the price (or canon) concession system.

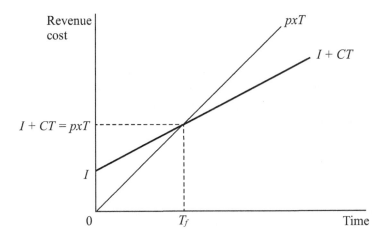

Figure 10.9 Concessionaire's revenues and costs with financial equilibrium

$$T_f = \frac{I}{px - C},$$ (10.23)

where T_f represents the duration of the concession determined ex ante by the regulator.

With perfect information on demand, the regulator will have set a value of T_f and the concessionaire (assuming perfect competition) will have submitted the best bid (canon paid, lower price to charge the users, etc.) that makes it possible for expression (10.22) to be satisfied as an equality. Figure 10.9 shows the equilibrium situation.

With the concession term T_f it can be seen how the total costs are covered by commercial revenue. At the same time Figure 10.9 shows that the compatibility of a fixed concession period and the financial equilibrium of the company rest on unrealistic assumptions: perfect information about demand and efficient behaviour by the concessionaire.

Demand uncertainty is common during the life of the project. One can argue that it is virtually impossible to predict demand accurately over a 30-year horizon. On the cost side there are also information problems. The bidder knows the costs, but the regulator does not (asymmetric information). Therefore, if we abandon the assumption of perfect information and allow the possibility of losses and profits over the life of a long-term concession, one should analyse the implications of the type of contract chosen.

Suppose that the concession goes to the bidder that, for the same quality, offers to charge the users the lowest price for a given T_f. The basic idea behind this auction is that firms interested in obtaining the concession will offer the lowest possible price consistent with their costs. Since there is no information on the costs of rival firms, the efficient bidder (who is identified with the subscript i) will try, like others, to increase the probability of winning the contract by offering a price that allows it to receive normal benefits:

$$p_i = \frac{I_i + C_i T_f}{x T_f} . \tag{10.24}$$

In expression (10.24) it can be observed that if the level of demand x were known, a lowest price auction with a fixed-term concession T_f would achieve its goal: the concession would be won by the firm that has the lowest total cost to implement the project. However, given the problem of uncertainty about demand x and the various estimates that companies can use when preparing their offers, the award mechanism based on a fixed-term concession does not guarantee that the outcome is the best possible.

Because of factors completely exogenous to the concessionaire, demand may significantly fluctuate over the life of a concession. For simplicity, consider that there are only two possibilities for the number of users during the lifetime of the project: high demand (x_h) with probability π or low (x_l) with probability $1 - \pi$.

Since bidders are not sure about future demand they will work with an expected value of demand (x_e), which we define as $x_e = \pi x_h + (1 - \pi)x_l$. Once the concession has been awarded and the infrastructure has been built, the demand is x_h or x_l and the company may be in a position of profits or losses.

Figure 10.10 shows a situation where, given a concession term T_f, the financial equilibrium would be achieved for the expected volume of demand x_e but not for the situations of high or low demand. In the case of high demand, revenues are higher than costs in the distance af; and if the demand is low, costs are not covered and losses are equal to fb. In practice, both cases are common and a renegotiation of the concession contract is often required to restore the financial equilibrium.

In the case of inelastic demand, if the demand scenario is low and there is no minimum income guarantee, the adjusting variable is p. By authorizing an increase in the price, the revenue function $px_l T$ shifts upward to cut the cost function at point f, so the financial equilibrium is ensured. Another possibility is to extend the concession period to T_l.

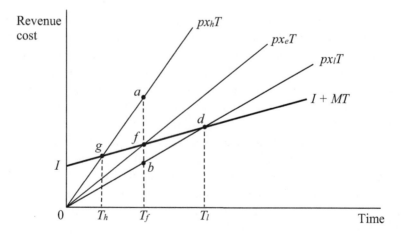

Figure 10.10 Financial equilibrium in a concession with unknown demand

If, on the contrary, the demand is high, the economic profits will be politically undesirable since they would appear to the public as a situation of unjustified privilege, the
reduction in price being an easy adjustment. The fall in price moves px_hT downward,
reducing the profits to zero if the movement is carried to point f. Another possibility is
to reduce the concession period to T_h.

This is roughly what has been happening in most fixed-term concessions in the
world, especially in cases where demand is lower than expected. In fact, this concession
contract, with virtually assured renegotiation, becomes a rate of return regulation of
the private firm that has invested in infrastructure construction and operation, with its
negative impact in terms of the incentives to minimize costs.

An additional problem is that with demand uncertainty it is quite likely that the most
optimistic bidder will be selected instead of the most efficient. A bidder with high costs
could win a contract if his beliefs about the number of users are optimistic enough to
offset its cost disadvantage compared with the other firms with lower costs. This is easy
to see from expression (10.24), which indicates how companies make their calculations
to submit their bids.

Let us consider the case of two firms i and j, which compete in an auction awarded to
the bid charging users the lowest price. Assuming that firm i is more efficient than j (i.e.,
it has lower costs, $I_i + C_i T_f < I_j + C_j T_f$), company i should win the contest. However,
it is possible that firm j is more optimistic about the expected demand, and this led
firm j to make an offer with a lower price ($p_j < p_i$), thereby obtaining the concession.
From expression (10.24), for the inefficient company j to win the contract, it would be
sufficient that the following condition is satisfied:

$$\frac{I_i + C_i T_f}{x_i^e T_f} > \frac{I_j + C_j T_f}{x_j^e T_f},$$
(10.25)

or, equivalently,

$$\frac{x_j^e}{x_i^e} > \frac{I_j + C_j T_f}{I_i + C_i T_f}.$$
(10.26)

Expression (10.26) shows that the less efficient firm can win the contract if it is optimistic ($x_j^e > x_i^e$) enough to offset its cost disadvantage. It can be seen that the condition
(10.26) can be met if the inefficient firm j is inefficient either in absolute terms (both
construction and maintenance costs are greater than those of i) or in relative terms
(its total cost $I_j + C_j T_f$ is higher for a fixed duration, although it might be $I_j < I_i$ or
$C_j < C_i$).

In conclusion one can note three major negative economic consequences of the conventional fixed-term concession system based on auctions with bids for the minimum
price to charge the users:

•   In the absence of perfect information on demand, this type of auction does not
      guarantee the selection of the firm with the lowest costs since the existence of

different beliefs about future demand may cause an inefficient and optimistic firm to win the contract.

- If firms anticipate that it may be possible to renegotiate the concession contract in the future because of changes in the volume of users, the incentives to operate at minimum cost are weak since efforts to operate efficiently can be substituted by negotiation with the regulator requiring a price change to restore the normal benefits.

- With the fixed-term contract and inelastic demand, price becomes an accounting adjustment variable, tending to rise when demand is low and decline when demand is high, which can lead to an inefficient use of the infrastructure, contrary to what would be desirable from an economic perspective. In general, there will be no pressure on existing capacity when demand is low, and it would be an undesirable pricing policy discouraging the use of infrastructure. On the contrary, when demand is high and there is congestion, the price should rise to ration the available capacity.

The three consequences of this type of contract reduce the ex post NPV of the project. The problems of private participation in infrastructure with fixed-term concession contracts are a result of the economic characteristics of these projects, and especially the uncertainty of demand. High costs, long life and asset specificity, coupled with the inability to predict the demand for the life of the concession, are the elements that cause the renegotiation of contracts and the loss of the essence of a public tender.

An alternative contract to avoid these problems is to change the mechanism of financial adjustment of the concession system. According to our analysis above, the problem of demand uncertainty translates into uncertainty about the revenue the firm expects from the concession. This is the fundamental point that generates the risk of failure of concessions (in the case of low demand) or of inadequate price reductions (in the case of high demand). One possible solution is for the government to fix the price, the level of quality and the discount rate, and for firms to make offers on the revenue they want to receive during the life of the concession, thus eliminating revenue uncertainty, and letting the contract last as long as it takes to earn the revenue included in the winning bid.[15]

If the concession period is allowed to be variable instead of fixed (remember that T_f is predetermined in the case of the traditional concession), it would be possible to accommodate situations of high or low demand without the need to renegotiate the contract or having to make unwanted changes in prices. For example, in Figure 10.10, in a situation of low demand (x_l) the length of the concession is automatically extended to T_l, thus allowing the recovery of the total costs. By contrast, in a case of high demand,

---

[15] This system was first applied in the UK in the construction and operation of a bridge. Later, it was used in the road concession Santiago–Valparaíso–Viña del Mar in Chile. For an analysis of variable-term concessions, see Engel et al. (2001) and Nombela and de Rus (2004). For the economics of public-private partnerships (PPP), see Engel et al. (2014); and for the use of PPP in infrastructure, Engel et al. (2020).

in a period T_h such recovery of total costs would have been realized earlier and ending the concession at that time would avoid economic profits.

THINGS TO REMEMBER

1. Even assuming that privatization results in net benefits for society, these benefits may not be well distributed. It may well be that producers are better off with privatization, but consumers and workers are worse off. Therefore, to assess a privatization project in practice, the practitioner should make a detailed assessment of winners and losers. This will be necessary to design the compensation mechanisms, for reasons of equity and political acceptability.

2. Working exclusively with expected values may neglect some valuable information. Risk analysis provides the decision maker with a more complete picture. Too much aggregation hides useful information.

3. It is impossible to foresee all the circumstances a project must go through during its lifespan. Ex ante demand and costs do not necessarily coincide with ex post values; hence, the economic evaluation of project should examine the facts that explain this divergence.

4. Actual demand depends on some unpredictable contingencies but also, to some extent, on decisions taken by economic agents. Contract designs both allocate risk and affect the level of effort exerted by firms to reduce costs. There are two basic types of contracts, the cost-plus and the fixed-price, and different combinations in the middle depending on the degree of risk and incentives.

5. The effects of public support by supranational agencies on the investment decision taken by national governments vary with the institutional design. The existence of two levels of government, in which supranational and national governments (or national and regional governments) can modify the incentives in the selection of projects, affects the value of cost–benefit analysis as a tool for informed decision taking.

6. Private participation requires the design of contracts. The government wants to select the most efficient contractor and to offer a contract that keeps the firm interested in minimizing costs. To achieve their objectives, the government and the firms must work in a world of uncertainty and asymmetric information. The type of contract can have profound effects on the ex post net present value of projects.

11

Microeconomic foundations of cost–benefit analysis[1]

One summer, a colleague asked me why I have not bought a parking permit. I replied that not having a convenient place to park made me more likely to ride my bike. He accused me of inconsistency: As a believer in rationality, I should be able to make the correct choice between sloth and exercise without first rigging the game. My response was that rationality is an assumption I made about other people. I know myself well enough to allow for the consequences of my own irrationality. But for the vast mass of my fellow humans, about whom I know very little, rationality is the best predictive assumption available.

(David Friedman, 1996, p. 5)

11.1 INTRODUCTION

This chapter covers the basic theoretical framework of cost–benefit analysis. The objective is to give a clearer picture of what is behind the concept of social welfare and the decision criteria based on the net present value. The approach is theoretical but neither exhaustive nor extremely technical.

The way from individual preferences to social welfare is the content of Section 11.2. Section 11.3 addresses the measurement of producer surplus in the product and factor markets. Section 11.4 analyses the three money measures of changes in individual utility most frequently used to evaluate economic changes: compensating variation, equivalent variation and consumer surplus. Section 11.5 deals with uncertainty.

11.2 FROM INDIVIDUAL UTILITY TO SOCIAL WELFARE

Given the social welfare function in expression (11.1), assuming independent utilities and taking total differentials, the change in social welfare (W) can be expressed as

---

[1] For a review of the basic theory, see, for example, Varian (1999). More advanced treatment of the utility and profit functions and the theoretical justification of the measurements of welfare changes can be found in Adler and Posner (2001); Johansson (1993); Just et al. (1982); Mas-Colell et al. (1995); and Varian (1992).

expression (11.2): the sum of the variations in the utility (U) of the m individuals who form the society, weighted by the relative importance the society attaches to the utility of each individual (i.e., social marginal utility: $\partial W/\partial U_i$).[2]

$$W = W\left(U_1, U_2, \ldots, U_m\right), \tag{11.1}$$

$$dW = \sum_{i=1}^{m} \frac{\partial W}{\partial U_i} dU_i. \tag{11.2}$$

The utility of individuals depends on the quantities of the n goods and services (x) available for consumption. In the case of individual i:

$$U_i = U_i\left(x_{i1}, x_{i2}, \ldots, x_{in}\right). \tag{11.3}$$

Assuming that individual i maximizes utility, subject to the constraint that aggregate expenditure cannot be greater than his income, we have the following expression:

$$\underset{x_{i1}, x_{i2}, \ldots, x_{in}}{Max} \quad U_i\left(x_{i1}, x_{i2}, \ldots, x_{in}\right) - \mu_i \left(\sum_{j=1}^{n} p_j x_{ij} - M_i\right), \tag{11.4}$$

where:

x_{ij}: quantity of good j consumed by individual i;
M_i: income of individual i;
p_j: price of good j;
μ_i: Lagrange multiplier.

First-order conditions are as follows:

$$\frac{\partial U_i}{\partial x_{ij}} - \mu_i p_j = 0, j = 1, \ldots, n, \tag{11.5}$$

$$\sum_{j=1}^{n} p_j x_{ij} - M_i = 0. \tag{11.6}$$

The economic interpretation of the first-order conditions is the following: to maximize utility, the individual allocates his income so that, at the optimum and for the selected goods, the marginal utility of consuming the last unit of the good ($\partial U_i/\partial x_{ij}$) is equal to the disutility of paying the price ($\mu_i p_j$) as μ_i is the marginal utility of income. Moreover, the spending on all the chosen goods exhausts the individual's income.

---

[2] Note that expression (11.2) does not specify the procedure for aggregating the benefits of the m individuals. It is compatible with any external criterion imposed by the analyst.

Solving for p_j in expression (11.5):

$$p_j = \frac{\dfrac{\partial U_i}{\partial x_{ij}}}{\mu_i}. \tag{11.7}$$

At the optimum, the individual consumes additional units of good j until the price is equal to the marginal valuation of the good (the ratio of expression (11.7)). Whenever the marginal valuation of the good is greater than its price, the individual increases the consumption of the good until the budget constraint is binding. It may happen that the price is higher than the marginal valuation of the good for some goods and the individual does not consume them. In this case the first-order condition is satisfied as a strict inequality (corner solution).

By differentiating expression (11.3) we obtain expression (11.8), where the variation in the total utility of individuals depends on the marginal utility of each good and the variation in the quantity consumed of that good:

$$dU_i = \sum_{j=1}^{n} \frac{\partial U_i}{\partial x_{ij}} dx_{ij}. \tag{11.8}$$

Substituting the first-order condition (11.5) in expression (11.8) we obtain the variation in individual welfare:

$$dU_i = \sum_{j=1}^{n} \mu_i p_j dx_{ij}. \tag{11.9}$$

Equation (11.9) contemplates utility as a function of quantities consumed, given the prices of goods and services and the income of the individual. The variation of the utility of individual i depends on the marginal variation in the quantities of the n goods consumed, multiplied by their price (which we assume to be constant) and converted to utilities by multiplying by the marginal utility of income (μ_i).

A useful concept for money measures of changes in individual utilities is the indirect utility function. Individual utility used in its original functional form (11.3) is a function of the quantities of goods and services consumed by the individuals, given prices and income. Going back to the first-order conditions (11.5) and (11.6), and obtaining the values of x that maximize the utility function as a function of the vector of prices (P) and income (M), the indirect utility function is the utility function expressed as $U = U(X(P, M))$, or:

$$V_i\left(p_1, p_2, \ldots, p_n, M_i\right) = U_i\left(x_{i1}\left(p_1, p_2, \ldots, p_n, M_i\right), x_{i2}\left(\cdot\right), \ldots, x_{in}\left(\cdot\right)\right). \tag{11.10}$$

Adding the budget constraint to (11.10) we can use the indirect utility function to express the utility maximization as a function of prices and income:

$$V_i\left(p_1, p_2, \ldots, p_n, M_i\right) = U_i\left(x_{i1}\left(p_1, p_2, \ldots, p_n, M_i\right), x_{i2}\left(\cdot\right), \ldots, x_{in}\left(\cdot\right)\right)$$

$$- \mu_i\left(\sum_{h=1}^{n} p_h x_{ih}\left(p_1, \ldots, p_n, M_i\right) - M_i\right). \tag{11.11}$$

At the optimum, differentiating with respect to p_j and noting that $V(P, M) = U(X(P, M))$, we obtain how the utility varies with an infinitesimal variation of price:

$$\frac{\partial V_i}{\partial p_j} = \sum_{h=1}^{n} \frac{\partial U_i}{\partial x_{ih}} \frac{\partial x_{ih}}{\partial p_j} - \mu_i\left(x_{ij} + \sum_{h=1}^{n} \frac{\partial x_{ih}}{\partial p_j} p_h\right), \tag{11.12}$$

$$\frac{\partial V_i}{\partial p_j} = \sum_{h=1}^{n} \left(\frac{\partial U_i}{\partial x_{ih}} - \mu_i p_h\right) \frac{\partial x_{ih}}{\partial p_j} - \mu_i x_{ij} = -\mu_i x_{ij}, \tag{11.13}$$

because at the optimum (see first-order condition (11.5)),

$$\left(\frac{\partial U_i}{\partial x_{ih}} - \mu_i p_h\right) \frac{\partial x_{ih}}{\partial p_j} = 0; \quad h = 1, 2 \ldots n. \tag{11.14}$$

The result obtained in (11.13) is well known in microeconomic theory as Roy's Identity. As we have seen, it is easily derived by applying the envelope theorem.[3]

By totally differentiating expression (11.10) we obtain expression (11.15), where the variation in the total utility of the individual depends on the marginal utility with respect to each change in price multiplied by the price changes, plus the marginal utility of income multiplied by the change in income:

$$dV_i = \sum_{j=1}^{n} \frac{\partial V_i}{\partial p_j} dp_j + \frac{\partial V_i}{\partial M_i} dM_i. \tag{11.15}$$

Keeping income constant ($dM_i = 0$) and using the result in (11.13):

$$dV_i = -\sum_{j=1}^{n} \mu_i x_{ij} dp_j. \tag{11.16}$$

This expression is equivalent to (11.9) for projects with price changes (keeping quantities constant). In this chapter we only deal with changes either in the quantities of goods (11.9) or in the prices (11.16) without changes in the costs. In Chapter 2 we deal with situations in which prices and quantities change simultaneously.[4]

---

[3] The derivative of the value of an objective function at the optimum with respect to an exogenous parameter is equal to the derivative of the objective function with respect to the parameter. Only the direct effect must be considered.

[4] Utility, and profits, can also be affected through a change in the level of an environmental good (e.g., air quality). This is covered in Chapters 5 and 6.

Expressions (11.9) and (11.16) show how to assess the change in individual utility as a result of a change in quantities and prices. The change in prices is multiplied by the quantity and the change in quantities is multiplied by prices. To convert this change in utility, expressed in monetary units, we need μ_i to be constant and, unless μ_i is constant, we cannot directly associate the monetary changes with changes in utility. Identical increases in income result in different changes in utility if the marginal utility of income is not constant.

With utility increasing with income ($\partial U/\partial M > 0$) but less than proportionately ($\partial^2 U/\partial M^2 < 0$), unless we know the value of the marginal utility of income for individuals with different income levels, it is not possible to convert the aggregate changes in quantities or prices of goods in utility changes.

The above argument is useful for understanding the economic rationale of the measurement of social benefits arising from the implementation of a project. As the utility is not observable, we use monetary measures that reflect the change in the utility of individuals. We are not directly measuring the change in utility, but the change in the willingness to pay or accept, with monetary measures that, despite their limitations, allow us to gain approximations of what we win and lose with the project.

Returning to the social welfare function (11.1) and its total differential (11.2), and using the results derived in this section, we can express the effect of a small change in quantities (11.17) and prices (11.18) on social welfare:

$$dW = \sum_{j=1}^{n}\sum_{i=1}^{m} \frac{\partial W}{\partial U_i} \frac{\partial U_i}{\partial M_i} p_j dx_{ij}, \tag{11.17}$$

$$dW = -\sum_{j=1}^{n}\sum_{i=1}^{m} \frac{\partial W}{\partial U_i} \frac{\partial U_i}{\partial M_i} x_{ij} dp_j. \tag{11.18}$$

For the economic interpretation of both expressions it is useful to read them from right to left. The project may involve a change in quantities (with p constant) or a change in prices (with x constant). In both cases these changes are converted into monetary units, multiplying by price or quantity, respectively.

For such monetary changes to be converted into changes in social welfare there are two types of weights. First, the marginal utility of income for each individual ($\partial U_i/\partial M_i$), which depends on the income level of the individual. This weight transforms income into individual utility. The second weight ($\partial W/\partial U_i$) converts individual utility into social welfare.

For society to improve, with the increase in individual utility, $\partial W/\partial U_i$ must be positive. The partial derivative $\partial W/\partial U_i$ can be different for different individuals. The society may give more weight to social groups with different income levels, health conditions or any other relevant characteristic. The two weights interpreted together are the social marginal utility of income.

Expressions (11.17) and (11.18) aggregate the change experienced by the m individuals, initially measured in monetary units, using the weights described. In (11.17) and (11.18) there is an implicit social welfare function that determines how to proceed with regard to the weighting scheme. The simplest case is the potential compensation, or Kaldor–Hicks criterion, in which benefits and costs are added unweighted (i.e., it is implicitly assumed that the two weights in (11.17) and (11.18) are equal to one). The potential compensation criterion implies that the marginal utility of income is constant, and society gives the same weight to the utility changes of all individuals regardless of income, health status, and so on.

Other approaches are possible with equations (11.17) and (11.18). One possibility is to correct for the marginal utility of income and add the changes in utility, giving the same social value to the utility of any individual. In this way, if the marginal utility of income is decreasing, we will outweigh the benefits and costs of those with lower income. It should be emphasized that this correction does not have any redistributive basis, although it may seem so if we compare it with the potential compensation criterion.

Another possibility is a welfare function that introduces the social aversion to inequality. In this case, once the net benefits of each individual are corrected according to their marginal utility of income, it introduces an additional weight (the social marginal utility) that varies inversely with the income of the individual in higher or lower proportions depending on the degree of egalitarianism.

11.3 MEASUREMENT OF PRODUCER SURPLUS

The difference between a firm's revenues and variable costs is called producer surplus. This surplus is the gross profit in the sense that fixed costs have not been deducted. Suppose a company has an annual revenue of $100 million and its total costs are equal to $100 million, of which $50 million are variable and $50 million fixed. Variable costs are by definition avoidable if the firm produces nothing. Assume that the fixed costs are sunk costs. With this information the firm has zero profits and a producer surplus equal to $50 million.

Suppose the owner of the company is asked for the maximum he is willing to pay to keep the firm open once production has started. Excluding any strategic consideration his answer is $50 million. Though the company earns a profit of zero, the producer surplus indicates the maximum he is willing to pay to stay open. If it closes he loses $50 million; if it remains open he covers costs. The fixed cost could be higher and the response would not change. The producer surplus is positive, so the owner would be willing to pay for continued production. Producing with a positive surplus contributes to the recovery of fixed costs. Depending on the size of the surplus, the fixed costs could be partially or wholly covered or the company could even make a profit.

What happens if the question about willingness to pay to avoid the closure was made to the owner before spending on the fixed factor? Would the producer surplus be the highest potential payment for avoiding closure? The answer is yes, and this maximum is now zero. Before starting the production, all the factors are variable and with the numbers of our example the surplus is zero. In general, if there are no fixed costs, the profit and producer surplus are identical.

More often the analyst needs to know the changes in the producer surplus rather than the absolute value of the surplus; for example, the change caused because the price or the production costs have changed.

Consider the case of a firm operating in competitive markets of factors and products that supplies a good x, with a well-behaved production function, $x = x(L, K)$, with a variable factor of production L with price w and a fixed factor K whose price is assumed to be one. The company's profit in the short term is equal to:

$$\pi = px(L) - wL - K. \tag{11.19}$$

As a decision rule to start production we can say that the firm will not invest unless the producer surplus (PS) is equal to or greater than the fixed cost:

$$PS = px(L) - wL \geq K. \tag{11.20}$$

In the short term, deriving (11.19) with respect to L, we obtain the first order condition of profit maximization:

$$p\frac{dx(L)}{dL} - w = 0, \tag{11.21}$$

which indicates that, to maximize profit, we should further increase production as long as the value of the marginal productivity of the variable factor is greater than the price of that factor.

With a fixed factor, under standard assumptions, the marginal productivity of L will eventually decrease, so that for the given prices (p, w) equality (11.21) must be met. The profit function depends therefore on the price of the good (p) and the price factor (w).

The profit equation (11.19) can be expressed as a value function, which depends indirectly on p and w (we use the same idea as in the case of the indirect utility function):

$$V(p, w) = px(p, w) - wL(p, w) - K. \tag{11.22}$$

The derivative of the function (11.22) with respect to the price of the good (a parameter for the competitive firm) shows the variation that occurs in the firm's profit at the maximum. Therefore it should not be interpreted as a first-order condition, but the effect on profits of a change in the price at the optimum:

$$\frac{\partial V}{\partial p} = x(p, w) + p\frac{\partial x}{\partial L}\frac{\partial L}{\partial p} - w\frac{\partial L}{\partial p} = x(p, w). \tag{11.23}$$

The increase in the benefit of an infinitesimal change in price is equal to the quantity sold by the firm (the envelope theorem) since, as the firm is located at the optimal production level, we know that:

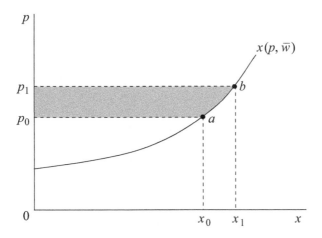

Figure 11.1 Producer surplus in the product market

$$\left(p\frac{\partial x}{\partial L} - w \right)\frac{\partial L}{\partial p} = 0. \tag{11.24}$$

The result obtained in (11.23) is very useful for calculating the change in producer surplus when the price changes, because we simply need to integrate the function $x(p, w)$, which is the supply function of the company, using as integration limits the initial and the final prices:

$$\Delta PS = \int_{p_0}^{p_1} x(p, w)\, dp. \tag{11.25}$$

Figure 11.1 shows the change in producer surplus when the price increases from p_0 to p_1. This change, represented by the area $p_1 b a p_0$, coincides with the change in the firm's profit. Note that for a very small price increase the surplus reduces to x_0 – that is, to the results stated in (11.23).

Deriving expression (11.22) with respect to the factor price (exogenous to the firm), we obtain the variation that occurs in the firm's profit when the factor price changes; just as happens with the price of a good, the idea is not to obtain a condition of maximization but to calculate the change in profits at the optimum when a parameter changes:

$$\frac{\partial V}{\partial w} = p\frac{\partial x}{\partial L}\frac{\partial L}{\partial w} - L(p, w) - w\frac{\partial L}{\partial w} = -L(p, w). \tag{11.26}$$

The variation in profits resulting from a change in the factor price is equal to the amount of a variable factor (with a negative sign) used by the company (the envelope theorem) because, given that the firm is maximizing profit, we know that:

$$\left(p\frac{\partial x}{\partial L} - w \right)\frac{\partial L}{\partial w} = 0. \tag{11.27}$$

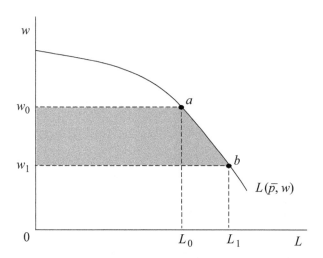

Figure 11.2 Producer surplus in the factor market

Integrating the demand function of the factor $L(p, w)$, with a negative sign, between the initial and the final price factor, we obtain the following expression that gives the change in the producer surplus:

$$\Delta PS = -\int_{w_0}^{w_1} L(p, w)\, dw. \tag{11.28}$$

The representation of this change is reflected by the area $w_0 abw_1$ in Figure 11.2.

Figure 11.1 shows the variation in producer surplus in the market for goods when the price changes, while Figure 11.2 represents the change in producer surplus on the market factor when the price of that factor changes. Alternatively, the surplus arising from the change in the price of the good can be measured in the market for the factor, and the surplus arising from a change in the factor price can be measured in the market for goods. Figures 11.3 and 11.4 capture the areas of Figures 11.1 and 11.2 respectively.

An increase in the price from p_0 to p_1 in the product market (Figure 11.1) leads to an upward shift of the labour demand curve in Figure 11.3, which represents the value of the marginal productivity of labour. As the price of the factor (w) remains constant in w_0, the condition (11.21) is not satisfied, so more labour will be hired until the condition is satisfied. The change in producer surplus in the factor market equals the area $bdfa$, between the two curves of factor demand limited by the factor price that remains constant at the new equilibrium.

Similarly, a price reduction in the factor market (Figure 11.2) results in a downward shift of the supply curve in the product market (Figure 11.4), which represents the reduction in the marginal cost of production. As the price of the good is kept constant, reducing the marginal cost makes an increase in production profitable. The

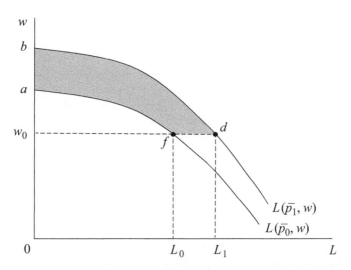

Figure 11.3 Effect of a change in the price of the good, measured in the factor market

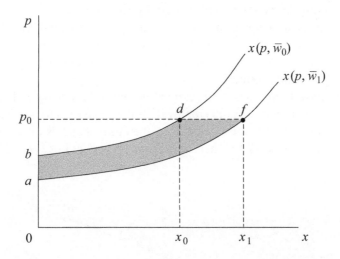

Figure 11.4 Effect of a change in the price of the factor, measured in the product market

change in producer surplus in the market for goods equals the area *bdfa*, between the two supply curves of the good limited by the constant price at the new level of production.[5]

---

[5] The previous analysis is generalized for multiple goods and factors (see Just et al., 1982).

Producer surplus and the surplus of the owners of the production factors

The change in producer surplus as a result of the implementation of a project does not show who the beneficiaries of this surplus are. The producer surplus is a little confusing because eventually this change in the surplus may be a change in the income of the company owners, the owners of land and other fixed factors, the taxpayers or the workers.

Suppose factor L is an imported raw material. In this case the reduction in the cost of production increases producer surplus and this is the change in social surplus (given that p does not change, the consumer surplus remains constant). By contrast, if L is domestic labour, the change in the surplus of workers must be taken into account like the surplus of any other social agent. A reduction in w as a result of the privatization of a public company represents a reduction in the worker surplus, which for constant x offsets the increase in producer surplus, leaving social welfare unaffected.

Workers offer their labour if they are paid wages at least equal to their opportunity costs. Quite often, in the economic evaluation of projects, worker surplus obtained by subtracting the opportunity cost of working (for example, the value of leisure) from the wages is not included, principally because many projects do not produce significant changes in the labour market, changing the equilibrium wage.

Figure 11.5 represents a function of labour supply $S_L (w)$. The minimum reservation wage is w_r, below which no one is willing to work in the market represented in the figure. This might be because there is an unemployment benefit or because the informal economy offers jobs paid around w_r.

Suppose that the labour market represented in Figure 11.5 is in equilibrium at point d, so that at wage w_0, L_0 workers are employed. If the wage rises to w_1, the change from d to b generates new jobs (from L_0 to L_1). In the event that b is an equilibrium, new employees are willing to work for their opportunity cost (area dbL_1L_0). However, they

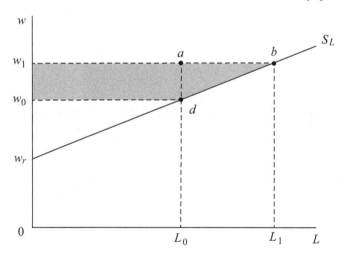

Figure 11.5 Worker surplus

receive as wages the area abL_1L_0, resulting in a surplus for the new employees equal to the area abd. Existing workers also benefit from the wage increase and their surplus goes from w_0dw_r to w_1adw_r; or, which is the same, the surplus of existing workers increases in the area w_1adw_0.

It should be emphasized that we could ignore the concept of producer surplus and simply add up the surpluses of the social agents: landowners, shareholders, consumers, workers and taxpayers. Although any individual belongs to more than one category, this functional classification is useful in cost–benefit analysis.

In practice, it is interesting to distinguish between fixed factors that persist in the long term, such as the available land in a particular urban area or the agricultural land of particular characteristics, and fixed factors by law, such as some licences that restrict the entry of new suppliers into the market.

Although it is straightforward to sum the surpluses of the agents, including the owners of fixed factors, the use of the producer surplus can be suitable when information is scarce and one must work with assumptions about what happens in the market at a very aggregate level.

Finally, a note of caution to avoid double counting. Suppose that Figure 11.1 represents an increase in the surplus of farmers as a result of rising agricultural prices. In assessing the change that has occurred in the market, we can use the producer surplus represented in Figure 11.1 or the income of the landowners if we expect land rents to be updated to absorb the benefits of farmers, but not both.

11.4 COMPENSATING VARIATION, EQUIVALENT VARIATION AND CONSUMER SURPLUS

A price reduction or an increase in product quality allows the individual to reach a higher level of utility. The individual has improved, although we do not know the magnitude of improvement since the value that is assigned to both levels of utility is completely arbitrary.

In cost–benefit analysis we aim to go further and want to know the change in the social welfare of such individual improvements and this requires aggregating the changes in individual utilities. If the magnitude of the differences in utility is arbitrary (it only matters that the utility in one state is higher than in the other), it makes even less sense to add the changes in utility for different individuals.

One way out of these problems is to rely on the monetary valuation that individuals give to the utility change, and then add these individual values (remember that the aggregation of individual valuations requires, for conversion to social welfare, to weight them according to the marginal social utility of income).

The three money measures of changes in individual utility most frequently used to evaluate economic changes are the compensating variation, the equivalent variation and consumer surplus.

The *compensating variation (CV)* can be defined as the income that can be taken from the individual once the change occurs, leaving him at the same level of utility as before the change.[6] The *equivalent variation* (*EV*) can be defined as the income to be given to the individual to attain the same level of utility reached with the change, but without the change (that is the amount of income that is equivalent to the change). The advantage of the *CV* and the *EV* is that they are money measures of the change in the individual's utility. The *consumer surplus* (*CS*) can be defined as the sum of the willingness to pay of each unit consumed (the area under the demand function between zero and the last unit consumed) minus the total expenditure on the good. The change in *CS* is therefore the difference in surplus before and after the change.

To see the theoretical justification of these money measures of utility, we start by minimizing the expenditure of an individual subject to a constant level of utility $\bar{U}$ (for simplicity of notation we omit the subscript i):

$$\underset{x_1,\dots,x_n}{Min} \ \sum_{j=1}^{n} p_j x_j - \mu \left(U\left(x_1,\dots,x_n\right) - \bar{U} \right). \tag{11.29}$$

The first-order conditions are:

$$p_j - \mu \frac{\partial U}{\partial x_j} = 0, j = 1,\dots,n, \tag{11.30}$$

$$U\left(x_1,\dots,x_n\right) = \bar{U}. \tag{11.31}$$

Obtaining from (11.30) and (11.31) the values x_j that minimize (11.29), we obtain an expenditure function at the optimal $e(P, \bar{U})$ in which P is the vector of prices $(p_1, \dots, p_n)$:

$$e = \sum_{j=1}^{n} p_j x_j (P, \bar{U}) - \mu \left[(U(x(P,\bar{U})) - \bar{U} \right]. \tag{11.32}$$

Deriving this value function with respect to p_j:

$$\frac{\partial e}{\partial p_j} = x_j \left(P, \bar{U} \right) + \sum_{h=1}^{n} p_h \frac{\partial x_h}{\partial p_j} - \mu \sum_{h=1}^{n} \frac{\partial U}{\partial x_h} \frac{\partial x_h}{\partial p_j} = x_j \left(P, \bar{U} \right). \tag{11.33}$$

Expression (11.33) shows that the variation in expenditure when the price of a good is changed infinitesimally is equal to the compensated demand $x_j (P, \bar{U})$ because, at the optimum, according to (11.30):

$$\left(p_h - \mu \frac{\partial U}{\partial x_h} \right) \frac{\partial x_h}{\partial p_j} = 0; \quad h = 1, 2 \dots, n. \tag{11.34}$$

---

[6] To define the *CV* as the income 'taken' or 'given' is arbitrary. Here it is defined as the amount of income to be taken from the individual after the change to bring him back to the initial level of utility, so an increase in utility will be associated with a *CV* with a positive sign, whereas a loss of utility will have a *CV* with a negative sign ('taken' with a negative sign is the same as 'given').

The demand function x_j $(P, \bar{U})$ is called compensated or Hicksian demand and the utility is constant, while with the market demand x_j $(P, \bar{M})$ income is constant. The compensated demand function shows how the demanded quantity changes when the price of the good changes, while the income is adjusted so that the utility remains constant.

Using the indirect utility function $V(P, M) = \bar{U}$, where $\bar{U}$ is the level of utility that minimizes the expenditure in (11.32), and two levels of utility for $\bar{U}$, the one before the change U^0 and the one obtained after the change U^1, we see that the individual improves when the sign of (11.35) is positive and is worse off when the sign is negative:

$$V(P^1, M^0) - V(P^0, M^0). \tag{11.35}$$

Expression (11.35) tells us the sign of the change, but it does not give us any information on the magnitude of the change.[7] In cost–benefit analysis, it is not enough to know that some individuals improve and others become worse off. If the money measure for taxpayers is a reduction of \$1000 with the project, it is not enough for the decision maker to know that workers, employers and consumers will be better off. She also needs to know the magnitude of the improvement to compare it with the costs incurred, and to know whether the benefits of the beneficiaries of the project are high enough to offset the costs.

We need money measures of changes in the utility. The compensating variation (CV) is one of them (see Jara-Díaz and Farah, 1988). Suppose that income remains constant and prices fall. In expression (11.36) we see how the CV measures the improvement, expressed in monetary terms, experienced by the individual:

$$U^0 = V(P^0, M^0) = V(P^1, M^0 - CV). \tag{11.36}$$

With initial prices and income (P^0, M^0), the utility is equal to U^0 (we are at the point of departure, before the change). Expression (11.36) shows the income that should be taken (CV) from the individual in order to preserve the utility at the initial level in the new situation. If the change was an increase in prices, the CV would be negative (we would increase the income of the individual). Inverting (11.36):

$$M^0 = e(P^0, U^0) \text{ and } M^0 - CV = e(P^1, U^0), \tag{11.37}$$

---

[7] Recall that any monotonic increasing transformation of the original utility function is also valid. If a utility function, which represents the preferences of an individual before the project is implemented, has a value of $U^0 = 1$ and after the project $U^1 = 3$, we know that the individual has improved. If transforming the original function, the new values were $U^0 = 1$ and $U^1 = 9$, the economic interpretation has not changed. The ranking of the basket of goods of the individual is identical. In U^1 the individual is better off than in U^0, but we do not know the magnitude of the change because the scale is arbitrary.

so that the CV can be expressed as:

$$CV = e(P^0, U^0) - e(P^1, U^0), \tag{11.38}$$

which in the case of independent goods can be expressed as:

$$CV = \sum_{j=1}^{n} \int_{p_j^1}^{p_j^0} x_j \left(P, U^0 \right) dp_j. \tag{11.39}$$

In equation (11.38) the CV appears as the difference in the minimum amount of income required to achieve the level of utility U^0 given the initial and final prices. If the difference is positive, the individual has improved (as you can take income to leave him at the same level of utility). If the difference is negative, the individual is worse off because we have to give him income to compensate for the change.

The CV in (11.39) is valid for the case of independent goods and uses the result in (11.33), where the derivative of the expenditure at the optimum with respect to price is the compensated demand function $x_j (P, U^0)$. If we integrate the compensated demand function, using the initial and final prices as integration limits, we obtain an area equal to the CV, since the compensated demand does not incorporate the income effect.

We can proceed in the same way for the equivalent variation:

$$U^1 = V(P^1, M^0) = V(P^0, M^0 + EV). \tag{11.40}$$

With the income constant and the final prices (P^1, M^0) the utility is equal to U^1 (the level of utility after the change). Suppose that at this utility level U^1 the individual has improved because the prices P^1 are lower than P^0. Expression (11.40) shows that the EV consists of giving income to the individual in order, with the initial prices (P^0) and without the change, to make him as well off as in the level of utility U^1, equivalent to the change. If the change was an increase in prices, the EV would be negative (income will be taken from the individual). Inverting (11.40):

$$M^0 = e(P^1, U^1) \text{ and } M^0 + EV = e(P^0, U^1), \tag{11.41}$$

and the EV can be expressed as:

$$EV = e(P^0, U^1) - e(P^1, U^1), \tag{11.42}$$

which in the case of independent goods can be expressed as:

$$EV = \sum_{j=1}^{n} \int_{p_j^1}^{p_j^0} x_j \left(P, U^1 \right) dp_j. \tag{11.43}$$

In expression (11.42), the *EV* appears as the minimum income required for attaining the level of utility U^1 with the initial and final prices. If the difference is positive, the individual has improved (as an increase in income is equal to a change that leads to a higher level of utility). If the difference is negative, the individual is worse off since the change is equivalent to a loss of income.

In the same way as with the *CV*, expression (11.43) is only valid for independent goods and uses the result in expression (11.33) where the derivative of the expenditure in the optimum with respect to price is the compensated demand function, though now at a different level of utility $x_j(P, U^1)$. By integrating the compensated demand function for a level of utility U^1 and using the initial and final price of the good j as limits of integration, an area equal to the *EV* is obtained.

The *CV* and the *EV* do not necessarily coincide. They both measure changes in the value of the individual's utility in terms of money, with respect to the initial level in the case of *CV* and the final level in the case of *EV*.

Figure 11.6 represents, in the upper part, the indifference curves and the budget constraint of a consumer who chooses between good x_1 (in the vertical axis) and other goods, or income (in the horizontal axis). Initially, the individual is located at point *b*, where the indifference curve U^0 is tangent to the budget constraint zM_2. Their income level is equal to M_2, which is the maximum amount of other goods that the individual could consume if he does not consume x_1. Suppose that we reduce the price of x_1, shifting the budget constraint to hM_2, and now the individual chooses point *l*. The *CV* consists of taking away income from the individual such that he reaches the same level of utility enjoyed in *b* but once the price of x_1 has changed. Point *d* is the new location, and is achieved by reducing income by $M_2 - M_1$. Applying the definition of *EV*, we should give income to the individual at the initial price in order to obtain the same level of utility as at point *l* (point *f*), which is achieved with an income increase of $M_3 - M_2$.

Figure 11.6 allows us to link the movements of income of *CV* and *EV* in the upper part of the figure with changes in the utility and its representation as areas in the bottom part. Let us look at this in more detail.

As can be observed, changes in income are not equal on the horizontal axis $(M_2 - M_1) < (M_3 - M_2)$; however, changes in utility are identical: from U^1 to U^0 in the *CV* and from U^0 to U^1 in the *EV*. If the changes in utility are identical, why are changes in income not equal? The bottom part of the figure represents in the vertical axis the marginal utility of income, and in the horizontal axis the income. The area between the different levels of income and the curve, which represents the marginal utility of income, is the change in utility due to changes in income.

Under the assumption of decreasing marginal utility of income, which implies that when the income is lower its marginal utility is higher and vice versa, areas A and B must be equal, because these areas represent the change in utility from U^1 to U^0 and from U^0 to U^1 (integral defined between the income levels of the corresponding curve of marginal utility of income). The absolute magnitude of the income is lower when the individual moves to a lower level of income (from M_2 to M_1) than when moving to a higher one (from M_2 to M_3).

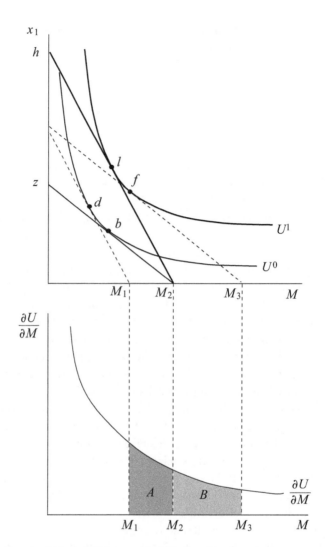

Figure 11.6 Why do CV and EV not coincide?

Figure 11.7 shows a compensated demand function and a reduction in the price of the good x_j from p_0 to p_1. The area between the two prices and the compensated demand can be the compensating variation or the equivalent variation depending on which level of utility is used as a reference (initial or final). In the special case of zero income effect the area is common to the CV, the EV and the change in CS, which we address below.

From the market demand function $x(P, \bar{M})$ we can calculate the change in consumer surplus as a result of a change in the price of one or several goods. Let p_0 be the initial price of good j and p_1 the final price; since consumer surplus is the difference between what individuals are willing to pay and what they actually pay, the change in consumer surplus (ΔCS) as a result of the change in prices is equal to:

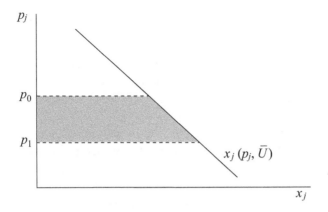

Figure 11.7 Valuation of a change in price with compensated demand

$$\Delta CS = \sum_{j=1}^{n} \int_{p_j^1}^{p_j^0} x_j \left(P, \bar{M} \right) dp_j. \tag{11.44}$$

The change in consumer surplus presents several problems; for example, we do not always obtain a single number because if several prices change, or prices and income change, the result depends on the path of integration. Another drawback of expression (11.44) is that, although consumer surplus has a unique value, regardless of the order in which the changes in prices are integrated, it does not measure changes in the utility unless the marginal utility of income is constant.[8] Consider this last point in more detail. From expression (11.13) we know that

$$x_j = -\frac{\dfrac{\partial V}{\partial p_j}}{\mu}, \tag{11.45}$$

and substituting in (11.44):

$$\Delta CS = -\sum_{j=1}^{n} \int_{p_j^1}^{p_j^0} \frac{1}{\mu} \frac{\partial V}{\partial p_j} dp_j. \tag{11.46}$$

If we want to relate the change in CS to changes in the utility, it is required that the marginal utility of income is constant. If μ is not constant, it can even happen that the change in CS has a different sign to the change in utility if the price changes have different signs (see Just et al., 1982). The representation of expression (11.44) for the change in one price is the area between the initial price and the final price and the market demand function (see Figure 11.8).

---

[8] For a rigorous treatment of the limitations of consumer surplus as a money measure of utility see for example Just et al. (1982) or Varian (1992). For a concise and clear treatment see Jara-Díaz and Farah (1988).

Market demand and compensated demand

In most economic evaluations of projects, market demand functions are required. Market demand allows us to calculate changes in consumer surplus and even the total surplus if there is available information to approximate the maximum reservation price. The use of the market demand function to estimate the change in the welfare of individuals has the disadvantage of including the income effect.

Market demand is the horizontal sum of individual demands. Figure 11.8 shows a consumer maximizing her utility, with the good x on the horizontal axis and the other goods (or income) on the vertical axis. Located initially at point a she consumes the quantity x_a of good x and M_1 of the other goods, reaching a level of utility U_0, represented by the indifference curve. The bottom part of the figure represents the inverse

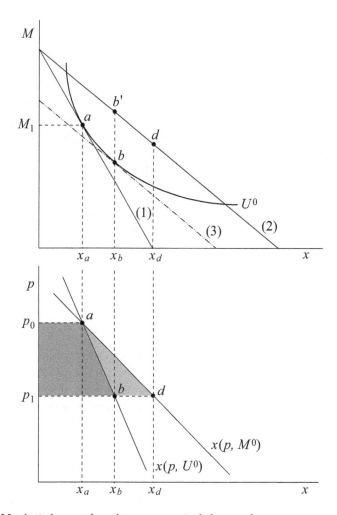

Figure 11.8 Market demand and compensated demand

market demand function of good x, $x(p, M^0)$. Point a in the bottom part of the figure shows that at price p_0 the consumer demands the quantity x_a.

Consider that, as a result of launching a public project, the price of good x changes from p_0 to p_1, which is represented in Figure 11.8 by reducing the slope of the budget constraint (which goes from (1) to (2)) while maintaining the same intersect on the vertical axis (the price of other goods does not change).

How has the individual improved with the change? One way of answering this question is to ask the consumer how much money she would be willing to pay in order to leave her at the level of utility at which she was located before the change in price (U^0 indifference curve). Recall that this concept is the compensating variation.

The problem with the above question is that indifference curves are not observable. It is difficult and expensive to obtain the information through consumer surveys, especially if there is an observable ordinary demand function in the market from which we can estimate the improvement. Can we get the measurement of the improvement with the consumer demand observed in the market? Consider two possible equilibria (d and b') once the change in price happens and the consumer adjusts her basket of consumption. The reason why the individual chooses point d or b' depends entirely on her preferences, since both points are on the budget constraint line.

Suppose that d is the point through which the new indifference curve is tangent to (2), increasing consumption of good x to x_d and reducing the consumption of other goods. At the bottom of the figure, the market demand function shows the shift from a to d as a result of reducing the price to p_1. The change in consumer surplus equals the area p_0adp_1. Compare this surplus with the compensating variation, taking away income from the individual in the upper part of the figure to leave her indifferent to the situation prior to the completion of the project (point b and quantity x_b). We leave the individual with only the substitution effect (budget constraint line (3) parallel to (2)) by removing the income effect. The demand function that goes from a to b is the compensated demand (without income effect) and the area p_0abp_1 measures the compensating variation. What does the area adb represent?

To answer this question, imagine that the new indifference curve tangent to (2) passed through b' instead of d. The quantity chosen is now x_b. In order to obtain the compensating variation we would lead the individual to point b (the same as above), but now we see that the functions of market demand and compensated demand coincide. The explanation is in the income effect. When the individual is at b after taking away income from her budget (regardless of whether she comes from d or b'), the improvement experienced by the individual as a result of the price reduction is measured by the area p_0abp_1.

This is the improvement that we want to measure and not what the consumer is going to spend this improvement on. When the individual chooses b' the income effect derived from the improvement is entirely dedicated to good M (the income effect in good x is zero); but if the individual spends part of the improvement represented in the area p_0abp_1 on consuming more x (at point d with quantity x_d), the area of the demand function p_0adp_1 would overestimate the change in the welfare of the individual by the amount adb, which is simply part of the area p_0abp_1 now spent on good x rather than on other goods.

The magnitude of the error

In the practice of cost–benefit analysis it is unusual to work with the compensated demand function. It has been shown that the bias resulting from the use of the ordinary demand curve can be insignificant when the expenditure on the good or goods affected by the project does not represent a high percentage of the budget of the individual, in which case the consumer surplus estimated with the ordinary demand is a good approx-imation in most cases (see Willig, 1976). On the other hand, it should not be forgotten that in the evaluation of the project we only know the initial price and the initial quan-tity; therefore, the price reduction and the demand response are only estimates. Errors associated with poor data quality are probably more important than those derived from calculating the change in consumer utility in money terms with the market demand instead of the compensated demand.

Let us very briefly analyse why we can use consumer surplus as a monetary measure of changes in the welfare of individuals. Returning to Figure 11.8, where the ordinary demand $x(p, M^0)$ is represented, we want to evaluate the improvement experienced by the consumer after the price drops from p_0 to p_1. The change in consumer surplus (ΔCS) is equal to the area p_0adp_1 and the compensating variation is equal to the area p_0abp_1. The difference between the two areas is adb. This is the overestimation of the benefits if we use ΔCS instead of the CV. What is the magnitude of this error?

The area adb is triangular and for small price changes it is approximately equal to the area $1/2 \, \Delta p \Delta x$, where Δp is the change in the price and Δx is the income effect (shift from x_b to x_d).

The elasticity of demand with respect to income is:

$$\eta = \frac{dx}{dM} \frac{M}{x}. \tag{11.47}$$

For small changes:

$$\Delta x = \eta x \frac{\Delta M}{M}. \tag{11.48}$$

and also $\Delta M \simeq \Delta CS$. Substituting into (11.48):

$$\Delta x = \eta x \frac{\Delta CS}{M}, \tag{11.49}$$

so that the area adb is equal to:

$$\frac{1}{2} \Delta p \Delta x = \frac{1}{2} \eta \Delta CS x \frac{\Delta p}{M}. \tag{11.50}$$

The CV is equal to the change in consumer surplus minus the overestimation represented by the area adb. We know that for a small change in the price $\Delta CS \simeq x\Delta p$. Solving for Δp and substituting into (11.50):

$$CV = \Delta CS - \frac{\eta}{2M}(\Delta CS)^2. \tag{11.51}$$

Operating in (11.51):

$$\frac{CV - \Delta CS}{\Delta CS} = -\frac{1}{2}\eta\frac{\Delta CS}{M}. \tag{11.52}$$

According to (11.52), the relative error of using the CS instead of the CV is low if η or $\Delta CS/M$ are low enough. For example, with a high income elasticity of demand ($\eta = 2$) and $\Delta CS/M \le 0.05$, or for $\eta = 1$ and $\Delta CS/M \le 0.1$, the error is less than or equal to 5 per cent.

In the case of non-marketed goods, the compensating and equivalent variations are quite useful and their estimation is carried out with consumer surveys through which the analyst tries to measure the willingness to pay or willingness to accept of an impact that changes the utility of the individual.

Theoretically these measurements do not bear the drawbacks of consumer surplus; however, the responses that individuals give to the interviewer are not necessarily the true EV or CV if the individual has no preferences (is able to realize the trade-off) on this kind of goods, or the individual suspects that his response may influence the outcome of the evaluation. Furthermore, we are implicitly assuming that the individual fully understands the questions in the survey, and that what is asked exactly reflects what we want to know, among other possible problems (see Chapters 5 and 6).

11.5 UNCERTAINTY

Assuming that consumers and firms maximize their utility, their choices are taken in relation to the results that are associated with these decisions. The problem is that there are often several possible outcomes associated with the same decision. The purchase of shares in a company can produce profits or losses for shareholders depending on the 'states of nature'; that is, the circumstances in the world that affect the profitability of the shares and in which the shareholder is unable to intervene.

The uncertainty is associated with the existence of different possible states of nature. If the individual buys a financial asset whose profitability depends on the state of nature, the risk is present in his decisions. The challenge now is to make decisions that involve risk.

Most individuals do not like the variability in the results. They are risk averse and they typically buy insurance to ensure a stable pattern of consumption (or profits) not subject to the uncertain states of nature.

An action subject to risk is the investment in infrastructure. Long life, specific assets, sunk costs and uncertain demand make the net present value of these investments very

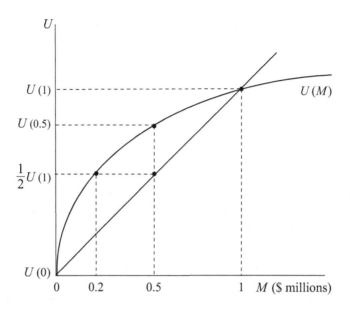

Figure 11.9 Uncertainty

difficult to predict. If the demand rises or falls over the life of the investment project, profitability can change dramatically.

There are a number of useful concepts for the analysis and understanding of the economic consequences of uncertainty: decreasing marginal utility, expected value, utility of the expected value, expected utility and certainty equivalent. Figure 11.9 can help with the definitions and the subsequent explanation.

The total utility (U) represented in Figure 11.9 is increasing and positive. When the individual receives income (M on the horizontal axis) his utility is positive; when he receives more income his utility increases. The concavity of the total utility curve adds a third assumption, that the utility increases with income but less than proportionately; that is, the marginal utility of income is positive but decreasing.

Positive and increasing income and total utility mean that the higher the income, the happier the individual. Positive and diminishing marginal utility means that when you receive additional income, your happiness increases more when you are 'poor' than when you are 'rich'. Suppose the individual whose utility curve is represented in Figure 11.9 is offered, for no payment, the following game:[9] a coin is thrown; if it is heads he wins a million dollars, if it is tails he wins nothing. Before throwing the coin he is offered an amount of money for not playing. The individual may abandon the game and accept the money or reject the money and play.

---

[9] Although the individual enters the game with a positive level of income and a positive level of total utility, we assume for simplicity, as Figure 11.9 shows, that $U(0)$ is the point corresponding to his original position before playing the game.

The expected value of the game is equal to half a million dollars ($\frac{1}{2}0 + \frac{1}{2}1$) but if the individual plays, this result will never occur. The result will be either heads and he wins a million, or tails and he wins nothing. The expected value (0.5) is the approximate result that would occur if the game is repeated a sufficiently large number of times, but the individual plays only once. What is the minimum amount we should offer him for not playing?

The minimum we would have to offer (his reservation price for not playing) should correspond to a similar level of utility to the one attained if he accepts the game. It is the amount of income that leaves the individual indifferent between playing and not playing. This level of income varies among individuals and is related, in addition to the initial level of income, to the degree of risk aversion.

Individuals with similar incomes may have different reservation prices. In the case of the individual in Figure 11.9 the reservation price is $200 000. If he is offered a lower amount, he will play. The value 0.2 on the horizontal axis corresponds to a level of utility that is identical to the level he would achieve if he accepts the game.

It should be emphasized that the level of utility of accepting the game is an expected level of utility ($\frac{1}{2}U(0) + \frac{1}{2}U(1)$). This expected level of utility corresponds to the option 'accept the game' and not the utility obtained after playing it, which is either $U(0)$ or $U(1)$. The individual is indifferent between playing the game with the same probability of obtaining the level of utility $U(0)$ or $U(1)$ and not playing if the offer is at least $200 000. This amount of money, which gives the same level of utility as the one obtained by playing the game, is denominated the 'certainty equivalent'.

It can be seen that the risk aversion of the individual makes the utility of the expected value $U(0.5)$ higher than the expected utility ($\frac{1}{2}U(0) + \frac{1}{2}U(1)$). This individual would be willing to pay a maximum of $800 000 for insurance before playing. If he ensures the guarantee of 1 million dollars whatever the result of the coin tossing, he will always gain the level of utility 0.2. If it is heads, he wins 1 million, less the premium of 0.8, he has 0.2. If it is tails he has zero but the insurance will compensate him with 1, and this 1 minus the premium of 0.8 is again 0.2.

As the expected value is what would be obtained if the game is repeated many times, an insurance company (which might also be thought of as an agreement among the large group of individuals identical to the one represented in Figure 11.9) could offer an insurance policy at a premium for which it would have to charge each individual at least 0.5 (which is called a fair premium[10]), and the individuals would pay a maximum of 0.8.

---

[10] Assuming that there are no operating costs of the insurance company or transaction costs between individuals to reach an agreement and compliance are zero.

References

Adamowicz, W.J., J. Louviere and J. Swait (1998), *Introduction to Attribute-Based Stated Choice Methods*, final report to National Oceanic and Atmospheric Administration (NOAA), US Department of Commerce, Washington, DC: NOAA.

Adler, M.D. and E.A. Posner (2001), 'Implementing cost–benefit analysis when preferences are distorted', in M.D. Adler and E.A Posner (eds), *Cost–Benefit Analysis: Legal, Economic and Philosophical Perspectives*, Chicago, IL: University of Chicago Press.

Angrist, J.D. and J.-S. Pischke (2014), *Mastering 'Metrics: The Path from Cause to Effect*, Princeton, NJ: Princeton University Press.

Anguera, R. (2006), 'The Channel Tunnel – an ex post economic evaluation', *Transportation Research Part A*, **40** (4), 291–315.

Arrow, K.J. and A.C. Fisher (1974), 'Environmental preservation, uncertainty, and irreversibility', *Quarterly Journal of Economics*, **88** (2), 312–19.

Arrow, K.J. and R.C. Lind (1970), 'Uncertainty and the evaluation of public investment decisions', *American Economic Review*, **60** (3), 364–78.

Asian Development Bank (ADB) (2017), *Guidelines for the Economic Analysis of Projects*, Manila: ADB.

Athey, S. and G.W. Imbens (2017), 'The state of applied econometrics: causality and policy evaluation', *Journal of Economic Perspectives*, **31** (2), 3–32.

Atkinson, A.B. and J.E. Stiglitz (2015), *Lectures on Public Economics*, updated edition, Princeton, NJ: Princeton University Press.

Bajari, P. and S. Tadelis (2001), 'Incentives versus transactions costs: a theory of procurement contracts', *RAND Journal of Economics*, **32** (3), 387–407.

Bazelon, C. and K. Smetters (1999), 'Discounting inside the Washington D.C. Beltway', *The Journal of Economic Perspectives*, **13** (4), 213–28.

Becker, G.S. (1983), 'A theory of competition among pressure groups for political influence', *The Quarterly Journal of Economics*, **98** (3), 371–400.

Becker, G.S. (2001), 'A comment on the conference on cost–benefit analysis', in M.D. Adler and E.A Posner (eds), *Cost–Benefit Analysis: Legal, Economic and Philosophical Perspectives*, Chicago, IL: University of Chicago Press, pp. 313–16.

Bergstrom, T.C. (2006), 'Benefit–cost in a benevolent society', *American Economic Review*, **96** (1), 339–51.

Bernstein, P.L. (1996), *Against the Gods: A Remarkable Story of Risk*, Toronto: Wiley.

Boadway, R. (1974), 'The welfare foundations of cost–benefit analysis', *Economic Journal*, **84** (336), 926–39.

Bonnafous, A. (1987), 'The regional impact of the TGV', *Transportation*, **14** (2), 127–37.

Bradford, D.F. (1975), 'Constraints on government investment opportunities and the choice of discount rate', *American Economic Review*, **65** (5), 887–99.

Brealey, R.A. and S.C. Myers (1996), *Principles of Corporate Finance*, 5th edition, New York: McGraw-Hill.

Carson, R., N. Flores and N. Meade (2001), 'Contingent valuation: controversies and evidence', *Environmental and Resource Economics*, **19** (2), 173–210.

Collier, P. and A.J. Venables (2018), 'Who gets the urban surplus?', *Journal of Economic Geography*, **18** (3), 523–38.

Cropper, M.L., S.K. Aydede and P.R. Portney (1992), 'Rate of time preference for saving lives', *American Economic Review (Papers and Proceedings)*, **82** (2), 469–72.

Dahlby, B (2008), *The Marginal Cost of Public Funds: Theory and Applications*, Cambridge, MA: MIT Press.

Dalhuisen, J.M., J.R. Florax, H.L. de Groot and P. Nijkamp (2003), 'Price and income elasticities of residential water demand: a meta-analysis', *Land Economics*, **79** (2), 292–308.

de Rus, G. (2008), 'The economic effects of high-speed rail investment', *Discussion Paper No. 2008–16*, OECD ITF, Joint Transport Research Centre.

de Rus, G. (2009), 'Interurban passenger transport: economic assessment of major infrastructure projects', *Discussion Paper No. 2009–18*, OECD ITF, Joint Transport Research Centre.

de Rus, G. (2011), 'The BCA of HSR: should the government invest in high speed rail infrastructure?', *Journal of Benefit-Cost Analysis*, **2** (1), 1–28.

de Rus, G. and G. Nombela (2007), 'Is investment in high speed rail socially profitable?', *Journal of Transport Economics and Policy*, **41** (1), 3–23.

de Rus, G. and M.P. Socorro (2010), 'Infrastructure investment and incentives with supranational funding', *Transition Studies Review*, **17** (3), 551–67.

Desvousges, W.H., F.R. Johnson and R.W. Dunford (1993), 'Measuring natural resource damages with contingent valuation: tests of validity and reliability', in J.A. Hausman (ed.), *Contingent Valuation: A Critical Assessment*, Amsterdam: North-Holland, pp. 91–164.

Diamond, P.A. and J.A. Hausman (1994), 'Contingent valuation: is some number better than no number?', *Journal of Economic Perspectives*, **8** (4), 45–64.

Dixit, A.K. and R.S. Pindyck (1994), *Investment under Uncertainty*, Princeton, NJ: Princeton University Press.

Domenich, T. and D. McFadden (1975), *Urban Travel Demand: A Behavioral Analysis*, Amsterdam: North-Holland.

Downs, A. (1957), *An Economic Analysis of Democracy*, New York: Harper & Row.

Duranton, G. and D. Puga (2004), 'Microfoundations of urban agglomeration economies', in J.V. Henderson and J.-F. Thisse (eds), *Handbook of Urban and Regional Economics, Vol. 4: Cities and Geography*, Amsterdam: North-Holland, pp. 2063–117.

Economics for the Environment Consultancy (EFTEC) (2003), *The Thames Tideway: Stated Preference Survey*, report to Thames Water, plc, London: EFTEC.

Engel, E., R. Fischer and A. Galetovic (2001), 'Least-present-value-of-revenue auctions and highway franchising', *Journal of Political Economy*, **109** (5), 993–1020.

Engel, E., R. Fischer and A. Galetovic (2014), *The Economics of Public-Private Partnerships*, Cambridge, UK: Cambridge University Press.

Engel, E., R. Fischer and A. Galetovic (2020), 'When and how to use public-private partnerships in infrastructure: lessons from the international experience', *NBER Working Paper No. 26766*.

Espey, M., J. Espey and W.D. Shaw (1997), 'Price elasticity of residential demand for water: a meta-analysis', *Water Resources Research*, **33** (6), 1369–74.

European Commission (2015), *Guide to Cost–Benefit Analysis of Investment Projects: Economic Appraisal Tool for Cohesion Policy 2014–2020*, Brussels: Directorate General Regional Policy, EU.

Evans, D. (2007), 'Social discount rates for the European Union: new estimates', in M. Florio (ed.), *Cost–Benefit Analysis and Incentives in Evaluation: The Structural Funds of the European Union*, Cheltenham, UK and Northampton, MA, USA: Edward Elgar Publishing, pp. 280–94.

Ferraro, P.J. and L.O. Taylor (2005), 'Do economists recognize an opportunity cost when they see one? A dismal performance from the dismal science', *Contributions to Economic Analysis and Policy*, **4** (1), 1–12.

Fisher, A.C. and W.M. Hanemann (1987), 'Quasi-option value: some misconceptions dispelled', *Journal of Environmental Economics and Management*, **14** (2), 183–90.

Flyvbjerg, B. (2014), 'What you should know about megaprojects and why: an overview', *Project Management Journal*, **45** (2), 6–19.

Flyvbjerg, B., N. Bruzelius and W. Rothengatter (2003), *Megaprojects and Risk: An Anatomy of Ambition*, Cambridge, UK: Cambridge University Press.

Fogel, R.W. (1962), 'A quantitative approach to the study of railroads in American economic growth: a report of some preliminary findings', *The Journal of Economic History*, **22** (2), 163–97.

Frederick, S. and B. Fischhoff (1998), 'Scope (in)sensitivity in elicited valuations', *Risk, Decision, and Policy*, **3** (2), 109–23.

Frederick, S., G. Loewenstein and T. O'Donoghue (2002), 'Time discounting and time preference: a critical review', *Journal of Economic Literature*, **40** (2), 351–401.

Freeman III, A.M. (2003), *The Measurement of Environmental and Resource Values: Theory and Methods*, Washington, DC: Resources for the Future.

Friedman, D. (1996), *Hidden Order. The Economics of Everyday Life*, New York: HarperBusiness.

Glaeser, E.L. and J.D. Gottlieb (2009), 'The wealth of cities: agglomeration economies and spatial equilibrium in the United States', *Journal of Economic Literature*, **47** (4), 983–1028.

Graham, D. (2007), 'Agglomeration, productivity and transport investment', *Journal of Transport Economics and Policy*, **41** (3), 317–43.

Graham, D. (2014), 'Causal influence for ex post evaluation of transport interventions', *Discussion Paper No. 2014–13*, paper prepared for the Roundtable: Ex-post Assessment of Transport Investments and Policy Interventions, 15–16 September, OECD, Paris.

Graham, D. and P.C. Melo (2011), 'Assessment of wider economic impacts of high-speed rail for Great Britain', *Transportation Research Record: Journal of the Transportation Research Board*, No. 2261, 15–24.

Guasch, J.L. (2004), *Granting and Renegotiating Infrastructure Concessions:*

Doing it Right, Washington, DC: World Bank.

Hanemann, W.M. (1991), 'Willingness to pay and willingness to accept: how much can they differ?', *American Economic Review*, **81** (3), 635–47.

Hanemann, W.M. (1994), 'Valuing the environment through contingent valuation', *Journal of Economic Perspectives*, **8** (4), 19–43.

Harberger, A.C. ([1964] 1972), 'Techniques of project appraisal', paper presented at the Conference on Economic Planning, reprinted in A.C. Harberger, *Project Evaluation (Collected Papers)* (Midway Reprint), Chicago, IL: University of Chicago Press, pp. 1–22.

Harberger, A.C. ([1965] 1972), 'Survey of literature on cost–benefit analysis for industrial project evaluation', paper prepared for the Inter-Regional Symposium in Industrial Project Evaluation, reprinted in A.C. Harberger, *Project Evaluation (Collected Papers)* (Midway Reprint), Chicago, IL: University of Chicago Press, pp. 23–69.

Harberger, A.C. (1972), *Project Evaluation (Collected Papers)* (Midway Reprint), Chicago, IL: University of Chicago Press.

Heal, G. (1997), 'Valuing our future: cost–benefit analysis of sustainability', *Discussion Papers Series No. 13*, United Nations Development Programme.

Henry, C. (1974), 'Investment decisions under uncertainty: the irreversibility effect', *American Economic Review*, **64** (6), 1006–12.

Hirshleifer, J. and J.G. Riley (1992), *The Analytics of Uncertainty and Information*, Cambridge, UK: Cambridge University Press.

HM Treasury (2018), *The Green Book: Central Government Guidance on Appraisal and Evaluation*, London: HM Stationery Office.

Horowitz, J. and K. McConnell (2002), 'A review of WTA/WTP studies', *Journal of Environmental Economics and Management*, **44** (3), 426–47.

Jara-Díaz, S.R. and M. Farah (1988), 'Valuation of users' benefits in transport systems', *Transport Reviews*, **8** (3), 197–218.

Johansson, P.-O. (1991), *An Introduction to Modern Welfare Economics*, Cambridge, UK: Cambridge University Press.

Johansson, P.-O. (1993), *Cost-Benefit Analysis of Environmental Change*, Cambridge, UK: Cambridge University Press.

Johansson, P.-O. and G. de Rus (2019), 'On the treatment of foreigners and foreign-owned firms in the cost-benefit analysis of transport projects', *Journal of Transport Economics and Policy*, **53** (3), 275–87.

Johansson, P.-O. and B. Kriström (2009), 'A blueprint for a cost–benefit analysis of a water use conflict: hydroelectricity versus other uses', working paper.

Johansson, P.-O. and B. Kriström (2016), *Cost–Benefit Analysis for Project Appraisal*, Cambridge, UK: Cambridge University Press.

Jones, C. (2002), 'The Boadway Paradox revisited', *Working Paper No. 421*, School of Economics, Australian National University.

Jones, L.P., P. Tandon and I. Vogelsang (1990), *Selling Public Enterprises: A Cost–Benefit Methodology*, Cambridge, MA: MIT Press.

Jones-Lee, M.W. (1992), 'Paternalistic altruism and the value of statistical life', *The Economic Journal*, **102** (410), 80–90.

Just, R.E., D.L. Hueth and A. Schmitz (1982), *Applied Welfare Economics and Public Policy*, Englewood Cliffs, NJ: Prentice Hall.

Kahnemann, D. and A. Tversky (eds) (2000), *Choice, Values and Frames*, Cambridge, UK: Cambridge University Press.

Klemperer, P. (1999), 'Auction theory: a guide to the literature', *Journal of Economic Surveys*, **13** (3), 227–86.

Krugman, P.R. (1991), 'Increasing returns and economic geography', *Journal of Political Economy*, **99** (3), 483–99.

Krugman, P.R. and A.J. Venables (1996), 'Integration, specialization and adjustment', *European Economic Review*, **40** (3–5), 959–67.

Laffont, J.J. and J. Tirole (1993), *A Theory of Incentives in Procurement and Regulation*, Cambridge, MA: MIT Press.

Lancaster, K. (1966), 'A new approach to consumer theory', *Journal of Political Economy*, **74** (2), 132–57.

Landsburg, S.E. (1993), *The Armchair Economist*, New York: The Free Press.

Lind, R.C. (1982), 'A primer on the major issues relating to the discount rate for evaluating national energy options', in R.C. Lind, K.L. Arrow and G.R. Corey (eds), *Discounting for Time and Risk in Energy Policy*, Baltimore, MD: Johns Hopkins University Press, pp. 21–94.

Little, I.M.D. and J.A. Mirrlees (1974), *Project Appraisal and Planning for Developing Countries*, London: Heinemann.

Lypsey, R.G. and K. Lancaster (1956), 'The general theory of second best', *Review of Economic Studies*, **24** (1), 11–32.

Mas-Colell, A., M.D. Whinston and J.R. Green (1995), *Microeconomic Theory*, New York: Oxford University Press.

Mensink, P. and T. Requate (2005), 'The Dixit–Pindyck and the Arrow–Fisher–Hanemann–Henry option values are not equivalent: a note on Fisher (2000)', *Resource and Energy Economics*, **27** (1), 83–8.

Nash, C.A. (2009), 'When to invest in high-speed rail links and networks?', *Discussion Paper No. 2009–16*, OECD ITF Joint Transport Research Centre.

National Oceanic and Atmospheric Administration (NOAA) (1993), 'Report of the NOAA panel on contingent valuation', *Federal Register*, **58** (10), 4602–14.

Niskanen, W.A. (1971), *Bureaucracy and Representative Government*, Chicago, IL: Aldine-Atherton.

Nombela, G. and G. de Rus (2004), 'Flexible-term contracts for road franchising', *Transportation Research A*, **38** (3), 163–247.

Olsen, T. and P. Osmundsen (2005), 'Sharing of endogenous risk in construction', *Journal of Economic Behavior and Organization*, **58** (4), 511–26.

Organisation for Economic Co-operation (OECD) (2007), 'Macro-, meso- and micro-economics planning and investment tools', paper presented at the Joint Transport Research Centre Round Table, 25–26 October, Boston, MA.

Pearce, D.W., G. Atkinson and S. Mourato (2006), *Cost–Benefit Analysis and the Environment: Recent Developments*, Paris: OECD Publishing.

Pearce, D.W. and R. Turner (1990), *Economics of Natural Resources and the Environment*, Baltimore, MD: Johns Hopkins University Press.

Pearce, D.W. and D. Ulph (1999), 'A social discount rate for the United Kingdom', in D.W. Pearce (ed.), *Economics and Environment: Essays on Ecological Economics and Sustainable Development*, Cheltenham, UK and Northampton, MA, USA: Edward Elgar.

Pindyck, R.S. (1991), 'Irreversibility, uncertainty, and investment', *Journal of Economic Literature*, **29** (3), 1110–48.

Puga, D. (2002), 'European regional policies in light of recent location theories', *Journal of Economic Geography*, **2** (4), 373–406.

Robinson, J.A. and R. Torvik (2005), 'White elephants', *Journal of Public Economics*, **89** (2–3), 197–210.

Savvides, S. (1994), 'Risk analysis in investment appraisal', *Project Appraisal*, **9** (1), 3–18.

Sobel, R.S. (1998), 'The political costs of tax increases and expenditure reductions: evidence from state legislative turnover', *Public Choice*, **96** (1–2), 61–80.

Stigler, G. (1988), *Memoirs of an Unregulated Economist*, New York: Basic Books.

Sunstein, C.R. (2014), *Valuing Life: Humanizing the Regulatory State*, Chicago, IL: University of Chicago Press.

Varian, H.R. (1992), *Microeconomic Analysis*, New York: W.W. Norton & Co.

Varian, H.R. (1999), *Intermediate Microeconomics: A Modern Approach*, New York: W.W. Norton & Co.

Venables, A. (2007), 'Evaluating urban transport improvements: cost–benefit analysis in the presence of agglomeration and income taxation', *Journal of Transport Economics and Policy*, **41** (2), 173–88.

Venables, A. (2019), 'Transport appraisal: wider economic benefits', paper presented at the CBA Workshop on the Assessment of Large Cross-border Transport Projects, Innovation and Networks Executive Agency (INEA), European Commission.

Venables, A.J. and M. Gasoriek (1999), *The Welfare Implications of Transport Improvements in the Presence of Market Failure*, London: Department of the Environment, Transport and the Regions.

Viscusi, W.K. (2018), 'Pricing lives: international guideposts for safety', *Economic Records*, **94**, June, 1–10.

Weitzman, M.L. (2001), 'Gamma discounting', *American Economic Review*, **91** (1), 260–71.

Willig, R. (1976), 'Consumer's surplus without apology', *American Economic Review*, **66** (4), 589–97.

Zerbe, R.O. (2018), 'The concept of standing in benefit-cost analysis' in S. Farrow (ed), *Teaching Benefit-Cost Analysis*, Edward Elgar, pp. 58–68.

Zhao, J. and C. Kling (2001), 'A new explanation for the WTP/WTA disparity', *Economics Letters*, **73** (3), 293–300.

Index